CW01368545

Parnall Aircraft

since 1914

The only surviving Parnall aeroplane. Parnall Elf G-AAIN at Old Warden in 1981 after restoration by the Shuttleworth Trust. It has a 120 hp Cirrus Hermes II engine. (*John A Long LRPS*)

Parnall Aircraft
since 1914

Kenneth E Wixey

NAVAL
INSTITUTE
PRESS

© Kenneth E Wixey 1990

First published in Great Britain by
Putnam Aeronautical Books, an imprint of
Conway Maritime Press Ltd,
24 Bride Lane, Fleet Street
London EC4Y 8DR

Published and distributed in the United States
of America and Canada by the Naval Institute Press
Annapolis, Maryland 21402
Library of Congress Catalog Card No. 89-64220
ISBN 1-55750-930-1
This edition is authorized for sale only in
the United States and its territories and possessions,
and Canada

All rights reserved. Unauthorised duplication contravenes
applicable laws.

Manufactured in Great Britain

Contents

Introduction	7
Acknowledgements	11
Parnall Works Lineage Chart	12
Family Business	13
The Fishponds Connection	25
George Parnall and Company	36
Parnall Aircraft Limited	53
Parnall and Sons Limited — Aircraft Built under Contract 1914–1918	69
Avro 504	69
Short 827	74
Short Bomber	77
Hamble Baby	80
Parnall Scout/Zepp-Chaser	85
Parnall Panther	88
George Parnall and Company 1920–1935	100
Parnall Puffin	100
Parnall Plover	105
Parnall Possum	112
Parnall Pixie Series	118
Parnall Perch	133
Autogiros	137
De Havilland D.H.9A Contracts	142
Parnall Peto	146
Parnall Pike	160
Parnall Imp	164
Parnall Pipit	167
Parnall Parasol	175
Parnall Elf	181
Parnall Prawn	190
Parnall G.4/31	193
Hendy 302/302A	197
Miles M.1 Satyr	200
Percival Gull Four	203
Parnall F.5/33 Project	207
Parnall Aircraft Limited 1935–1939	214
Parnall Heck	214
Parnall Type 382 (Heck Mk.III)	220

Appendix A: Individual Aircraft Notes
Appendix B: Dispositions of Certain
  Parnall-Built Aircraft on Naval Duty 1918
Bibliography
Index

Introduction

When Great Britain went to war with Germany in August 1914, the aeroplane was still at a very rudimentary stage in its development. Indeed even as the hostile nations clashed, there persisted a school of thought among some military officers that those flimsy contraptions of linen and spruce, which would admittedly carry a man aloft, would nevertheless be of little strategic value in the ensuing conflict. It was conceded that aeroplanes made excellent reconnaissance vehicles from which observation reports on enemy troop movements could be obtained, but other than that quite a number of the more short-sighted generals and admirals could foresee no advantage in the employment of aeroplanes as a key weapon in contemporary warfare.

Before the First World War the apathy of the majority of British politicians towards supporting the development of military aviation in the United Kingdom was hard to understand in view of the rapidly worsening political situation in Europe. While Germany proceeded with the construction of her giant Zeppelin airships, together with the less impressive but numerically superior Military Aviation Service, the British Government was extremely reluctant to give financial backing to the country's aviation industry such as it was. Had it not been for the initiative of private enterprise, Britain would undoubtedly have been in even worse straits regarding her military aviation requirements when the war started. As it was, thanks to the more far-sighted military pundits such as Maj Brooke-Popham, Capt Hugh Trenchard (later a Viscount and Marshal of the Royal Air Force), Capt (later Rear Admiral Sir) Murray Sueter, Capt (later Air Chief Marshal Sir) Philip Joubert de la Ferté, and Cmdr Charles Rumney Samson RN, to name but a few, Britain was able to prepare more readily in the field of air power.

Politically one member of Parliament in particular had the tenacity of purpose and firm belief in the aeroplane as a military weapon, enough to continuously warn the British Government of the day that they neglected the development of British military air power at their peril. That politician was Winston Churchill, First Lord of the Admiralty, a keen airman, and first member of the British Government to pilot his own aeroplane.

Eventually Prime Minister Herbert Asquith requested that the Imperial Defence Committee put forward proposals for the creation of an efficient British air force. As a result the Royal Flying Corps (RFC) came into being on 13 April, 1912. The new Service was at first divided into a

Military Wing and a Naval Wing, but under the auspicious eye of Winston Churchill, who was already setting up a system of seaplane stations around Britain's coasts, the Naval Wing developed its own specialist techniques, and on 1 July, 1914, became the Royal Naval Air Service (RNAS).

Meanwhile the seething cauldron of political unrest in Europe finally spilled over on 28 June, 1914, when the Austrian Archduke Franz Ferdinand and his wife Sophie were assassinated in the town of Sarajevo in Serbia. This event had within two months spread its political consequences across the nations, and inflicted upon the world its first experience of global conflict.

On the outbreak of this first world war, Britain possessed few British-built military aeroplanes, the majority in service being of French origin. This state of affairs was soon rectified when British aeroplane manufacturers began producing an increasing number of their own products. Indeed, Great Britain became a major producer of military aeroplanes, and during four years of war her aircraft industry grew in proportion until, by the time of the Armistice in November 1918, it was employing 350,000 men and women.

During the four years of war from 1914 to 1918, this growing body of aircraft workers between them produced 55,000 aeroplanes of all types for military service. This rapid expansion of the aviation industry was due not only to the more prominent manufacturers such as the Royal Aircraft Factory (RAF) at Farnborough, A V Roe & Co Ltd (Avro), the British & Colonial Aeroplane Co Ltd (later Bristol Aeroplane Co Ltd), Aircraft Manufacturing Co Ltd (Airco and later de Havilland Aircraft Co Ltd), Sopwith Aviation Co Ltd, Short Brothers, and Vickers (Aviation) Ltd, but also to the numerous smaller firms throughout Britain which undertook sub-contract work on behalf of aeroplane manufacturers and government departments to produce aeroplanes and their many components.

The majority of these early military aircraft were constructed mainly from wood, so it was not surprising when companies renowned for their expertise and skill in cabinet-making, woodworking and joinery, were called upon to consider the construction of wooden aeroplanes and parts.

A number of these sub-contractors became so successful at aeroplane manufacture that it was not long before they had continuous production lines of complete new aeroplanes awaiting delivery to the squadrons. The significance of the effect some of the contractors were having by their inroads into the aircraft industry was soon made apparent. For example, Samuel Waring (later Lord Waring) of the Waring and Gillow partnership was responsible for founding the British Nieuport & General Aircraft Co Ltd at Cricklewood, an event which followed an agreement with the French Nieuport concern to construct that company's aeroplanes in Great Britain. At Cheltenham, the high-class woodworking firm of H H Martyn & Co Ltd, became part of a new venture when it helped form the Gloucestershire Aircraft Co Ltd (later Gloster Aircraft).

This company eventually acquired the design rights of the aforementioned British Nieuport & General Aircraft, when that concern was forced to close down in 1920, an arrangement which also included the services of H P Folland, British Nieuport & General's design engineer who would become chief designer to the Gloster Aircraft company.

Meanwhile an equally well-known company in the West Country, recognised for its woodworking skills, was Parnall & Sons Ltd of Bristol. This firm, which specialised in shopfitting and allied equipment, was requested by the Admiralty to undertake the manufacture and reconditioning of naval aeroplanes. The contracts covered types designed by Avro, Sopwith, Fairey Aviation and Short Brothers, and before the end of the war, two designs created by Parnall's themselves after encouragement from the Admiralty. This progressive development in the company's history was to result in a lengthy association which Parnall's enjoyed with the Admiralty, Air Ministry and the British aircraft industry.

This relationship induced the production of a series of naval aeroplanes, albeit mostly prototypes and experimental machines for the Air Ministry, as well as a number of civil types, including Parnall's own designs and those built under contract for other aeroplane manufacturers. The earlier types of aircraft originated in Bristol both with Parnall & Sons Ltd, and with George Parnall's own company after its formation at the Coliseum works in Park Row, Bristol. However, the majority of aeroplanes produced by George Parnall & Co were designed and built at Yate in Gloucestershire, after the company moved there in the mid-1920s.

Parnall & Sons Ltd of Fishponds, Bristol (until recently a member of the Avery Group, but now part of GEC), still flourish as manufacturers of high-class shopfittings and other components.

This firm owes its origins to Parnall's nineteenth-century family business, a concern from which were to evolve two entirely separate companies bearing the names of Parnall. Both establishments would accomplish much to further the cause of British aviation over three decades from 1915 until 1945. Indeed Parnall & Sons of Fishponds continued producing aircraft components well into the 1960s for both the civil and military market.

It should, perhaps, be explained that George Parnall sold his Yate aircraft works in 1935, but the concern which took it over still retained the name of Parnall in its title when it became Parnall Aircraft Ltd, and this company's part in the history of Parnall's is fully described in the main text.

The primary aim of this book is to firmly establish the name of Parnall in its richly deserved niche in the annals of British aeronautical achievements. It is intended also as a tribute to a comparatively small, but nevertheless, proud pair of family businesses which, through their largely unsung efforts, managed to uphold that hallmark of quality one expects from British companies steeped in traditions of craftsmanship.

The first section of the book relates to the historical background and environment surrounding Parnall & Sons at Bristol, from the firm's early beginnings. This includes the historical association of the Fishponds factory with early aviation, its acquisition by Parnall's and the company's involvement with various aircraft work at the site from 1939 until the mid-1960s.

This first part also covers the story of George Parnall's break with Avery's, the forming of his own company in Park Row, the move to Yate, a summary of the years at Yate until 1935, his retirement and untimely death. It contains too the story of Yate's continuing involvement with the aircraft industry from 1935 until the end of the Second World War, and what followed.

The second part of the book is devoted mainly to those aeroplanes designed and built by Parnall, and to types designed by other aircraft manufacturers which were produced by Parnall under contract for both military and civil use.

Each aircraft type, including those built under contract, is described and available data given. Numerous photographs (a number previously unpublished) and available drawings serve to portray the various subjects.

Much of the technical data and details appertaining to certain Parnall-designed aeroplanes were lost in the German air attacks on the Yate works in 1941, and as a consequence, despite the exhaustive research by a number of very helpful individuals and the author, information regarding a few machines is unavoidably sparse. Also in one or two cases, very few suitable illustrations exist of a particular aeroplane, thus accounting for the poor quality photographs which may occasionally depict a certain machine. The inclusion of details extracted from the personal flight log of the late Capt Frank T Courtney are by kind permission of Capt Courtney himself.

Acknowledgements

The author wishes to express his sincere gratitude to the following official establishments, private companies and individuals without whose ready help this book would never have materialised.

Aircraft and Armament Experimental Establishment, Boscombe Down; Beaumont Aviation Literature; British Aerospace (Aircraft Group), Kingston-upon Thames and Filton; J M Bruce; L Callaway (ex-works manager, George Parnall & Co, Yate); Ian Carnochan (one time PRO, T I Jackson Ltd, Yate); Ted Chapman; the late Capt Frank T Courtney (one time free-lance test pilot); Doubleday & Co Inc; E Draycott (ex-ground engineer, works inspector at George Parnall & Co, Yate); Fleet Air Arm Museum, Yeovilton; Mrs Margaret Fry (ex-women's supervisor, George Parnall & Co, Yate); Norman Hall-Warren (ex-design staff, George Parnall & Co, Yate); Eric Harlin; Imperial War Museum; the late A J Jackson; T I Jackson Ltd, Yate; Philip Jarrett; George Jenks (Avro Historical Research Group); John A Long (Parnall & Sons Ltd) Fishponds, Bristol; Macdonald & Janes; David Male; Ministry of Defence (Air Historical Branch); Mark Parnall of Launceston, Cornwall; Brian Pickering, Military Aircraft Photographs; the late Stephen Piercey (*Flight International*); Putnam & Co; Elfan Ap Rees (British Rotorcraft Museum); Richard Riding (*Aeroplane Monthly*); Bruce Robertson; Rolls-Royce (Aero-engine division), Bristol; Royal Aeronautical Society; Royal Aircraft Establishment, Farnborough (Main Library); Royal Air Force Museum, Hendon; Shell UK (Aviation division); G Stuart-Leslie; Westland Helicopters Ltd, Yeovil; J W Williamson (Parnall & Sons Ltd), Fishponds, Bristol.

Finally I would like to record an appreciation of my wife's forbearance during those periods of research when silence was golden!

Kenneth E Wixey
Brockworth
Gloucestershire.

Parnall Works Lineage Chart

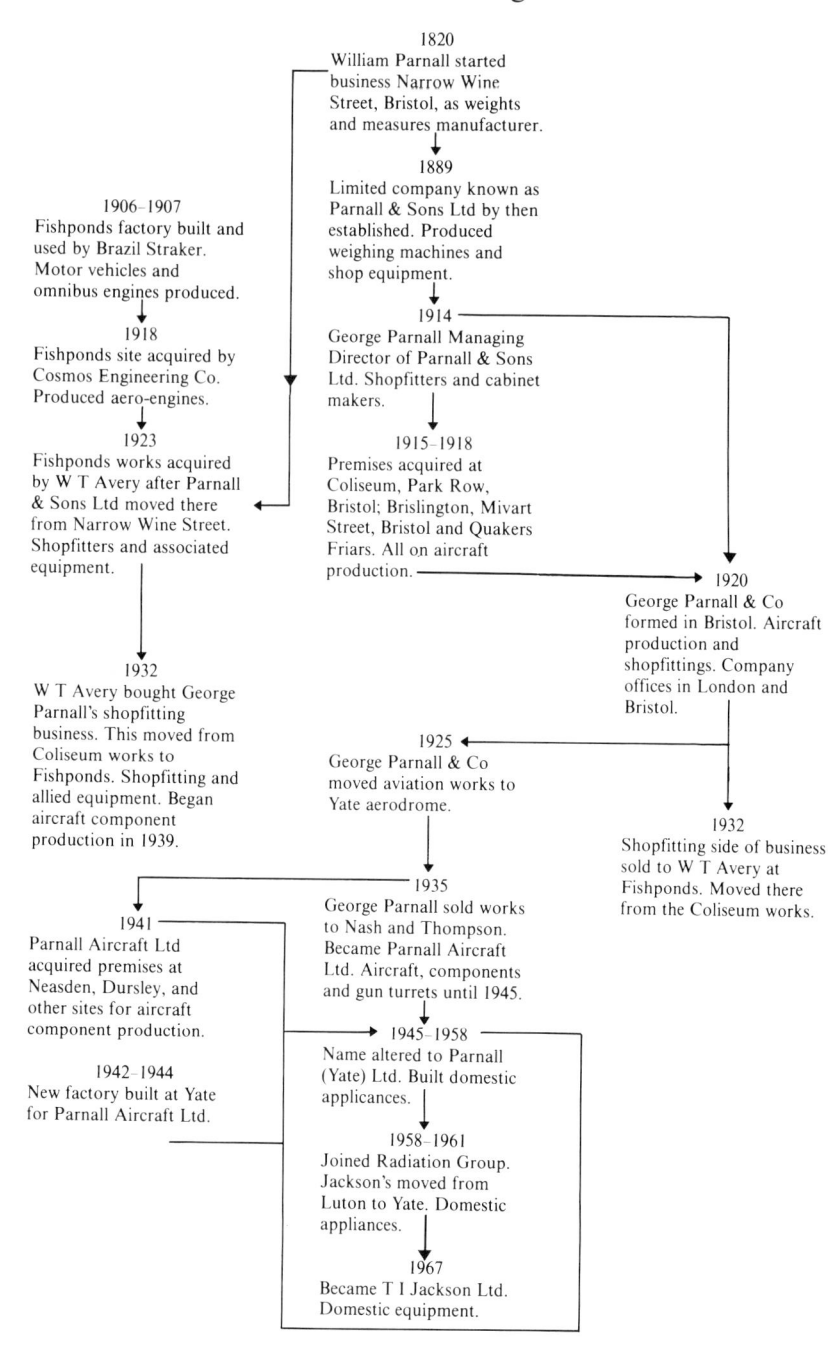

1820
William Parnall started business Narrow Wine Street, Bristol, as weights and measures manufacturer.

1889
Limited company known as Parnall & Sons Ltd by then established. Produced weighing machines and shop equipment.

1906–1907
Fishponds factory built and used by Brazil Straker. Motor vehicles and omnibus engines produced.

1914
George Parnall Managing Director of Parnall & Sons Ltd. Shopfitters and cabinet makers.

1918
Fishponds site acquired by Cosmos Engineering Co. Produced aero-engines.

1915–1918
Premises acquired at Coliseum, Park Row, Bristol; Brislington, Mivart Street, Bristol and Quakers Friars. All on aircraft production.

1923
Fishponds works acquired by W T Avery after Parnall & Sons Ltd moved there from Narrow Wine Street. Shopfitters and associated equipment.

1920
George Parnall & Co formed in Bristol. Aircraft production and shopfittings. Company offices in London and Bristol.

1925
George Parnall & Co moved aviation works to Yate aerodrome.

1932
W T Avery bought George Parnall's shopfitting business. This moved from Coliseum works to Fishponds. Shopfitting and allied equipment. Began aircraft component production in 1939.

1932
Shopfitting side of business sold to W T Avery at Fishponds. Moved there from the Coliseum works.

1935
George Parnall sold works to Nash and Thompson. Became Parnall Aircraft Ltd. Aircraft, components and gun turrets until 1945.

1941
Parnall Aircraft Ltd acquired premises at Neasden, Dursley, and other sites for aircraft component production.

1942–1944
New factory built at Yate for Parnall Aircraft Ltd.

1945–1958
Name altered to Parnall (Yate) Ltd. Built domestic applicances.

1958–1961
Joined Radiation Group. Jackson's moved from Luton to Yate. Domestic appliances.

1967
Became T I Jackson Ltd. Domestic equipment.

This Avro 504K (F8748) is believed to be one of the final batch of this type built by Parnall & Sons at Bristol during the First World War. (*MAP*)

Family Business

In the year 1337 a dukedom was created for Edward the Black Prince. The area chosen was a beautiful expanse of countryside forming the extreme southwestern peninsula of England, tapering from the River Tamar – a natural boundary with Devonshire – to Land's End and the Lizard Point, respectively the westernmost and southernmost points of the mainland. This, one of England's most beautiful counties, still retains its title of the Royal Duchy of Cornwall.

On the west side of the Cornish peninsula, amidst a magnificent stretch of coastline overlooking the Atlantic near Bude, lies the parish of St Gennys. A section of this coast at St Gennys, about one and a half miles in length, and including what is possibly the highest coastal cliff in England, is the property of the National Trust. The Trust was presented with the land by the Parnall family whose ancestral home is situated in the parish, and was given to the Nation as a memorial to Dennis Parnall, an RAF fighter pilot and one of the immortal 'few' who fought in the Battle of Britain in 1940. Like so many of Britain's young men, Dennis Parnall paid the supreme sacrifice when his fighter was shot down over the Channel.

Dennis was one of three sons born to George Parnall, the other two being Basil, who unfortunately died as a boy, and Alan, also a pilot with the RAF who attained the rank of Wing Commander. Alan Parnall died in 1967.

George Parnall himself, although of true Cornish ancestry, was a Bristolian by birth, and firmly established the name of Parnall, not only in Bristol's commercial world, but later in the field of aviation.

PARNALL & SONS', Ltd., COFFEE BOXES.

Black supplied unless ordered otherwise.

All Coffee Box Lids (except 350 & 350A) open from front to back, unless ordered otherwise.

350   COUNTER COFFEE BOX.
Japanned and ornamented with gold letters and borders.
Three compartments ... 18-in. 15/-   21-in. 17/6   24-in. 20/-   27-in. 22/6

351   COUNTER COFFEE BOX.
With three compartments, handsomely ornamented, with large gold beading
21-in. 25/-   24-in. 30/-   27-in. 35/-   30-in. 40/-

353   NEW COUNTER COFFEE BOX.
Handsome ornamental raised foot, large double gold beading all round, elaborately finished in gold and colours, three divisions.
24-in. 47/6   27-in. 57/6   30-in. 67/6
If done in burnished gold, very effective—
24-in. 52/6   27-in. 62/6   30-in. 72/6
This Box is very convenient to serve from, and is specially recommended.

353a   PERFECTION COFFEE BOX.
Handsome and highly finished, with polished mahogany O.G. moulded covers, new shaped body, with O.G. moulded foot, richly ornamented with Coffee plant, scroll and leaf border, and written in burnished gold, lettering highly shaded in colours.   Very effective.
24-in. 55/-   27-in. 62/6   30-in. 70/-   If 4 compartments to larger sizes, 7/6 extra
The covers stand against a ledge when open. Any colour to order, but black sent unless otherwise desired.

358a   TEA OR COFFEE BOX.
With three compartments, desk-shaped sloping lids, the front fitted with beading all round, handsomely written, and decorated in gold.
If four compartments to larger sizes, 5/- extra.
20-in. 30/-   24-in. 35/-   28-in. 40/-

358b   IMPROVED COFFEE BOX.
Desk-shaped, with polished mahogany O.G. moulded covers, strongly made and well finished, with gold lettering and borders. Specially adapted for rough wear.   24-in. 35/-   27-in. 42/6   30-in. 50/-
If 4 compartments to larger sizes, 7/6 extra.   Covers stand against a ledge when open.

353b
The Show Case has moveable compartments

COFFEE BOX AND SHOW CASE COMBINED.
Effective in appearance and very useful. The Sample Show Case is fitted with plate glass, with polished brass beading, and is dust-tight. Japanned and ornamented in gold in very best style, and of superior quality and finish.
Three compartments ... 24-in. 65/-   27-in. 75/-   30-in. 85/-

358c

TEA, COFFEE, OR COCOA BOX.
Useful for displaying goods on the counter, and to serve or weigh from. Japanned and ornamented in gold, and fitted with polished brass beading around the top, or plainer style without brass beading.
With brass beading, 22 × 10, 25/-   24 × 11, 30/-   27 × 12, 35/-   30 × 13, 40/-
With gilt beading, 22 × 10, 15/-   24 × 11, 18/-   27 × 12, 21/-   30 × 13, 25/-

DON'T FORGET our full Name and Address:—

The Old Firm. { **PARNALL & SONS, LTD., NARROW WINE STREET, BRISTOL.** } Established 1820.

COPYRIGHT CATALOGUE No. 26.   And at 10 ROOD LANE, LONDON, E.C.

These eight illustrations depict a variety of counter-type containers, advertised in an early Parnall & Sons catalogue. (*K E Wixey Parnall collection*)

To establish the events which finally resulted in the establishment of two entirely separate concerns under the name of Parnall, both of which evolved from the original family business, it is first necessary to render an account of the history of Parnall & Sons Ltd, from which the firm of George Parnall & Co eventually branched out.

In the year 1820 a certain William Parnall made arrangements to open a business in Narrow Wine Street, Bristol, from where he began trading as a 'weights and measures manufacturer'. Over the ensuing years the business expanded, eventually progressing to cabinet making, the fabrication of shopfronts, shopfittings and their associated equipment. By the year 1889 the firm was established as a limited company known as Parnall & Sons Ltd. During the following decade the company gained a reputation second to none for its quality of workmanship in the field of shopfitting and ancillary apparatus, including a very fine range of weighing and measuring machines. In 1898 the attention of W & T Avery, the well-known weights and measures manufacturers, was drawn to the weighing machine side of Parnall's business. Avery made a successful take-over bid which resulted in it becoming involved with the manufacture of Parnall-designed weighing and measuring contrivances. The name of Parnall & Sons Ltd was, however, retained for trading purposes.

The head of Parnall's at the time of the Avery take-over was John Parnall, who through his Cornish ancestry and business connections in Bristol, would, in 1903, be elected as president of the Bristol Cornish Association. On the first day of February 1873 John Parnall's wife had given birth to a son – George Geach Parnall – and he in turn was

Hamble Baby Convert N2059 nearing completion in the Coliseum works of Parnall at Park Row, Bristol. The Parnall c/n P.1/74 appears beneath serial number. An Avro 504 is under construction in the background. (*K E Wixey Parnall collection*)

eventually to become managing director of the Avery-owned Parnall company, a position he still held when Britain went to war with Germany on 4 August, 1914.

George Parnall had continued to uphold and develop further the family business in Narrow Wine Street, and after the start of the war it was not long before the firm's expertise in woodcraft was sought after in connection with the manufacturer of wooden aeroplane structures.

A number of contracts were awarded to the Parnall company for the construction of aeroplanes for the Admiralty, and a variety of types were produced. These included Avro 504s, Sopwith (Fairey) Hamble Baby seaplanes and landplanes, Short seaplanes and Short bombers. In addition Parnall & Sons designed and built two aircraft of their own creation before the cessation of hostilities, the single-seat Scout (Zepp-Chaser) and two-seat Panther, the Panther reaching eventual production status albeit with another aeroplane manufacturer.

Obviously the undertaking of such an influx of aviation work necessitated the acquisition of additional premises by Parnall, and sites were taken over at the Coliseum works, Park Row, in Bristol; at Eastville (Mivart Street), in Brislington; and at Quakers Friars.

The Coliseum works (the building itself was originally a roller-skating rink and later site for several trade exhibitions) and the Mivart Street factory became responsible mainly for constructional work; Mivart Street concentrated on propeller production. Older Bristolians have recalled

This rare print purports to be an in-flight view of the Parnall Panther prototype N.91. It is in fact a faked picture; nevertheless it depicts well the Panther's pronounced humped profile. (*K E Wixey Parnall collection*)

scenes during the First World War when aeroplanes were 'wheeled' out onto the street awaiting despatch!

The Brislington factory was concerned chiefly with experimental work, and it was there that the first Panther prototype was developed. Propeller

Harold Bolas, chief designer with Parnall & Sons and later George Parnall & Co, from 1917 until 1929, is seen in front of Parnall Elf G-AAFH. The Elf was Bolas's last design for Parnall before leaving for the United States. (*Norman Hall-Warren*)

production was transferred from Mivart Street to Brislington in 1916, while staff at Quakers Friars involved themselves mainly in covering and doping the various aeroplanes components.

By the time of the Armistice in November 1918, the Parnall works had between them completed at least 600 military aeroplanes, a substantial contribution to the expansion of the Royal Naval Air Service, Royal Flying Corps and consequently the Royal Air Force (RAF), which was formed by the amalgamation of the RNAS and RFC on 1 April, 1918.

During the First World War Parnall & Sons acquired the services of Harold Bolas, a young man who was quickly promoted to chief aircraft designer, and who was eventually to join George Parnall's own company and remain with them until 1929. Harold Bolas was a graduate of Manchester University, a first class lacrosse player, and who in 1910 began an aviation career with the AID at the Army Aircraft Factory at Farnborough. The work was mainly concerned with making modifications to some of the Army airships then under construction at Farnborough, and Bolas found himself assigned to tasks alongside such men as F M Green, S W Hiscocks and Geoffrey de Havilland.

With the start of the war Bolas was commissioned in the RNAS and appointed to a position with the Admiralty's Air Department. He there became involved with detailed design work on the A.D. Flying-Boat, a project in which he was closely associated with Harold Yendall and Clifford W Tinson. Lieut Linton Hope was responsible for designing the flying-boat's hull, and the complete aircraft was built by Pemberton-Billing Ltd.

Harold Bolas undertook next the design of a two-seat, two-bay, biplane mounted on floats and powered by a pusher engine. He worked on this

The Army airship *Gamma II* represents the type of vessels on which Harold Bolas began work at Farnborough in 1919. (*Hampshire County Library*)

Once installed at the Admiralty, Harold Bolas became involved with design of the first A.D. flying-boat, a production version of which is shown here; N1522 of the RNAS. *(J M Bruce/G S Leslie collection)*

project with Reginald J Mitchell (later of Schneider Trophy and Spitfire fame); the result of the two men's ideas was the A.D. Navyplane, with a tailplane supported by four booms and, like the flying-boat, incorporating a wooden monocoque structure.

This embodied a crew nacelle weighing only about 80lb complete with seat and floor fittings. It was this form of monocoque construction which was to influence Harold Bolas later, when he designed the Parnall Panther.

The A.D. Navyplane was not a success chiefly because of the inferior types of powerplant installed. The Admiralty did place an order for six machines, but only one (9095) was completed, the rest of the contract being cancelled after tests held in 1917 proved unsatisfactory.

Harold Bolas was released by the Admiralty on a loan basis to Parnall & Sons, joining the firm in 1917, and quickly finding himself in the position of chief designer. Bolas was mostly concerned with the Brislington factory and, although priority was being given to Government contract work on aircraft designed by other manufacturers, it was not long before plans were developed for the building of his first design for Parnall. This was the N.2A, later named Panther, a two-seater spotter reconnaissance biplane for the Royal Navy. Six prototypes were completed, but two production orders awarded to the company by the Air Ministry were cancelled after Parnall's controlling group, W T Avery, disagreed with the Ministry over the cancellation of the second contract.

After the war the company readjusted itself to the requirements of peace, and under Avery's jurisdiction Parnall returned to the business of manufacturing shopfittings and associated equipment. George Parnall, however, was not at all happy with the way things were being run, and he

Powered by a 230 hp Bentley B.R.2 rotary engine, the Panther was Harold Bolas's first design for Parnall. Seen here is the prototype N.91. It has the .303-in Vickers machine-gun fitted to the upper port side and hydrovane had not been fitted at that time. (*J M Bruce/G S Leslie collection*)

proposed to Avery that the firm should concentrate more on supplying shopfronts and fittings for the larger shops and department stores, which was where George Parnall felt the future lay.

Even more important was his passionate enthusiasm for the future of aviation, and it is to his credit that George Parnall put much effort into trying to persuade W T Avery to continue with, indeed expand, the company's aviation interests.

Avery's as the controlling body did not agree with either of George Parnall's ideas however, and decided against accepting his proposals. As a consequence George Parnall resigned from his position with the Avery Group in 1919, thus relinquishing his managing directorship of Parnall & Sons. However, the name of George Parnall would later become highly respected in the field of shopfitting and more especially in British aviation circles.

Meanwhile in 1923, the Avery Group moved Parnall's shopfitting concern from Narrow Wine Street to Fishponds, the new site being at Lodge Causeway. It consisted of a group of factory and office buildings that had been vacated in 1919 by a company known as Cosmos Engineering, which had manufactured aero-engines. Under Avery's control Parnall & Sons Ltd continued to flourish as a high-class firm of shopfitters, but ironically in the late 1920s it began to face stiff competition from none other than George Parnall himself who had opened a business in 1920 under the name of George Parnall & Co. This situation became such an embarrassment to the Avery Group that, when the world recession in trade began to affect shopfitting businesses, its Board of Directors decided to make an offer to George Parnall for the shopfitting side of his

PARNALL & SONS', Ltd., SHOP FRONTS.

EXPERTS & SPECIALISTS
IN MODERN SHOP FRONTS, INTERIOR FITTINGS, STRUCTURAL AND COMPLETE ALTERATIONS.

Under Avery's control, Parnall & Sons Ltd continued to produce ornate and high-class shopfronts and fittings during the 1920s. This is typical of the workmanship involved in a large provisions store of the period. (*K E Wixey Parnall collection*)

business. This was running side-by-side with the aviation interests at the Coliseum works in Park Row, George Parnall having leased the premises on forming his own company. In 1932 he accepted Avery's terms and sold them the shopfitting side of the business, a move which allowed George Parnall to concentrate more on the aircraft manufacturing part of the company which had by then moved to Yate in Gloucestershire.

Once Avery had control of the shopfitting business at the Coliseum works, the staff there were transferred together with equipment to the Lodge Causeway factory at Fishponds. There the Avery Group continued to produce its equipment and apparatus under the trading name of Parnall & Sons Ltd, an arrangement that has survived to this day.

Meanwhile during the late 1930s, the RAF was undergoing a rapid expansion programme and, in similar circumstances to the First World War, the British Government chose a number of firms to complement the main aircraft manufacturing companies on a sub-contract basis. Among these contractors was Parnall's at Fishponds. The company's previous record of aircraft production in the First World War had induced the Air Ministry to award it several contracts for the construction of wooden

The Lodge Causeway works at Fishponds, Bristol, where Parnall & Sons became permanently established. (*K E Wixey Parnall collection*)

airframes and components for de Havilland Tiger Moth training biplanes. Further orders followed during 1939 and 1940 for more Tiger Moth airframes, and a year later a large contract was awarded the Fishponds works for the production of wings for Airspeed Oxfords.

During 1942 Parnall produced wing flaps for the Fairey Barracuda carrier-borne torpedo/dive-bomber, and complete fins for the Short Stirling heavy bomber. In 1943 the company built wing flaps for another four-engined heavy bomber, the Handley Page Halifax, as well as tailplanes for Bristol Beaufighters, and numerous components for de Havilland Mosquitos.

Another important usage of the Fishponds factory was in the production of many fuselages for the large troop-carrying Airspeed Horsa glider, a type used extensively at Arnhem and before that in the landings in France in June 1944.

Parnall constructed de Havilland Tiger Moth airframes and components. K4288 served with No.18 ERFTS in 1938. (*MAP*)

After the Second World War Parnall's Fishponds factory, with its fabrication methods in metal by then well in evidence, continued to supply components to the aircraft industry. In 1952 the company built fuselages for de Havilland Venom jet fighters, and later were responsible for the production of tailplanes for the de Havilland Heron as well as wing ribs for the Dove.

Parnall built wing ribs for the de Havilland Dove. This example was owned by Smiths Aircraft Instruments. (*de Havilland Aircraft*)

Interior fittings for the Bristol Freighter were manufactured at Parnall's, Fishponds, as were the wings, fins, rudders and ailerons for the large Bristol Britannia propeller-turbine transports.

During 1955 the company produced interior fittings for the de Havilland Comet, and a decade later was manufacturing metal parts for the Hawker Siddeley 125 executive jet aircraft. The firm also produced items of furniture for the mock-up and prototype of the Concorde.

At the time of writing Parnall & Sons at Fishponds has no aviation work on hand, but the company continue to flourish in other very competitive markets.

The Fishponds Connection

The premises in which Parnall & Sons Ltd undertook its lucrative business under Avery's after the company had moved there in 1923 had, on previous occasions, been very much associated with British engineering and aeronautical developments. In view of its use by the Parnall concern for well over sixty years, as well as the site's significant aviation background, the Fishponds factory deserves detailed examination.

The works at Lodge Causeway, Fishponds, owes its inception to the enterprise of a young Irishman named Joseph Peter Brazil. Born in 1868, young Brazil found little scope for his engineering talents in his native Ireland and, like many of his countrymen, decided to seek a career in England. He served an apprenticeship with the Gloucester Wagon Company (later the Gloucester Railway Carriage and Wagon Company), and in the ensuing years developed his interests until, by 1893, he was able to enter into partnership with Messrs Owen and Holborow. Under the trading name of Owen, Brazil & Holborow, they manufactured cigarette processing machinery, hydraulic railway buffers, special castings to order and machined parts for Straker steam buses.

The business was conducted at the Vulcan Iron Works in St Philips Marsh, Bristol, and it was not long before the Straker steam buses were being built at the Vulcan works. Sidney Straker himself became a partner in the firm after the retirement of Owen in 1901, and he also founded the Straker Steam Vehicle Company in London where his partner was a man named Squire. However, the internal combustion engine became firmly established in conjunction with the progression of the motor car, and the steam bus with its noise and dirt was superseded by the motor omnibus.

This change in events Peter Brazil and Sidney Straker took in their stride. Together with Squire, who had been controlling the selling and servicing of the steam buses at Bush Lane in London, they decided to design and produce a new type of motor omnibus built around the Bussing engine.

While the London end of the business moved to larger premises at Nelson Street, Blackfriars, where it operated under the trading name of Sidney Straker & Squire, it was agreed that this site was inadequate for the purposes of selling and servicing buses, and it was decided to erect a new works in Bristol where the latest range of vehicles could be built. In consequence a four-acre site was acquired at the Lodge Causeway, Fishponds, and construction of the new factory began in January 1906. Four months later, on 7 May, the Fishponds works was officially declared open, and it was not long before a workforce of some 300 men was employed there to produce bus engines under Bussing patents. Construction of the vehicle bodies was undertaken at the London premises, and by the start of the war the Bristol and London works had, between them, supplied London with three-quarters of its omnibus fleet.

The first company to run a 24 hp Straker-Squire-Bussing motor omnibus had been the London Road-Car Company (LRCC), which began operating No.6 on 6 March, 1905. Just under three months later, on 29 May, the London General Omnibus Company (LGOC) introduced the type on its Kilburn to Marble Arch service via Maida Vale and Edgware Road. By then at least one hundred of this type of omnibus were operating in London, another concern using them being London & District Motor Bus Company Ltd, which ran under the fleet name of *Arrow*. By July 1907, more than 300 Straker-Squire motor buses were in service.

The Great Western Railway purchased a number of the buses, some with charabanc bodies, while at least one was built as a double-decker with a front-entrance stairway. One of the charabanc type worked a service between Torquay and Brixham in Devonshire. A batch of six double-deckers was sold to Bath Electric Tramways, which required them to work feeder services from the tram terminus at Bathford.

A revised engine was installed in the Straker-Squire buses from 1907, developing 30 hp and later 40 hp. By 1911 redesigned double-deckers were

This 1905/6 Straker-Squire (EH-J) is seen in service with the LGOC on its Cricklewood route. (*R W Kidner*)

being produced and ran with such companies as Worthing Motor Services; Great Eastern; London Motor Omnibus Company; Brighton, Hove & Preston United Omnibus Company; Ortona of Cambridge; and of course LRCC and LGOC in London. An improved version of the bus was produced in 1913.

Meanwhile in 1907 one of the original partners (Holborow) had retired and the Bristol firm became the Brazil Straker Company. Strangely an agreement between Straker and the Bristol-based company prevented the Brazil Straker concern gaining any credit for the Straker-Squire buses or more famous motor cars which followed. The arrangement did not appear to do justice to Peter Brazil who, it was thought, should have had his name included in the trading title, especially as Squire was not, apparently, a very active partner in the London end of the business.

Peter Brazil himself was, however, a shareholder in the Bristol tobacco manufacturing company of W D & H O Wills, and the production of Brazil's cigarette processing machinery was transferred from the Vulcan works to the new factory at Fishponds.

The Lodge Causeway works were well-planned, quite modern and airy by contemporary standards, while the new gear grinding and cutting machinery installed was considered an innovation at the time. The majority of the machines were self-contained, contrasting greatly with the outdated, steam-driven overhead belting systems then in vogue.

During 1907 the company, which was then producing nearly seventy bus engines a month, acquired the services of a young engineer and designer named Roy Fedden. As a tribute to his Irish sponsor – Peter Brazil – Fedden designed a new motor car which he named the Shamrock, and this became the prototype for a range of the well known Straker-Squire cars. As a result of this success Fedden was appointed chief engineer at the Fishponds works where all Straker-Squire motor car engines were eventually produced.

Roy Fedden was a keen competition driver in Straker-Squire cars, and often participated in motoring events before the First World War. One of Fedden's designs, the 25 hp Straker-Squire, had in fact competed in July 1907 at Brooklands first motor racing season. This trend continued after the war. Fedden designed a new car for the racing circuits. This was a 4-litre, overhead-camshaft, six-cylinder design based on a Rolls-Royce Hawk aero-engine being installed in a two-seat racing body. This car did well in the immediate postwar meetings, and after modifications was driven by Kensington-Moir on the Brooklands circuit. The fastest lap speed of the Fedden-designed Straker-Squire was 103.76 mph at a May meeting in 1921.

In addition to his motoring interests, however, Roy Fedden had developed an overwhelming enthusiasm for aeroplane engines, his main interests involving the air-cooled types such as were built in the early days by Anzani and Robert Esnault-Pelterie (REP).

Fedden convinced Brazil Straker that it would be in its interests to

One of the first contracts undertaken by Brazil Straker for the Admiralty was the overhauling of Curtiss OX-5 engines for RNAS Curtiss JN-4 'Jenny' trainers. This JN-4 is seen at RNAS Redcar. (*MAP*)

undertake work on aero-engines, and his decision stood the company in good stead when the war began in August 1914. Under Admiralty jurisdiction Brazil Straker began refurbishing engines used in aeroplanes serving mainly with the RNAS. The first contracts were for the overhauling of Curtiss OX-5 engines, an American inline type used to power the famous Curtiss JN-4 'Jenny' training biplanes, a number of which saw service with the RNAS during the 1914–18 war.

Large contracts followed for the Brazil Straker company to produce Rolls-Royce Hawk and Falcon engines; no less than 2,500 of these types were built at the Fishponds factory under Fedden's supervision. The Rolls-Royce Hawk powered airships and several types of aircraft including, the Avro 504F, Grahame-White two-seat experimental trainer, Phoenix-built Maurice Farman Longhorns, B.E.2e RNAS trainers, and the Sage Type 3 prototype (N5280).

Rolls-Royce Falcon I, II and III series engines were installed in the Avro 529, Bristol F.2A and F.2B, Fairey F.2 and F.127, the Martinsyde R.G., Martinsyde F.3 and F.4 Buzzard, Blackburn Kangaroo, Sopwith Cuckoo and the R.E.7.

R.E.7s were among the aircraft fitted with Rolls-Royce Falcons built by Brazil Straker. (*K E Wixey Parnall Collection*)

Left to right – Roy Fedden, C F Uwins and Rex Pierson with the altitude record Vickers Vespa VI in 1932. Pierson designed the Vespa, Fedden designed its supercharged Bristol Pegasus S engine and Uwins was the pilot. (*Rolls-Royce, Bristol*)

Brazil Straker also produced a number of French-designed static V-8 air-cooled 80 hp Renault radial engines, a radical design at a time when air-cooled rotary engines were in vogue. It is thought in fact that it was the French engine which may, perhaps, have induced Roy Fedden to involve Brazil Straker in a naval competition to build an aero-engine weighing less than 600 lb which could produce 300 hp. Named Mercury, Fedden's engine was first tested in April 1918. It featured fourteen cylinders divided into two rows of seven, each cylinder being made from steel and capped with an aluminium head.

The total weight of this powerplant was only 587 lb, and it produced 315 hp at 1,800 rpm. For his tireless efforts and service to the British aircraft industry during the First World War, Roy Fedden (later Sir Roy) was awarded the MBE in 1919.

In addition to aero-engines the Fishponds factory also manufactured shells for the War Office between 1914 and 1918; over three-quarters of a million of these missiles were produced on the site. Brazil Straker were also responsible for the production of a number of staff cars and heavy lorries for use by the British forces.

During 1918 a financial group known as Cosmos Engineering made a successful take-over bid for the Brazil Straker company, their chief interest being the production of aeroplane engines. This move resulted in the

The 400/450 hp Cosmos Jupiter designed by Roy Fedden was developed as the Bristol Jupiter. (*Rolls-Royce*)

automobile side of the business going to Straker-Squire in London, while Peter Brazil himself joined the Cosmos Board of Directors, and the Fishponds factory concentrated on the building of aero-engines.

Together with a Siddeley design, Roy Fedden's lightweight Mercury engine was accepted by the Air Ministry, but with the end of the war in November 1918, both companies had their government contracts cancelled. By then Fedden had already started work on improving his design, and with the Cosmos take-over providing even further opportunities to investigate the possibilities and potential of air-cooled engines for aircraft, he designed a single-row radial having nine large-bore cylinders, each with four valves. This engine – named Jupiter – was

The Cosmos Jupiter was first flown in Bristol Badger Mk.II F3496. (*MAP*)

accepted by the Air Ministry after successful bench tests, but the war ended before it could be tried out in a combat aircraft.

The Cosmos Jupiter was eventually flown for the first time on 18 June, 1919, from Filton, where it had been installed in a Bristol Badger II F3496.

This Jupiter was later fitted in the Sopwith 107 biplane, G-EAKI entered in the 1919 Schneider Trophy Contest piloted by Harry Hawker. Later a second Bristol Badger (J6492) was employed also as a Jupiter test-bed and was experimentally fitted with a variety of engine cowlings.

Fedden started work on a new radial engine at Fishponds, his ideas for incorporating two rows of large cylinders in the new design being expected to produce an output of 1,000 hp at 1,750 rpm. His plans for this powerplant were, however, thwarted when Cosmos found itself in serious financial straits, a state of affairs brought about by a combination of factors including a rather grandiose scheme in which it was intended to set up a number of Cosmos works throughout the country. Part of this programme included the development of the Fishponds factory as a toolroom and experimental centre feeding the entire group.

One of the managing directors at Cosmos, a man named Taylor, had already objected strongly on religious grounds to the company's production of cigarette machinery. He was therefore, particularly pleased when his opinions appeared to be having some effect; the very lucrative tobacco manufacturing machinery section of the business was withdrawn from Cosmos, and Peter Brazil took his licence to manufacture tobacco machinery to Brecknell, Munro and Rogers, subsequently joining their Board of Directors.

This action deprived Cosmos Engineering of a constant source of

The Cosmos Jupiter installed in the Bristol Badger Mk.III J6492. (*Rolls-Royce, Bristol*)

revenue, funds which might have possibly been enough to carry the firm until Fedden's aero-engines attracted the government into placing a contract. Consequently with the lack of the commercial profit it had enjoyed, no hope of government financial support, and realising that funds for aero-engine development would have to be self-provided, Cosmos had no alternative but to go into voluntary liquidation.

Fortunately for Roy Fedden and other Cosmos employees, the Bristol Aeroplane Company Ltd had decided to form an aero-engine division, and immediately acquired the Cosmos assets (book value £60,000) for £15,000, plus the services of Roy Fedden, five Jupiter engines and the majority of Cosmos Engineering's staff. All were automatically transferred to the Filton works of the Bristol Aeroplane Company, where work continued as Fedden and his team further developed their family of air-cooled radial engines.

As for the Fishponds-born Jupiter engine, Fedden improved upon it until it became one of the most successful radial aero-engines in Great Britain during the late 1920s and early 1930s. This Bristol Jupiter gave excellent service for a number of years to Imperial Airways, which used it

Imperial Airways' Short Calcutta *City of Alexandria* was among the successful civil aircraft to be powered by Bristol Jupiters. (*Short Brothers*)

to power such well known types of aircraft as the de Havilland D.H.66 Hercules (three 420 hp Jupiter VI), Handley Page H.P. 42/45 Hannibal/ Heracles class (four 540/555 hp Jupiter XIF/XFBM), Short Calcutta flying-boats (three 540 hp Jupiter XIF), Short Kent flying-boats (four 555 hp Jupiter XFBM), and surely the 'granddaddy' of them all, the Handley Page W.9 Hampstead, an early three-engined airliner carrying fourteen passengers and a crew of two. This aircraft was fitted in April 1926 with three 420 hp Jupiter VIs, which were installed to prove their worth during a 250-hour trials period under airline conditions. The Jupiters were flown

The Gloster Gamecock had the Bristol Jupiter VI. (*Gloster Aircraft*)

Famous Bristol combination, the Bulldog IIA airframe and Jupiter VIIF engine. (*The Aeroplane*)

in competition with Armstrong Siddeley Jaguars, but because of their much lower maintenance costs and quicker turn around during overhaul, the Jupiters were chosen by Imperial Airways to power a number of their expanding fleet of commercial aeroplane types.

The British Air Ministry also showed much interest in the Bristol Jupiter engine, and Fedden's design was chosen to power quite a number of British military aircraft during the 1920s and early 1930s.

The agile Boulton Paul Sidestrand day bomber was another of the RAF's Jupiter-powered types. (*MAP*)

These included the Boulton Paul Sidestrand (two 460 hp Jupiter VIIIF), Bristol Bulldog (490 hp Jupiter VIIF), Gloucestershire Aircraft (Nieuport) Nighthawk/Mars VI (385 hp Jupiter III), Gloster Gamecock (425 hp Jupiter VI), Handley Page Hinaidi (two 440 hp Jupiter VIII), Handley Page Clive (two 460 hp Jupiter VIIIF), Hawker Woodcock (420 hp Jupiter IV), Parnall Plover (436 hp Jupiter VI), Short Rangoon (three 540 hp Jupiter XIF) and the Westland Wapiti (550 hp Jupiter VIII, VIIIF or XFA).

A number of lesser known types of aircraft were also powered by the Jupiter engine including, the Bristol Bulldog two-seat trainer, Fokker F.VIIa, Gloster A.S.31 Survey, Handley Page Hare (J8622), Hawker Hawfinch (J8776), Hawker Hedgehog (N187), Hawker Heron (J6989), Junkers-F 13fe (G-EBZV), Saunders Roe A.4 Medina (G-EBMG), Short S.7 Valetta (G-AAJY), Short L.17 Scylla, Westland P.V.3 and the following Vickers aircraft types: the 113 Vespa (G-EBLD), Type 131 Valiant (G-EBVM), Type 132 Vildebeest Mk.I civil demonstrator (G-ABGE), Type 134 Vellore I and III, Type 203 Viastra VI (G-ABVM), Type 210 Vespa VI (G-ABIL) and the Type 220 Viastra VIII (G-AAUB).

When it is remembered that all three aeroplanes were powered by an engine conceived, gestated and born within the Lodge Causeway works, to which can be added the important aviation work done under the same roof between 1939 and 1965, the significance of these premises to the annals of British aviation history can, perhaps, be better appreciated.

George Parnall and Company

It was said of the late George Parnall that he was a man of vision, competence and aggression when it came to commercial enterprise. He was endowed with a tenacity of purpose, possessed great determination, and was destined to have his own aviation business compete against the giants among contemporary British aircraft manufacturers.

After his resignation as head of the Avery-controlled firm of Parnall & Sons in 1919, George Parnall took up a lease on the Coliseum building in Park Row, Bristol. There he inaugurated his own shopfitting and aircraft manufacturing business under the trade name of George Parnall & Co. This was no reckless gamble, but a well planned scheme to introduce a programme of work in which innovative ideas could be applied practically in the fields of both shopfitting and aeroplane manufacture.

The Coliseum, having already been used for aircraft construction on behalf of the Admiralty during the First World War, presented no great problem when it came to setting up the necessary equipment for the

HRH The Duke of York (later HM King George VI) with George Parnall on the Parnall stand at the 1929 Olympia Aero Show. They are by the tail of the Elf with the Peto on the right. (*Mark Parnall*)

George Parnall at his desk in the Yate works during 1930. (*Mark Parnall*)

production of aeroplanes alongside that required to construct shopfittings. The walls of the Coliseum were soon resounding to the noise of skilled workmen creating, assembling and adjusting fittings, show cases and shop fronts for an increasing number of George Parnall's customers. One of the largest contracts awarded the firm was that to supply most of the fittings and equipment at Peter Robinson's large store then being erected in London's Oxford Circus.

Determined to fulfil his ambition to build aeroplanes, George Parnall took the first step in that direction by acquiring the services of Harold Bolas as his chief aircraft designer.

Bolas had remained at Parnall & Sons' Brislington factory after the war, but when George Parnall offered him the position as chief designer of aircraft at the Coliseum works with his own company, Bolas immediately accepted. His first design, the Puffin, was built at the Coliseum beside the shopfittings taking shape there, and made its first flight during November 1920. The Parnall Plover single-seat naval fighter followed in 1922, and the following year saw the appearance of the Possum triplane. It was also in 1923 that the first of the ultra-light Parnall Pixie series emerged from the Coliseum to make its maiden flight from the Bristol Aeroplane Company's Aerodrome at Filton; in the early 1920s all Parnall aircraft were test-flown from Filton.

As George Parnall's business interests spread, the main Coliseum works were supplemented by other sites previously used during the war by Parnall & Sons, these being the factories located at Mivart Street and Quakers Friars. Another works was acquired at Feeder Road, Bristol, where the fabrication of metal components accounted for most of the tasks performed. As well as those offices incorporated into the Coliseum works, others had been opened by George Parnall's company, one in London at

Comparison in sizes on Yate aerodrome with the Parnall Plover naval amphibian on the left, diminutive Pixie centre, and the larger Possum experimental triplane on the right. (*K E Wixey Parnall collection*)

Refurbishing and production of de Havilland D.H.9A general purpose biplanes provided Parnall with valuable government contracts in the 1920s. The two D.H.9As pictured here are from No. 39 Squadron RAF circa 1926. (*Hawker Siddeley Aviation*)

Evelyn House, 62 Oxford Street, and the other in Berkeley Square, Bristol. The Coliseum offices were situated along a gallery at one end of the building, and it was there that Bolas drew up his earlier designs for the company.

It was during the early 1920s that George Parnall accepted certain Air Ministry contracts for the refurbishing of a number of de Havilland D.H.9A general purpose biplanes for the RAF, and also for the production of a batch of new machines of the same type.

Realising the significance of these contacts to the expansion of his aircraft manufacturing business, while at the same time appreciating the limitations imposed by the Bristol works on any increase in aircraft construction work, George Parnall decided to acquire more suitable premises from which to conduct his aeronautical enterprises. His choice fell on Yate, a village in Gloucestershire (now part of Avon) nine miles

The B.E.2c was one of the types rebuilt at No. 3 (Western) Aircraft Repair Depot. (*MAP*)

from Bristol. The facilities appeared ideal and included brick-built engine repair shops, spacious flight sheds constructed of timber and asbestos sheeting, and a small aerodrome.

At one time Yate was part of a small agricultural community, but gained some prominence when coal was discovered beneath its fields. A mining company (Long's) soon had a coal mine operating and Yate village increased in size as the miners and their families moved into the area. The mine eventually closed down, but the old mine shaft remained and was used to supply water from its depths to the industrial site which grew up at Yate.

During the First World War it was decided to construct an aircraft maintenance base near the old Yate mine, where machines of the RFC could be brought for repairs and major overhaul. The site was known as Number 3 (Western) Aircraft Repair Depot and was the third aeroplane supply depot in the country. It was built during 1917 by German prisoners of war who were billeted at a camp on the Yate to Westerleigh Road by the entrance to Westerleigh Common.

At least 200 combat aircraft are recorded as having been rebuilt at Yate between the depot's completion and the end of the war. All of these machines, with the exception of four, were contained within the military serial block B8831–B9030, the four exceptions being B8837–B8840, which were allocated to Blackburn Kangaroos.

As a matter of interest, a few examples of individual aircraft known to have been rebuilt at No. 3 ARD, between 1917 and 1918 were as follows: B8874, B8876, B8880, B8881, B8883–B8887, B8889, B8900, B8907, B8909 (R.E.8); B8864, B8896 (B.E.2c/d); B8850–B8854, B8899 (B.E.2e); B8911–

Inside the planning office of George Parnall & Co, Yate, on 28 November, 1930. (*Mark Parnall*)

A team of draftsmen pose for the camera in the drawing office at Parnall's Yate works in 1930. (*Mark Parnall*)

B8912 (Sopwith 1½ Strutter); B8921 (Sopwith Camel); B8914 (Arab-powered Bristol F.2B); B8915 (Puma-powered Bristol F.2B); B8925, B8928, B8941, B8947 (Falcon-powered Bristol F.2B).

George Parnall's acquisition of the Yate site meant that not only was the design and construction of aircraft possible in a single concentrated area, but the test flying of aeroplanes could be carried out from the company's own aerodrome instead of at Filton. Although by the end of 1925 the transfer of George Parnall's aviation business from Bristol to Yate had been completed, the company's brochures continued to refer to the Coliseum works as well as Yate aerodrome and the London office in Oxford Street.

George Parnall's decision to branch out on his own and acquire the Yate site can, perhaps, be considered as the main contributory factor in the area's eventual development as an industrial centre. Even so, during Parnall's earlier days at Yate the surrounding countryside retained much of its rural character.

The company's main administration offices occupied the entire block of buildings at the western end of the aerodrome and, together with the works, were accessible by a road through the railway station yard and the cattle market!

At the opposite end of the aerodrome was located the old RFC and RAF headquarters, and it was within these premises that George Parnall had his design offices installed. From there one had, it appears, a

Typical 1930 office environment at Parnall's Yate factory. (*Mark Parnall*)

41

The cabinet-making shop at Yate in 1930, shows the amount of shopfitting being undertaken alongside Parnall's aviation work. (*Mark Parnall*)

'grandstand' view of the complete aerodrome with its rather undulating surface.

The longest take-off run was limited to 1,500 ft. Although this run was into the prevailing wind, at the end of it pilots were faced with a climb over the works and hangars, a main line railway, a group of railway sidings and a number of houses.

Some interesting facts relating to Yate aerodrome have come to light among old records, obviously intended as a guide for pilots and aircrew. The aerodrome itself was classed as a private, unlicensed and civil flying field not available for use, except in an emergency, without permission being previously obtained from the controlling authority – entered as George Parnall & Co, Coliseum Works, Park Row, Bristol.

Situated in the county of Gloucestershire, the position of Yate aerodrome was given as 51.33N and 2.25W, local position 9½ miles northeast of Bristol, immediately north of Yate and on the east side of Bristol–Gloucester railway. Landmarks by day were the railway crossing, loop-lines and triangular junction 1¼ miles south by west. The nature of the aerodrome surroundings was not very encouraging to the unfamiliar pilot, being described as undulating and somewhat enclosed with small fields and a warning that it was not very suitable for emergency landings!

The landing area was 700 yards north–south, 600 yards northeast–southwest, 600 yards east–west, and 750 yards southest–northwest. The

This view gives some idea of the extent to which the Yate works of George Parnall were developed from 1925. (*T I Jackson Ltd*)

altitude of Yate aerodrome above mean sea level was 250 ft, while the surface conditions were described as grass-covered with a fairly good surface in the southern portion, rough with an overgrown furrow in the northern portion, a northwest–southeast depression crossing the landing area and a slight slope down towards the northeast.

A number of obstructions were listed including, a hedge on the north side, a hedge on the east side, the aircraft works 20 ft high in the southeast corner, houses and trees alongside the road on the south side, and hangars 30 ft high plus buildings and railway telegraph wires on the west side. A warning note was also given that cattle grazed on the landing ground, and that one hour was required to clear the area of animals!

By day the marking to look out for was a concrete compass base in the southwest corner of the aerodrome. No signals were given and wind direction was indicated by a wind sleeve flown from a hangar situated in the centre of the west side. The aerodrome was, it appeared, unusable at night as there were no floodlights to show markings, signals or wind direction. The same non-operational conditions applied in fog.

Accommodation for aircraft at Yate comprised three hangars, all constructed of timber and each formed into two bays. Two of these hangars were 210 ft wide and 65 ft long with a door 65 ft wide and 14 ft 6 in high. The third hangar was 200 ft in width, 102 ft in length and had a door 95 ft wide and 19 ft high.

Aircraft handling facilities at Yate consisted of a landing party, repairs to aeroplanes in the works and refuelling arrangements. It was emphasised,

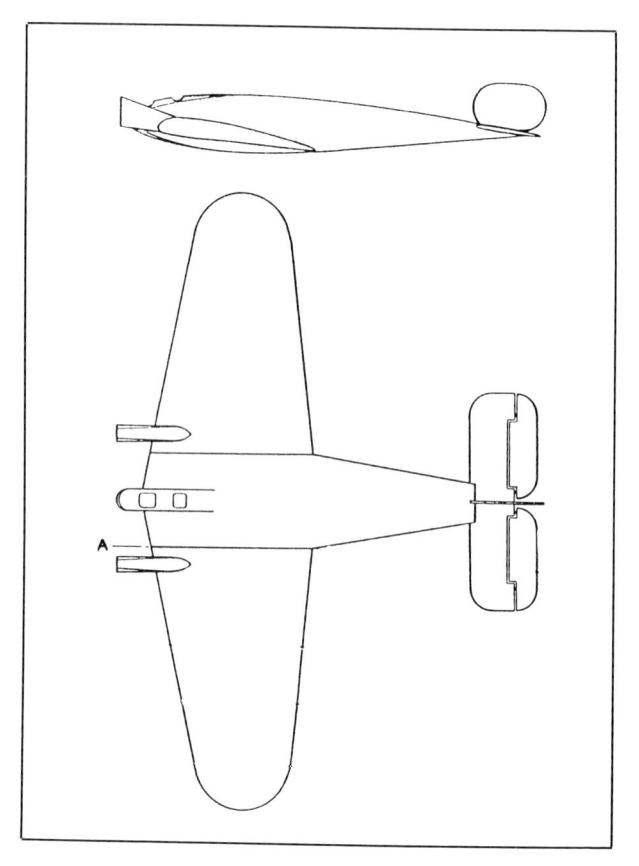

This drawing is of the 'Bodyless' monoplane designed by the Russian designer M Voevodskii, and upon which Harold Bolas based his ideas for projected Parnall 'bodyless' aircraft, but which came to nothing. (*K E Wixey Parnall collection*)

however, that only small stocks of fuel and oil were kept on the aerodrome. Flying hours were restricted to between sunrise and sunset, and charges for the use of facilities at Yate aerodrome were by arrangement with George Parnall & Co. However, despite the obstacles, a number of civil aircraft made use of the airfield, and among types observed at Yate were British Aircraft Eagles and Double Eagles, Short Scions and a de Havilland Gipsy Moth belonging to an AID inspector.

During his term of office at Yate as chief designer, Harold Bolas produced a number of varying military and civil types of aircraft, some of which were quite aesthetically pleasing in appearance, and they carried names including, Pixie, Perch, Pike, Peto, Pipit, Prawn, Parasol, Imp and Elf.

Bolas also made some initial design studies of his own which featured a

Two of Harold Bolas's designs for George Parnall included the tiny Pixie (top) and handsome Elf two-seat biplane. At the time of the photograph the Elf (G-AAFH) was flying with the Cornish Aviation Company of St Austell.
(*Mark Parnall and W E Chapman*)

'bodyless' monoplane. This design had the appearance of a giant Manta-Ray, and was based on the profound theories of the Russian aircraft designer M Voevodskii.* The idea was to marry what was virtually a flying-wing to a very wide fuselage, which resulted in a continuous aerofoil section for both the wing and body. External bracing for the wing areas was complete eliminated, and the extremely thick monoplane wing centre-section was contoured aerodynamically to provide a smooth profile devoid of any angular or sudden changes of form. Although this design was based on excellent theory, Bolas was disappointed when the eventual wind-tunnel tests on the model of his 'bodyless' monoplane indicated that, in practice, the aeroplane would have very little advantage in performance over the earlier biplane fighters that had appeared at the end of the First

*Frequently incorrectly given as Woyevodsky.

Parnall Pixie III G-EBJG, which Mrs Fry helped prepare for the 1926 Light Aeroplane Trials, held at Lympne. The engine was a 32 hp Bristol Cherub III. (*Eric Harlin*)

World War. As a result of these findings Harold Bolas gave up the whole idea of his 'bodyless' monoplane project, and continued to design more orthodox types of aeroplane for George Parnall.

In 1929 Harold Bolas left George Parnall to take up residence in the United States, where a new career was apparently in the offing.

When he left England there is little doubt that Harold Bolas bequeathed his native land with a legacy of technical achievements which undoubtedly contributed to the advancement of British aviation. Bolas returned to England many years later, and is believed to have been living in Bath during the 1950s.

Some interesting personal recollections of the early days at Yate have been passed on to the author by two ex-employees of George Parnall. First Mrs Margaret Fry, still living in Yate at the time of writing, joined the company on 3 December, 1925, and was their first female employee. At the age of sixteen (then Miss May) she can recall seeing the little Pixie III

Although of very poor quality, this photograph is extremely rare, and shows Parnall Plover naval fighters inside Yate works in the 1920s. The nearest machine is N9608. (*K E Wixey Parnall collection via F E Draycott*)

Although the quality of this photograph is poor, it shows Mrs Margaret Fry as forewoman at Parnalls at Yate. As Miss May, she was the first female employee taken on by George Parnall, late in 1925. (*Mrs Margaret Fry*)

G-EBJG being prepared for the 1926 Lympne Light Aeroplane Trials, and distinctly remembers noticing a number of Parnall Plovers in the works for servicing and minor modifications. Margaret Fry worked on the Parnall Pike, Peto, Pipit, Elf and other types and, at the age of twenty-five she was appointed forewoman. Later, as superintendent of the covering and doping shop, Margaret Fry became involved with Parnall's contract work on the Percival Gull Fours, and in 1934 supervised the covering on the G.4/31 general purpose biplane.

One unusual and rather sad story of Margaret Fry's concerned the Parnall Elf biplanes owned in succession by Lord Apsley. Both machines were, in turn, hangared in Parnall's flight shed, his Lordship's home being not far away at Petty France. Lady Apsley had broken her back in a riding accident, but despite her handicap still wanted to fly with her husband. In order that her wish could be fulfilled, Lady Apsley was hoisted into the cockpit by means of a crane with a special attachment.

George Parnall was referred to by Mrs Fry as 'a lovely gentleman', and she clearly recalls his friendly chats with the staff on the progress being made. He often brought his sons Dennis and Alan with him on these visits, and was particularly interested in the progress being made with the G.4/31 general purpose biplane and its prospects as a possible production aircraft.

Another old employee of George Parnall's is J E Draycott, who at the time of writing lives in Keighley, West Yorkshire. He can remember answering an advertisement in the *Bristol Evening Post* in which George

The Parnall Elf prototype, later registered G-AAFH, and owned by Lord Apsley. (*T I Jackson Ltd*)

Parnall & Co sought a licensed ground engineer who would be prepared to operate as a works inspector.

At that time Draycott was employed with Birmingham Aero Services as a licensed ground engineer, this company flying from Keynsham, near Bristol, from where they gave joy-rides to the public. However, the depression was beginning to hit numerous concerns throughout the country, and Birmingham Aero Services being no exception, they were forced to close down.

A much tidier working area (than in the previous views) is revealed in this photograph of the cabinet shop at Yate, where George Parnall's 'bread and butter' shopfitting business continued beside aeroplane manufacture. (*Mark Parnall*)

In the meantime, and in response to Mr Draycott's reply to the advertisement, Charlie Baker, a chief inspector on George Parnall's staff, went to Keynsham to see him and seemed only too pleased to engage Draycott there and then.

This amicable arrangement took place in 1929 when the first Parnall Elf was being built, and really came about because the AID, which supervised civil aviation in those days, insisted on George Parnall's company employing a licensed ground engineer. It appears that under the regulations then in force a competent engineer, in this case Mr Draycott, could certify the construction and airworthiness of any civil aeroplane before its issue of a Certificate of Airworthiness by the Air Ministry, and before each daily certificate of airworthiness was issued.

When he first started with George Parnall, Mr Draycott found the firm had very little in the way of Air Ministry contracts forthcoming, and was mainly engaged with work on the Elf, the Peto submarine-borne aircraft and the Pipit single-seat fighter. Other work being undertaken at that time included some special wings of an experimental nature being built for the Royal Aircraft Establishment at Farnborough, the construction of spare parts for the Air Ministry and initial work on the Prawn experimental single-seat flying-boat.

In those days the Parnall Works Inspection Department comprised just four men: Charlie Baker the chief, E Dowling, a man named Price, who

The machine shop in the Yate works of George Parnall & Co in 1930. The contemporary belt-driven machinery is visible. (*Mark Parnall*)

Extremely rare picture of the Parnall Plover naval fighter (N9610) in amphibious configuration, taken on Yate aerodrome in about 1922–23. (*K E Wixey Parnall collection via F E Draycott*)

was an ex-boxer and of course Mr Draycott. The AID inspector then was Reg Amey who lived at *Fir Tree Cottage* on the main road through Yate. He also had an office at Yate, and for his work was supplied with and travelled in an Air Ministry Trojan van with solid tyres. In this vehicle Reg Amey carried his calibrating and c of g equipment!

Among a number of well-known personalities who visited George Parnall's Yate works over the years were Sir Philip Sassoon, Sir Charles Kingsford Smith, the Earl of Limerick and Edgar Percival. Indeed it was Edgar Percival's contract awarded to Parnall for the construction of the first twenty-four production Percival Gull monoplanes that helped George Parnall to survive as long as it did.

George Parnall himself was a founder member of the Society of British Aircraft Constructors, one of the reasons why his company was selected, under approval, to supply aeroplanes designed for military purposes to the Air Ministry. Regrettably however, apart from a small batch of Plover naval fighters, none of George Parnall's aircraft designs reached production status.

With the exception of a few civil machines, most Parnall-designed aircraft were used for experimental purposes, and any quantity production involved aircraft designed by other companies and built under contract. This situation prompted George Parnall to sell the top works at Yate to Newman's the electrical engineers in 1932, the same year that Avery's bought the shopfitting business run by George Parnall in Bristol.

A year later the Nazis' rise to power in Germany was posing a new threat

The only Parnall-designed aeroplane on the Yate site in 1935 was the G.4/31 general purpose biplane, K2772. (*MAP*)

in Europe, and Britain's politicians became acutely aware of the dangers threatening across the Channel. One result was an expansion scheme for the Royal Air Force, a programme that was well under way by 1935. That

George Geach Parnall with his company's Elf biplane with its 105 hp Cirrus Hermes engine. (*Mark Parnall*)

same year the only Parnall aeroplane nearing completion at Yate was the G.4/31 general purpose biplane, already obsolete in its concept. Another project at Yate, the Parnall two-seat fighter designed to Air Ministry specification F.5/33, had only reached the drawing board stage, and despite a documented report being presented to the Air Ministry on this design in 1934, it did not attain even mock-up status.

George Parnall, realising the Government would be requiring his Yate works for further aviation contracts, decided to sell his aviation business, at the same time retiring from the aeronautical scene. As a result of this decision the Yate site was sold to Nash & Thompson Ltd (later Parnall Aircraft Limited), while George Parnall retired to live in Bristol. But alas, his well earned retirement was relatively short-lived for, on 23 May, 1936, he suffered a cerebral haemorrhage at his home at Clifton. Just under a month later, on 21 June, he died.

In its obituary of George Parnall *The Aeroplane* (24 June, 1936) said of him – 'George Parnall retired from business fortunately still a rich man. He was a cheery soul, always full of social and commercial as well as technical ideas, about which he loved to argue in a friendly way. He will be greatly missed wherever Trade people gather together.'

George Parnall was described by the Bristol newspapers as a very fine chess player. He won the championship of the Bristol and Clifton Chess Club several years in succession, became president of the Bristol Literary and University Club, and was indeed an exceedingly popular personality among his host of friends in and around the Bristol area.

Even so, despite his popularity as a Bristolian, George Parnall's body was returned to his native Cornwall where he was buried in the parish churchyard at St Gennys.

Parnall Aircraft Limited

It says much for George Parnall that the new group which formed at Yate decided to use the name Parnall in the company's new title of Parnall Aircraft Limited. This firm was established by the former racing motorist A G Frazer-Nash and Capt E Gratton-Thompson, both of whom were on the Board of Directors of the new company. Gratton-Thompson himself later became managing director, while Parnall Aircraft's chairman was Lieut-General Sir Ridley Vaughn KCB, KBE, DSO, who was also associated with Imperial Chemical Industries.

Frazer-Nash and Gratton-Thompson had invented and produced the Frazer-Nash hydraulically-operated aircraft gun turret, which was developed under the trading name of Nash & Thompson Ltd at Tolworth in Surrey. The continuing development and production of these turrets, together with the Vane oil motors which worked in conjunction with them, was transferred to the Yate works of the newly formed Parnall Aircraft company in 1935.

It is interesting to observe that, as a result of heavy over-subscribing, the subscription lists for 608,000 ordinary shares of five shillings each in

Close-up of the Frazer-Nash 'lobster-back' segmented gun-turret installed in a Hawker Demon two-seat fighter. These modified Demons were known as Turret Demons. (*British Aerospace*)

This very rare photograph shows one of the Parnall Heck 2C monoplanes at Yate. Standing on the left of the group of Parnall employees is Crosby Warren, a test pilot who was killed while testing a Gloster Meteor. (*K E Wixey Parnall collection via Margaret Fry*)

Parnall Aircraft, were closed at 09.05 hrs on the day of issue, 28 May, 1935.

Meanwhile the RAF had been having problems with its Hawker Demon two-seat fighters. In a 200 mph slipstream the gunner in his rear cockpit was having difficulty in operating efficiently the .303-in Lewis machine-gun, mounted on a gun-ring. To overcome this handicap Frazer-Nash designed a special hydraulically-operated open turret or shield known as the 'lobster-back', so named because of its segmented back-shield.

Normally the shield was 'closed', but the segments opened with the gunner's movements. Later production Demons were built with the 'lobster-back' incorporated from the start, and quite a number of machines

Although not accepted for service in the RAF, Parnall's Type 382 two-seat trainer, known as the Heck III, was quite an advanced concept for its day. The aircraft is seen here after roll-out at Yate. (*Parnall & Sons via John Long LRPS*)

were converted. The turrets were produced at Yate by Parnall Aircraft, and Margaret Fry could recall sixty-two Demons being converted at Yate where, she said – 'they were cut in half to have gun turrets fitted'.

All Demons fitted with these 'lobster-back' turrets or shields, including the later machines built new with the turrets fitted (built under contract by Boulton Paul Aircraft), were known as Hawker Turret Demons, and the type served with a number of RAF fighter squadrons until at least 1939.

In the covering shop at Yate, work was undertaken to produce drogue targets for air-gunnery practice, and several thousands of these, in assorted colours, were made at the works. In addition Parnall's began a certain amount of sub-contract work in conjunction with the RAF expansion programme, and numbers of components were produced for Armstrong Whitworth Whitley bombers, a type that bore the brunt of the early bombing raids over Germany in the Second World War.

Meanwhile when Nash & Thompson took over from George Parnall in 1935, only the G.4/31 biplane remained on the books and, although designed to a 1931 specification, was still only at the testing stage. This aeroplane, like the others built to the same Air Ministry specification by other companies, was unsuccessful. The new Parnall company did, however, undertake the construction of six Hendy Heck low-wing cabin monoplanes which were designated Parnall Heck 2c. A further development of the Heck, the Type 382 training monoplane, emerged from Yate in 1939, but it was not accepted for service by the Air Ministry.

Another contract at the Yate works was the construction of the large tailplane for the first Armstrong Whitworth Ensign airliner.

A nose gun turret built at Yate by Parnall for the Vickers Wellington Mk.IA.
(K E Wixey Parnall collection)

The Frazer-Nash front gun turret is prominent on this Whitley Mk.IV as its crew prepare to board for a raid on Germany in 1940. (*MAP*)

In the meantime considerable extensions were being made to the works at Yate in order that production of aircraft gun turrets could be increased. The Air Ministry orders for manually-operated gun-rings, which had been produced alongside the Demon 'lobster-back' shields, were now superseded by contracts for large numbers of enclosed turrets of the type with which an ever increasing quantity of Whitley and Wellington bombers were being equipped. At one time, records show that Whitleys and Harrows were observed at Yate in connection with gun turret developments for British bombers.

It was in fact the 1938 Mk. III version of the Whitley that first had a Nash & Thompson turret, this being a nose installation housing a single Vickers 'K' gun. Also fitted to this mark of the Whitley was a Nash & Thompson ventral retractable turret, with two .303-in Browning machine-guns and a 360 degree traverse. The turrets produced at Yate were complex assemblies of precision-machined metal components which were cowled in perspex to allow for the best possible field of view for the gunner. The ventral retractable type turrets as installed at first in the Whitley III, had perspex windows set into the metal skin.

It was not long before Frazer-Nash turrets for the Blackburn Botha, Short Sunderland and, later, Avro Lancaster, were rolling off Parnall's assembly lines. The company was also to produce large numbers of Supermarine Spitfire airframes and wing leading-edges, as a result of which it became one of the largest Spitfire airframe sub-contractors in Great Britain.

56

Spitfire wing leading-edges under construction at Parnall's Yate factory during the Second World War. (*K E Wixey Parnall collection*)

Meanwhile the political scene worsened in Europe, and on 3 September, 1939, Great Britain was once again at war with Germany.

It was later confirmed that, five days before the start of the Second World War, a German reconnaissance aircraft had flown over Yate. Documents recovered after the war from German archives proved this without doubt. An aerial photograph of Parnall's factory was taken on 22 August, 1939; the picture was taken from the German aircraft through light cloud. In the resulting negative both Parnall's and Newman's works were pinpointed (Newman's mainly produced artillery shells), the aerodrome being indicated by the reference number 10/284. Linked with the photograph was a copy of a section of the Ordnance survey map then covering Yate, including descriptions of the various buildings in the area.

A directive was later issued to German airmen emphasising the importance of Parnall, especially in relation to the production of bomber gun turrets. The document stated how destroying the Yate works could seriously affect British bomber output, and included the exact location of Parnall's factory beside the main Bristol to Wickwar railway line about two kilometres north of the double junction at Westerleigh. It was pointed out that a railway line branched north-westerly in an arc towards Thornbury and that immediately adjoining the factory was Yate aerodrome – 'der Flugplatz Yate (10/284)'.

After the Battle of Britain had been won by the RAF Fighter Command the Luftwaffe turned mainly to night attacks against Britain's towns and cities, but ironically, tragedy struck Parnall's Yate works in an unexpected daylight sortie by a lone German raider on the afternoon of 27 February, 1941. The bomber, a Heinkel He 111, was first observed by a Mr Blair of Tortworth who said he saw the enemy aircraft flying over the railway

```
GB 7451 b                                                                    Lfd.Nr.68
Nur für den Dienstgebrauch           Yate                    Genst. 5. Abt. Oktober 1940
Bild Nr.: 580 S 25      Flugzeugzellenfabrik Parnall Aircraft Co. Ltd.    Karte 1:100 000
Aufnahme vom 29.8.39     Länge (westl. Greenw.): 2° 25' 30"  Breite: 51° 32' 30"    GB/E 27
                         Mißweisung: —11° 21' (Mitte 1940)  Zielhöhe über NN 70 m
```

This view of Yate, on which Parnall Aircraft and Newman's works are outlined, was taken by a German reconnaissance aircraft on 29 August, 1939. (*K E Wixey Parnall collection*)

station at Charfield. It was low enough to him to see the swastika on the vertical tail surfaces.

It was simplicity itself for the German crew to comply with the Luftwaffe intelligence reports concerning Parnall's location. They just followed the railway tracks which gave them a direct bearing onto their target. As the Heinkel approached Yate not a shot was fired, and to confuse any anti-aircraft gunners in the area, the German pilot lowered his undercarriage as he approached the Yate factory, where many who saw the bomber thought it was a British aeroplane landing, precisely the impression the German pilot intended to make when lowering his wheels. Consequently, before anyone realised what was happening the bombs were falling at the same time as the alert sounded. The time was 14.30 hr and, within seconds, the

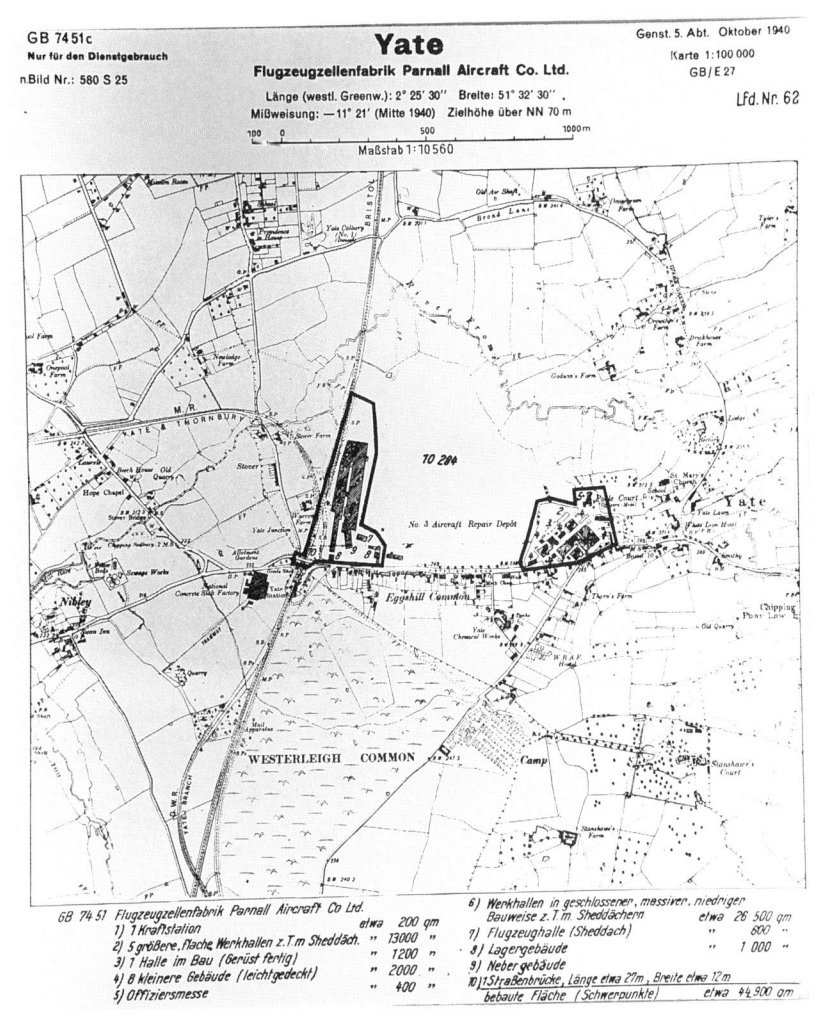

This Luftwaffe map, drawn in 1940, provides a good indication of the layout at Yate. Reference is still made here to No. 3 Aircraft Repair Depot. Parnall's works are on the left. (*Photocopy via T I Jackson Ltd, Yate*)

enemy bomber had vanished unscathed into low cloud.

The bombs consisted of a cluster of high-explosives and one oil-bomb, the latter dropping on the drawing office which swiftly became an inferno. One witness who was thrown clear by the blast suffered minor injuries when his office was demolished. He said – 'the stick-bombs appeared to literally "march" up the length of the works'. Another ex-Parnall employee, Ron Guy, recalled working in the turret assembly shop when the bombs fell. He said they missed the turret shop, but hit the main office and

Flugzeugzellenfabrik Parnall Aircraft Co. Ltd., Yate (74 51)

Das Werk ist Haupthersteller von „Doppel- und Vierling-MG-Türmen", die u. a. als Heckstände in englische Kampfflugzeuge eingebaut werden. Parnall ist außer der Firma Nash & Thompson, London-Tolworth (78 15, lfd. Nr. 63), der einzige Hersteller dieser Türme, jedoch von wesentlich größerer Leistungsfähigkeit.

Eine Zerstörung des Werkes würde die Kampfflugzeugausbringung stark beeinträchtigen.

Das Werk liegt an der Bahnlinie Bristol—Wickwar, etwa 2 km nördlich der Doppelkreuzung von Westerleigh. An dem Werk zweigt eine Bahnlinie im Bogen nach NW (Thornbury) ab. Unmittelbar am Werk liegt der Flugplatz Yate (10 284).

PARNALL AIRCRAFT FACTORY YATE (7451)

THIS FACTORY IS THE MAIN PRODUCER OF "2 x 4MG TURRETS" WHICH ARE FITTED IN ENGLISH FIGHTER PLANES.

PARNALL IS A SUBSIDIARY OF NASH & THOMPSON LONDON & TOLWORTH (78 15 REF NR. 63) & IS THE ONLY PRODUCER OF THESE TURRETS & ARE ABLE TO PRODUCE IN STILL LARGER QUANTITIES.

TO DESTROY THIS FACTORY WOULD RESTRICT PRODUCTION OF FIGHTER PLANES.

THE FACTORY IS BUILT ALONG THE RAILWAY LINE BRISTOL-WICKWAR APPROX 2 KILOM NORTH OF DOUBLE JUNCTION OF WESTERLEIGH.

ADJOINING THE FACTORY THE RAILWAY LINE BRANCHES OFF TO N.W. (THORNBURY).

ASSEMBLY (SHOPS) AT FACTORY NEAR YATE AIRFIELD (10 284).

TRANSLATION OF GERMAN TEXT.

◄ Instructions issued to Luftwaffe bomber crews in which the importance of Yate to the British war effort was explained, plus guidelines on how to approach the factory. The English translation is below. (*K E Wixey Parnall collection*)

assembly shop. Luckily three of the six high-explosive bombs failed to explode, or casualties would have been even higher. These three unexploded bombs fell on the erecting shop, one hitting a girder, ricocheting round the walls of the shops and ending up spinning in the centre of the floor. The second unexploded bomb was found later beneath a pile of debris, while the third was discovered the following morning propped up in one corner of the shop as though it had been carefully placed there.

Entrance to Parnall's main office block at Yate following the German air attacks of 1941. (*K E Wixey Parnall collection*)

The front of Parnall's Yate works after the German raid in February 1941.
(*T I Jackson Ltd*)

As it was, another bomb of the delayed-action type exploded ten minutes after rescue work had begun, causing considerable loss of life and injuries.

A vivid account of the bombing attacks on Parnall's at Yate was given to the author by, once again, Margaret Fry. She remembers the German

This view, taken after the German air attack in February 1941, shows the extent of the damage. The railway sidings are in the top half of the picture. (*T I Jackson Ltd*)

bomber swooping low over the factory with the gunner, who was clearly visible, 'popping away' with his machine-gun at the factory buildings. At that moment Margaret Fry was closing the doors of her department after the other women workers had run to the air-raid shelters, and she readily admits her luck in not having been hit by one of the enemy aircraft's bullets. The delayed-action bomb that exploded did so just as Mrs Fry was running for the shelter. As a result of the explosion she received injuries to her ears which unfortunately, despite an operation, necessitated her wearing a hearing-aid thereafter.

This first raid on Parnall's cost the lives of over fifty employees, while many others were injured. Nevertheless production was dispersed very quickly to eleven other sites. Despite inches of murky water covering the floor, by the morning after the attack, work had already started again in the turret shop! Just over a week later, on Friday, 7 March, the Luftwaffe struck again at the Yate works. Again the raider was a single Heinkel He 111.

Parnall had received notification that the Heinkel involved in the first raid on the factory had been shot down at Devizes in Wiltshire, but many of Parnall's employees were convinced the second attack was made by the same aircraft. The second raid did not cause as many casualties as the first (fortunately on this occasion the purple warning had been given and most workers had managed to reach the shelters), but it did create serious material damage to the factory causing production to temporarily cease. Twelve high-explosive bombs were dropped, and as a result the turret

Devastation in the main turret shop at Parnall after the second raid on the works by a German Heinkel on 7 March, 1941. (*T I Jackson Ltd*)

shop, which received a direct hit, was wrecked as were some of the other factory buildings. As the for German Heinkel, it once again escaped from the Yate area unscathed, despite the fact that it had been seen flying very low over the Sharpness Docks area by at least one eye-witness. Local reports did suggest, however, that the German bomber may have been flying too low for any anti-aircraft guns in the area to be effective!

Some of the Parnall employees killed in the two raids were buried in a common grave in the churchyard of the parish church of St Mary at Yate. These included a number of victims who could not be identified. Others who perished in the German attacks were buried elsewhere. A memorial plaque records the names of all those who died at Yate works as a result of the enemy action, and can be seen in the main entrance to the present works at Yate belonging to T I Jackson Ltd. On Sunday 26, February, 1950, a service of dedication and the unveiling of a memorial to the Parnall employees killed in the 1941 air raids on the Yate works was held in St Mary's church, and on the following day a similar ceremony was held in the company offices.

Meanwhile after the second air attack on Yate, the Ministry of Aircraft Production ordered immediate dispersal of the factory.

A mammoth round-the-clock operation began which was accomplished in one week! Much of the production machinery and equipment that was salvageable from Yate was transferred to Boulton Mills near Dursley, Gloucestershire, and during the week from 7 March, 1941, a cold period with a thick layer of snow carpeting the ground, lorries were busy trundling through the lanes around Dursley carrying lathes, drilling machinery and other production equipment to Boulton Mills. This traffic

Avro Lancaster rear fuselages under construction in the main structure jigs at the Temple Cloud works of Parnall in April 1945. (*K E Wixey Parnall collection*)

Lancaster fuselage assembly section, No. 1 Factory, Temple Cloud, about April 1945. (*K E Wixey Parnall collection*)

Two Parnall employees working on the fin of a Lancaster in the Temple Cloud No. 2 Factory. This section of the works contained the Lancaster and Lincoln fin structure assembly line. (*K E Wixey Parnall collection*)

In this view of the new Yate works, rebuilt after the German air raids of 1941, the main turret shop is in full production on Frazer-Nash F.N.121 rear turrets for Lancasters. (*K E Wixey Parnall collection*)

continued for days as hundreds of tons of machinery converged on Dursley, the town's streets some days being blocked from end to end with lorries loaded with Parnall's machinery as they waited their turn to enter the Boulton Mills site. As a result of all this effort, it was only eight days after the second German attack on the Yate works before the first section transferred to the Dursley area was operating, no mean feat under the difficult circumstances.

Soon busloads of workers were travelling to and from the Boulton Mills factory and many cars were to be seen parked in the area. It was after the works had been established at Boulton Mills that Parnall's received a visit from HRH The Duke of Kent.

Parnall also operated a number of other sites around the Bristol area as well as in different parts of the country, especially after the raids on Yate. These satellite factories were located temporarily at first in such unlikely surroundings as a cider factory (Wickwar), New Mills (Charfield), Abbey Mills (Kingswood near Wooton-under-Edge), Central Garage and Gough's Garage (Fishponds), the Slab Works (Yate), a corset factory (Kingswood, Bristol), Magnal Products (Warmley, near Bristol), Baughn's (Stroud, Glos) and the New Mendip Engineering Co (Melksham, Wilts).

The Boulton Mills site near Dursley was also one of those dispersed works classed as temporary, while later on Parnall's production was concentrated more into semi-permanent quarters located at Arnold's Field

Lancaster F.N.121 rear turret (left) and the same type of turret with a radar scanner/controller. (*K E Wixey Parnall collection*)

(Wickwar), The Ridge (Yate), the Polysulphin Soap Works (Keynsham), The Quarries (Temple Cloud), Lennard's boot factory (Soundwell), Barton Hill (Bristol) and the Old Mill (Wick). A much larger site was acquired by Parnall's in 1941, when the company began operations in the Ascot gas-water heater works at Neasden in north London. By the time production was at its height, Parnall Aircraft employed a workforce of some 10,000. In the latter stages of the war a comparatively large, modern factory was completed and began operations on the site of the old bombed-out works at Yate.

Production there involved mainly nose, tail and dorsal gun-turrets for Avro Lancasters, but other work resulted in components for the Lancaster's successor, the Lincoln, and of course substantial numbers of the aforementioned Spitfire airframes. One very important contract which had been awarded to Parnall's by the Ministry of Aircraft Production was for the production of jigs and components for Britain's new jet-propelled fighter, the Gloster F.9/40 (later named Meteor), but this order had to be cancelled after the German air raids destroyed Parnall's drawing offices at Yate. Later in the war, however, after the new factory at Yate was operational, Meteor components were a part of the sub-contract programme.

The administrative centre for Yate and Parnall's in general had to be transferred after the 1941 bombings, and went to Arnold Field at Wickwar, this becoming the turret administrative centre.

This site also contained a main turret machine shop and a small turret assembly line. Total area of the Arnold's Field works was 55,815 sq ft, while the workforce totalled 838. Another satellite works, The Ridge, Yate, covered an area of 43,000 sq ft, and 260 people were employed there on Vane Oil Motor production, turret assembly and the instruction of RAF personnel.

The rebuilt factory at Yate occupied an area of 324,920 sq ft and employed a total of 3,500. In Somerset, the Quarries site at Temple Cloud was responsible for mainly Lancaster major components such as rear fuselage sections, these being produced in number one factory, while number two, which was concerned with Lancaster and Lincoln fin and rudder construction, also contained the paint shop. The Lennard's boot factory at Soundwell, Bristol, had an area of 21,650 sq ft and 320 employees, and was responsible mainly for the production of bomb containers.

The end of the Second World War soon brought about the demise of Parnall Aircraft Ltd, the company rapidly severing its connections with the aircraft industry and launching into the world of domestic appliances.

Parnall and Sons Limited
Aircraft Built under Contract 1914–1918
Avro 504

About 10,000 Avro 504s were produced by the British aircraft industry between 1914 and 1932. Of this total 8,340 were completed during the four years of the 1914–18 war; 3,696 by the parent company (A V Roe & Co) and 4,644 by various sub-contractors, among which was Parnall & Sons at Bristol, which built at least 530 Avro 504s.

First appearing in 1913, the 504 was to become recognised as one of the great training aeroplanes of all time, although for a short period the type was employed on combat duties. The Avro 504 was intended as a civil sporting machine and was entered in the Aerial Derby at Hendon in September 1913, later achieving a speed of over 80 mph and a registered climb of 1,000 ft in under two minutes.

The British War office became interested in the type and twelve were ordered for the Army and one for the Admiralty. After evaluation trials both Services placed production orders for 504s, the Admiralty stipulating that those machines built for the RNAS should have different sized wing spars from those employed in the RFC aircraft. This variation in 504s existed until the RNAS and RFC were amalgamated to form the RAF on 1 April, 1918.

Those Avro 504s already in service at the start of the war were at first employed on reconnaissance and bombing missions, while a later version,

The elongated fin is noticeable on this RNAS Avro 504B (9826), a version built under contract at Bristol by Parnall & Sons (*MoD*)

Another 504 variant built by Parnall was the J with a 100 hp Gnome Monosoupape engine. C4364 seen here was an Avro-built machine. (*Real Photographs via MAP*)

the 504K, was in 1918 modified in a number of cases as a single-seat anti-Zeppelin fighter for home defence duties, a .303-in Lewis machine-gun being mounted on the upper wing and the front cockpit faired over.

An earlier version, the 504B, was recognised as the naval variant and differed mainly from other 504s in having a long extended fin and plain rudder, a distinct contrast to the comma-type rudder and absence of fin familiar on most other 504s. A pylon-style tailskid was also introduced on the 504B, and this set a pattern for the following variants.

A modified gunnery training version of the 504B, the 504G, was armed with a fixed forward-firing Vickers .303-in machine-gun synchronised to fire through the propeller arc, while a .303-in Lewis machine-gun was mounted on a Scarff gun-ring in the rear cockpit.

During 1916, the Avro 504J appeared powered by the 100 hp Gnome Monosoupape engine, this version becoming popularly known as the Mono-Avro. Many machines ordered as 504As subsequently emerged as 504Js, and did not possess the elongated vertical tail surfaces of earlier 504s of the RNAS.

Supplies of Monosoupape engines began to diminish however, and alternative powerplants were tried out on some 504s; these included the 130 hp Clerget, and 80 hp and 110 hp Le Rhône. Installing these different engines necessitated modifications being made to the front of existing airframes, which resulted in the 504K variant. This type could be fitted with a Gnome, Clerget or Le Rhône engine, and subsequently a number of machines were converted to 504K standard, among them some 504Js. Those aircraft already under construction by contractors as 504As and 504Js were modified in situ and delivered as 504Ks.

Naval 504s served with several RNAS units including, No.1 Squadron (Dover/Eastchurch), No.4 Squadron (Dover/Eastchurch) and at the

Included here for its rarity is this photograph of Parnall-built Avro 504B No.B396 (ex-N6027) at Spittlegate. The engine was an 80 hp Gnome rotary. The Parnall trade mark is aft of the serial number. (*C H Lattimer-Needham via Eric Harlin*)

RNAS Stations at Chingford, Cranwell, Fairlop, Frieston, Manston, Port Victoria and Redcar, all of which were training schools.

Parnall & Sons first became involved with the 504 when it received an Admiralty contract to build thirty Avro 504Bs (9861–9890). These aircraft had underwing bomb racks and could carry four 16 lb bombs. One machine from this batch (9890) was armed with a forward-firing .303-in Vickers machine-gun and interrupter gear.

Another extremely rare photograph showing Parnall-built Avro 504J B8593 at Newmarket in about 1917. The engine was a 100 hp Gnome Monosoupape. (*Eric Harlin*)

Believed to have been photographed on Bristol Downs, this Parnall-built Avro 504K, E3254, was the first from a batch of 150 machines (E3254-E3403) produced by Parnall for the RAF after that service was formed on 1 April, 1918. (*Parnall & Sons via John Long LRPS*)

Parnall's second Admiralty order for Avro 504s was to produce twenty 504Bs (N6010-N6029) intended for service with the RNAS. In the event, however, fifteen of these machines were transferred to the RFC and allotted Army serial numbers in the 'B' prefix series. Three other Parnall-built 504s (naval serials unknown) were also transferred to the RFC, where they were serialled A9975-A9977, but from which batch they came is not certain.

During 1917, Parnall received a contract for the construction of thirty Avro 504B armament trainers (N6650-N6679) powered by 80 hp Gnome engines. Seven of these aircraft were later transferred to the RFC. At one time it was believed that this particular batch of 504Bs was built by Avro, but independent Admiralty and Avro documents have now confirmed that this order was fulfilled by Parnall at Bristol.

By the same token, however, another batch of 504Bs (N5800-N5829) previously considered as Parnall-built, are now known to have been produced by Avro.

A further two hundred 504s were ordered later from Parnall (B8581-B8780), these being 504Js. From this batch at least two are confirmed as having survived to become civil machines after 1918.

Among the last aircraft with 'D' prefix serial numbers to be delivered to the RFC, before its amalgamation with the RNAS, was a batch of 100 Parnall-built Avro 504Ks (D9281-D9380) from which three at least survived to pursue civil careers.

Subsequently among new contracts for aircraft to serve with the newly formed RAF was one received by Parnall for the production of 150 Avro

This very rare picture is of Parnall-built Avro 504K E3345, on a training sortie during the early days of the RAF. (*Eric Harlin*)

504K trainers (E3254–E3403). From this batch quite a number later appeared in the British civil register.

Parnall is also believed to have built a number of 504Ks from another batch of 250 (F8696–F8945), but although it is known that F8864–F8882 were produced by Frederick Sage & Co, no confirmation of any machine being built by Parnall from this batch of 504Ks has been traced. One reliable source has recorded at one time that a number of 504Ks in this serial range were Parnall-built, and indeed mentions that aircraft F8812 and F8834 were later converted to 504N standards.

Avro 504B

Two-seat trainer. 80 hp Gnome seven-cylinder air-cooled rotary.

Span 36 ft; length 29 ft 5 in; height 10 ft 5 in; wing area 330 sq ft.

Empty weight 924 lb; loaded weight 1,574 lb.

Maximum speed 82 mph at sea level; climb to 3,500 ft 7 mins; service ceiling 12,000 ft; endurance 3 hr.

Provision for four 16/20 lb bombs

Avro 504K

Two-seat ab initio trainer. 110 hp Le Rhône, 130 hp Clerget or 110 hp Gnome Monosoupape.

Dimensions as Avro 504B.

Empty weight 1,231 lb; loaded weight 1,829 lb.

Maximum speed 95 mph at sea level, 85 mph at 10,000 ft; climb to 3,500 ft 7 min, to 10,000 ft, 16 min; service ceiling 16,000 ft; range 250 miles; endurance 3 hr.

One .303-in Lewis machine-gun on single-seat fighter conversions.

Weights and performance with Le Rhône engine.

Production (Parnall only)

504B: 50 confirmed; 504B armament trainers: 30 confirmed; 504A/J/K including As and Js modified to K standard: 200 confirmed; 504K: 250* confirmed.

For individual aircraft notes see Appendix A.

*An unknown number of 504Ks are believed to have been built by Parnall from a batch of 200 serialled F8696–F8945. These would have been in the F8696–F8863 range, as 504Ks serialled F8864–F8945 are known to have been produced by Frederick Sage.

In this picture one can almost hear the 150 hp Sunbeam Nubian engine being throttled back as Short Type 827, No.8255, is about to alight. This particular machine was one of eight produced by Parnall at Bristol during the First World War. (*Short Brothers via Parnall*)

Short 827

Having become established as sub-contractors to build naval aeroplanes for the Admiralty, Parnall undertook the construction of two types of machine designed by Short Brothers. The first of these was the Short Seaplane Admiralty Type 827, of which twenty were ordered from Parnall in two batches of twelve and eight respectively.

The Short 827 was a single-engined, two-seat twin-float seaplane designed for naval reconnaissance and bombing duties, and was identical to its contemporary, the Short 830, except for the powerplant installation. The Short 827 was powered by a 150 hp Sunbeam Nubian water-cooled vee-type engine, whereas the Short 830 was fitted with the 135 hp Salmson radial.

Identical to those machines built by Parnall at Bristol, this Short Type 827 seaplane, No.8230 of the RNAS, has suffered an alighting mishap. It was produced by the Brush Electrical Engineering. (*Fleet Air Arm Museum*)

In the event the Type 827 predominated, the Nubian being more or less standardised for the type with the result that comparatively few Type 830s were built. Indeed while the parent firm produced only nineteen Type 830s, the Type 827 of which more than 100 were ordered, was sub-contracted to four other companies, Short Brothers producing forty-eight.

The Type 827 was a two-bay biplane with steel-tube interplane struts and wire bracing, and the extended upper wings, which included inversely

A Short Type 827, identical to those produced by Parnall, being erected on the quayside at Kilwa during the First World War. This particular machine (8649) was built by the Sunbeam Motor Car Co. (*MAP*)

tapered ailerons, were cable-braced. Both sets of wings folded rearward to facilitate stowage. A rather large radiator was mounted above the Sunbeam Nubian engine forward of the wings. Provision was made for the carrying of a .303-in Lewis machine-gun for the observer's use, and small bombs could be carried on racks beneath the fuselage.

After the Short Type 827 began to appear in 1915, it remained in service until the Armistice, and was employed both at home and overseas. Those used in home waters flew patrol duties over the English Channel, and especially the North Sea. They were based at the RNAS coastal air stations at Calshot, Dundee, Killingholme, the Isle of Grain and Great Yarmouth. In fact it was one of the Great Yarmouth based Short Type 827s, which, at 04.05 on 25 April, 1916, bombed the German warships that had begun bombarding Lowestoft.

Short Type 827s also operated from the seaplane carriers *Ben-my-Chree*, *Manica* and *Raven II*, while the armed merchant ships *Laconia* and *Himalaya* operated one Short Type 827 each. During March 1916, four Short 827s, in company with four French Voisin pusher biplanes were shipped to Zanzibar for service in East Africa, where they eventually became No.8 Naval Squadron.

Four other Short Type 827s were handed over to the Belgian forces in East Africa, and in 1917, a further four went to the Mediterranean area, where they operated from a base at Otranto.

Parnall's first order for Short 827s was for twelve machines (8218–8229) one of which served with No.8 Naval Squadron in East Africa. This aircraft was one of four later handed over to the Belgian forces. Four other 827s from this batch were fitted with dual controls.

Although a little hazy, this photograph is quite rare, and shows to advantage the drooped ailerons on the upper wings of this Short Type 827 of the RNAS. Numbered 8638, it was built by Sunbeam and represents the type produced by Parnall. (*Fleet Air Arm Museum*)

An extension of the original contract for twelve Short 827s was undertaken by Parnall's, and involved the construction of a further eight.

Short 827

Two-seat reconnaissance and bomber seaplane. 150 hp Sunbeam Nubian eight-cylinder vee water-cooled engine.

Span 53 ft 11 in upper, 40 ft lower; length 35 ft 3 in; height 13 ft 6 in; wing area 506 sq ft.
Loaded weight 3,400 lb.
Maximum speed 61 mph at 2,000 ft.
Provision for one .303-in Lewis machine-gun and bombs.

Production (Parnall only)

Twenty confirmed
For individual aircraft notes see Appendix A.

In its original form the Short Bomber had two-bay wings but it was modified to three-bay configuration. (Short Brothers)

Short Bomber

In addition to the Type 827 and one Type 184 seaplane (No. 843) which it rebuilt in November 1916, Parnall became involved with one other Short-designed aeroplane during the First World War – the Short Bomber.

Bearing no official type designation the Short Bomber was planned as an adaptation of the highly successful Short Type 184 and was Short's response to the Admiralty's request for an aeroplane possessing good range and heavy bombing capabilities. Early production Short Bombers incorporated fuselages of the same dimensions as the Type 184 seaplane, but later machines had lengthened fuselages to improve longitudinal stability. All production machines had dual controls, the observer being housed in the rear cockpit as opposed to the original front cockpit position

One of the six Short Bombers built by Parnall. (*MAP*)

on the prototype. The fuel tanks on Short Bombers were armoured, but the airframe was composed mainly of wood which was fabric-covered. The extensive overhang to the upper mainplanes was braced by wires stretching from the king posts. A characteristic feature of the Short Bomber was its cumbersome four-wheeled undercarriage.

A total of eighty-three Short Bombers were built, thirty-six by Short Brothers, twenty by Mann, Egerton, fifteen by Sunbeam, six by Phoenix Dynamo and six by Parnall. All except those produced by Sunbeam, which installed its own 225 hp Mohawk engines, were powered by the 250 hp Rolls-Royce Eagle.

First production aircraft were available late in 1916 and on the night of 15 November the type saw action when four joined eighteen other bombers, mostly French Caudrons, from the 4th and 5th Naval Wings.

The Short Bombers were operating with No.7 Squadron of the RNAS 5th Wing based at Coudekerque, and the targets for the force of twenty-two bombers was Ateliers de la Marine, and the Slyken electric power station at Ostend. Each of the Short Bombers carried eight 65 lb bombs.

Short Bomber 9834 was built by Phoenix Dynamo and like the Parnall-built examples had the 250 hp Rolls-Royce Eagle III. (*MAP*)

Short Bomber No. 9771 (Parnall c/n 21) nearing completion in the Coliseum works of Parnall. Lower wings for another of the type are in the foreground, and the combined front and rear cockpit coaming. (*K E Wixey Parnall collection*)

Considered as an interim type, the Short Bomber was required to serve as a long-range heavy bomber until the arrival in service of the Handley Page O/100, Cmdr Murray Sueter's 'bloody paralyser of an aeroplane'. As a consequence the Short Bomber was never looked upon as a real operational success, but the type did, nevertheless, pave the way for the founding of the truly Independent Air Force of 1918.

Parnall received a contract to build ten Short Bombers (9771–9780), but this was later amended when the last four machines on the order were cancelled, as were a number of Short Bombers ordered from other manufacturers.

One of the Parnall-built Short Bombers flew with No. 5 Wing of the RNAS while another Parnall-built machine was transferred to the RFC from No. 3 Wing of the RNAS at Luxeuil.

Short Bomber

Two-seat long-range heavy bomber. 250 hp Rolls-Royce Eagle III twelve-cylinder vee water-cooled engine.

Span 85 ft; length 45 ft; height 15 ft; wing area 870 sq ft.

Empty weight 5,000 lb; loaded weight 6,800 lb.

Maximum speed 77.5 mph at 6,500 ft; climb to 6,500 ft 21 min 25 sec; to 10,000 ft 45 min; service ceiling 9,500 ft; endurance 6 hr.

One .303-in Lewis machine-gun. Bomb load four 230 lb or eight 112 lb on underwing racks.

Production (Parnall only)

Contract for ten, only six built and last four cancelled.
For individual aircraft notes see Appendix A.

Used as an anti-submarine patrol seaplane, the Hamble Baby played a mundane, but important part in the war at sea. This Fairey-built machine has two 65-lb bombs slung beneath the centre fuselage. (*Fleet Air Arm Museum*)

Hamble Baby

Perhaps the most important contract awarded to Parnall during the First World War was that for the construction of Hamble Baby seaplanes and landplanes.

The Hamble Baby evolved from the original Sopwith Baby, which was itself a direct descendant of the Sopwith Schneider seaplane of 1914. The Schneider had been fitted with a 100 hp Gnome Monosoupape rotary engine, almost entirely enclosed within a 'bull-nose' metal cowling. The Baby, however, was powered by a 110 hp Clerget, and the profile of the aircraft's nose was consequently altered to the familiar squat appearance characterised by the horse-shoe style front end of the cowling. Performance of the type was further improved when the 130 hp Clerget was fitted, but as modifications were involved, which Sopwith with their large Camel fighter commitments were unable to undertake, the task of improving the Baby design was allotted to Blackburn Aircraft and to Fairey Aviation.

The Blackburn machines differed little from the 110 hp version and were known simply as the Blackburn Baby, but Fairey modified the design to such an extent, it materialised as virtually a new type. This came about after a Sopwith-built Baby (8134) was delivered to the Fairey works at

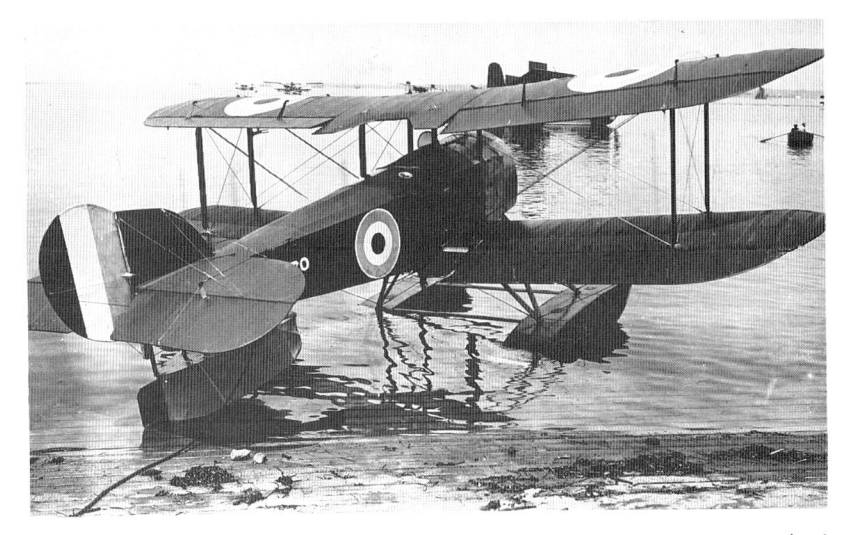

Believed to be N1970, this Parnall-built Hamble Baby reveals clearly the retained Sopwith design of vertical tail surfaces and floats. (*Imperial War Museum*)

Hayes in Middlesex, where the wings were completely redesigned, the squared-off wingtips of the original Baby being replaced by rounded tips. An innovation was the installation of the Fairey Camber Gear in tṇ revised wing form. This device consisted of hinged flaps attached to each mainplane and running the full length of the trailing edge.

This view of the Parnall Hamble Baby Convert shows to advantage the wide-track undercarriage and rounded wingtips. Most of these aeroplanes were used as trainers. (*Imperial War Museum*)

Acting as normal ailerons in flight, these flaps, when lowered together, gave increased lift, thus improving somewhat the load carrying capacity of the aeroplane.

Lateral control of the Fairey-built Baby (named Hamble Baby after Fairey's works at Hamble Point near Southampton) was maintained by tightening the operating cables and slackening the balancing cables simultaneously. A wheel and cable drum attached to the Baby's control column effectively tightened or loosened the aileron control cables. Use of Fairey's Camber Gear on Hamble Babies was the first occasion in which trailing-edge flaps to increase wing lift had been incorporated into a production aeroplane.

The Hamble Baby was tested by Sqn Cdr Maurice Wright, and its production was initially undertaken by the Fairey company, but the majority of Hamble Babies were constructed by Parnall at Bristol under contract.

The Parnall-built Babies were distinguished by their retention of the original Sopwith-type floats and fin and rudder. The last seventy-four machines of the type built by Parnall were, however, completed as landplanes, and were known as Hamble Baby Converts. In this variant horizontal skids replaced the floats, although the main N struts of the seaplane undercarriage were retained. This resulted in a very long axle for the wheels, the axle itself being bound to the skids by rubber cord. The Parnall-built Hamble Baby Converts (N1986–N2059) were used mostly for training, many of them serving at the RNAS Station at Cranwell.

In this view of Parnall Hamble Baby Convert N2002 (Parnall c/n P.1/17), the Sopwith lineage is obvious. Also noticeable is the Parnall trade mark on the side of the rear fuselage. (*Imperial War Museum*)

The original Sopwith tailplane and blunt wingtips denote a Blackburn-built Baby in this very rare flying view of a patrolling Baby with its bomb load. (*Fleet Air Arm Museum*)

Fairey-built Hamble Baby N1452 with 110/130 hp Clerget. The full-span trailing-edge flaps can be seen as well as the differences between Fairey- and Parnall-built examples. (*MAP*)

Of the 180 Hamble Babies produced, no less than 130 were built by Parnall at its Bristol works in two batches, the first comprising thirty machines (N1190–N1219) and the second 100 (N1960–N2059).

The first thirty machines were all seaplanes powered by the 110 hp Clerget while from the second batch of 100 machines, twenty-six were completed as seaplanes, the remaining seventy-four being Hamble Baby Convert landplanes. All Babies in this second batch were powered by the 130 hp Clerget.

Like other aircraft manufacturers during the 1914–18 war, Parnall added its trade name to many of the aircraft it built, the Hamble Baby being no exception. The legend Parnall & Sons Ltd., Bristol, England, formed an oval on the fuselage sides, while the words Aircraft Constructors were added one above the other in the centre of the oval. Included also was the individual aircraft company number, which was painted in small figures immediately below the main military serial number.

The single-seat Babies were employed on unspectacular but very useful and essential duties patrolling the waters around the coasts of Great Britain. They flew from a number of shore bases including, the RNAS Seaplane Stations at Calshot, Cattewater, Dundee, Great Yarmouth, Felixstowe, Scapa Flow, Westgate, Killingholme and Fishguard. Overseas the Baby seaplanes operated from the RNAS stations at Dunkirk, Otranto, Santa Maria di Leuca, Thasos, Suda Bay, Syra, Port Said and Alexandria. The type also flew from a number of seaplane and aircraft carriers as well as aboard the light cruisers *Arethusa* and *Undaunted*.

With its 130 hp Clerget and Fairey Patent Camber Gear, the Hamble Baby was the ultimate in the Baby series, and was capable of carrying two 65 lb bombs. Armament varied, earlier versions having a .303-in machine-gun mounted to fire obliquely upwards through an aperture in the upper centre-section. This arrangement was modified later so that the Lewis gun, fixed centrally above the fuselage, fired through the propeller arc by means of synchronising gear.

Some Babies carried Ranken anti-airship darts, while Le Prieur rockets, carried in racks attached to the interplane struts, were tried out on the type. Towards the end of the war Babies were giving way to more advanced types of aircraft, but even so on 31 October, 1918, there were still eighteen Hamble Baby seaplanes and Hamble Baby Converts on RAF charge.

Hamble Baby (Parnall-Built)

Single-seat anti-submarine, scout and bomber. 110 hp or 130 hp Clerget air-cooled rotary engine.

Span 27 ft 9¼ in; length 23 ft 4 in; height 9 ft 6 in; wing area 246 sq ft.

Empty weight, 1,386 lb; loaded weight 1,946 lb.

Maximum speed 100 mph at sea level, 90 mph at 2,000 ft; climb to 2,000 ft 5 min 30 sec, to 10,000 ft 35 min; service ceiling 7,600 ft; endurance 2 hr.

One .303-in Lewis machine-gun or Ranken darts. Bomb load two 65 lb on under-fuselage racks.

Production (Parnall only)

110 hp Clerget seaplane: 30 confirmed; 130 hp Clerget seaplane: 26 confirmed; 130 hp Clerget Convert: 74 confirmed. Total 130.

For individual aircraft notes see Appendix A.

The only known existing photograph of the Parnall Scout/Zepp-Chaser. Even in this poor quality, but extremely rare picture, the heaviness of the design is apparent even in the struts alone. Notice also the radiator slung beneath the nose and the large diameter propeller. (*Parnall & Sons*)

Parnall Scout/Zepp Chaser

On the evening of 19 January, 1915, the German Zeppelin airships L3 and L4 made the first air attack on Britain, when they bombed Great Yarmouth and King's Lynn killing four people, injuring 16 others, and causing damage to a number of houses and a power station.

As a result the government began organising home-defence units on a more effective basis, a move which necessarily involved the deployment of forces in Britain that would otherwise have proved strategically more valuable elsewhere. The possibility of the demoralisation of the civil population, which had never before been subjected to such terror from the skies, was another factor the authorities had to take into consideration.

It was decided that the most effective deterrent against the large airships was the aeroplane, and as a consequence B.E.2c and D.H.4 biplanes of the RNAS were sent up on anti-Zeppelin patrols, at times meeting with some success.

The Admiralty, having assumed the role of defender of Britain's coastline against air attacks, soon wished to procure an aircraft type of naval concept that would be capable of quickly intercepting any raiding German airships. As a result Parnall was invited to submit plans for such a type. The requirements were for a single-seat scouting aeroplane for service with the RNAS which would have the ability to rapidly attain the height of marauding Zeppelins and attack them.

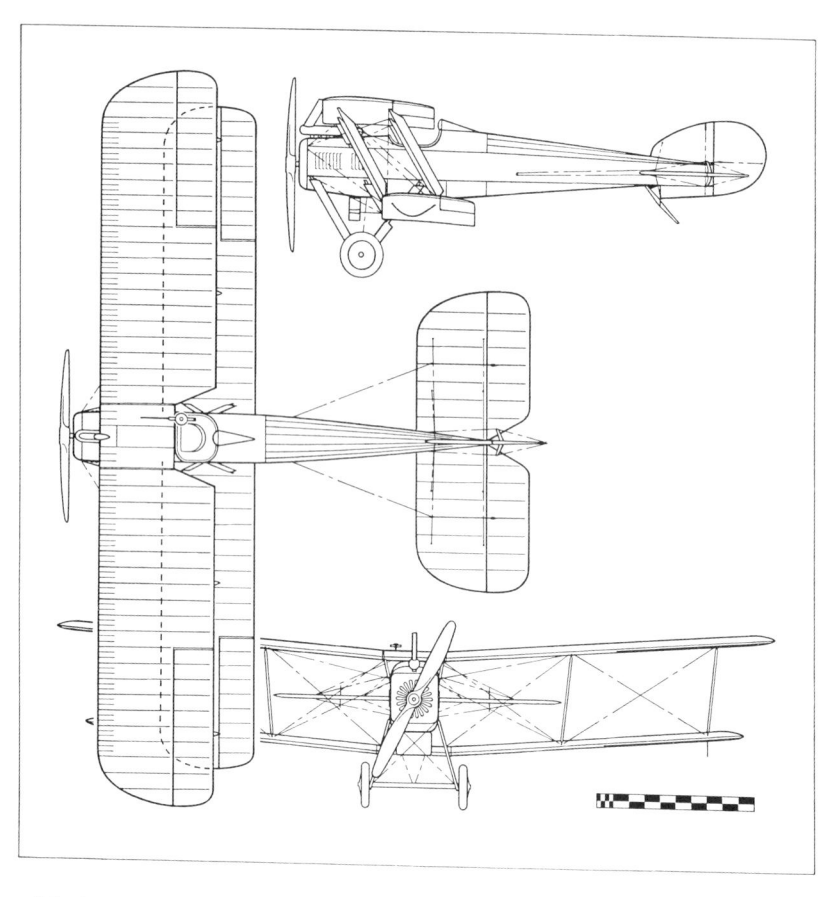

The response from Parnall was the Scout, or Zepp-Chaser as it was more popularly known, and it was the company's first aircraft design.

The Parnall Scout's creation was accredited to Adolf Camden Pratt (later to become head of Vickers Aviation stress section), but the idea for the aircraft was attributed to Keith Davies, who was a test pilot with the Parnall company at that time. Davies was born in London during 1885, trained as an engineer and became interested in aviation. He held RAC Aviator's Certificate No. 22, and flew with the early pioneers at Brooklands, where he was employed by Messrs Humber in connection with the Humber three-cylinder engine installed in a Blériot monoplane. Davies later went to India with Capt Windham and gave flying demonstrations in the Central Provinces Exhibition at Allahabad, thus becoming in 1910 the first man to make an official flight in India. In 1912, Keith Davies was the second officer to be gazetted to the RFC reserve, and later was attached to the Royal Aircraft Factory as an experimental pilot. He was one of the first pilots to undertake night-flying tests, and after being a member of the AID at Farnborough, Davies transferred to Parnall & Sons where it was intended that he should take on the duties of a test pilot flying both landplanes and seaplanes. Keith Davies joined Parnall in 1916, and after his work with the Zepp-Chaser, he eventually left the company's services to take over an aircraft factory in London until the end of the war.

Davies's ideas and Camden Pratt's interpretation of them in designing the Parnall Scout – sometimes referred to as the 'night flyer' – resulted in a large aeroplane incorporating a two-bay biplane layout with unequal span wings and considerable stagger. In order to provide the pilot with a good field of view, the upper mainplane was quite close to the top of the fuselage, the lower mainplane being set well below it and attached by N struts, the forward sections of which were symmetrical with the rear undercarriage legs.

The undercarriage was a cumbersome affair of the cross-axle type with thick front supporting members attached to the corners of the blunt nose. The 250 hp Sunbeam Maori II was cooled by a large square-shaped radiator slung between the undercarriage legs. The Zepp-Chaser's nose-heavy appearance was accentuated by the fitting of a large diameter two-bladed wooden propeller. The upper mainplane trailing-edge contained a large cut-out to enhance the pilot's upward field of view. Ailerons were fitted to all four wings while the relatively short fuselage necessitated a large tailplane.

The Parnall Scout was completed in an all-black factory finish in readiness for its role of Zeppelin interception at night.

Meanwhile a nocturnal attack system against enemy airships had already been tried out at Orfordness and applied with some success to a number of Home-Defence aircraft types. The idea was to fit a machine-gun at an angle to the side of the aircraft's cockpit, and when the pilot dived his machine at a predetermined attitude at the target, the machine-gun fired on a horizontal trajectory. As a consequence the Parnall Zepp-Chaser was fitted with a .303-in Lewis gun mounted on the starboard side of the cockpit at an angle of forty-five degrees.

The Parnall Scout was destined never to fire its gun in anger however, if it ever fired it at all! When the machine was sent to Upavon for its trials, the stress calculations proved the Zepp-Chaser to be excessively heavy and the aircraft's safety factor was declared as very low. Indeed after further ground tests had been made the machine was proclaimed as unsafe, and as far as is known, it was never flown.

Two Parnall Scouts were originally ordered (N505–N506), but only N505 was built.

The second Zepp-Chaser was to have been powered by a 190 hp Rolls-Royce Falcon engine, but work on this aircraft was never started. Parnall are believed to have scrapped the sole example of the Zepp-Chaser in 1917.

The following information was gleaned from the official Aeronautical Inspection Directorate (Preliminary Experiment Report) of 1916.

Parnall Scout (Zepp-Chaser)

Two-seat scout for defence against German airships. 250 hp Sunbeam Maori II twelve-cylinder vee water-cooled engine.

Span 44 ft upper, 40 ft lower; chord 7 ft upper, 5 ft 6 in lower; incidence 2 deg; dihedral 4 deg; stagger 4 ft; gap 5 ft 6 in; wing area 516 sq ft; aileron area 36 sq ft; tailplane span 18 ft; tailplane area 74 sq ft; elevator area 38 sq ft; fin area 6.5 sq ft; rudder area 12.75 sq ft.

Estimated maximum speed 113.5 mph at sea level, 101.5 mph at 10,000 ft.

Fuel 36 Imp Gal.

One .303-in Lewis machine-gun at 45 deg elevation.

Production

Two ordered, only one completed. See Appendix A.

A prototype Parnall Panther with inflated Isle of Grain style flotation bags. The hydrovane forward of the wheels, the humped fuselage and the starboard side strut carrying the propeller for actuating the wind-driven fuel pump are all visible. (*Parnall & Sons*)

Parnall Panther

During 1917 the British Admiralty issued Specification A.D./N.2A, which called for a two-seat reconnaissance and spotting aeroplane capable of operating with the RNAS from an aircraft-carrier.

In response designs were submitted from three sources: Handley Page with the Type 14 (R/200), the Isle of Grain (Port Victoria) Naval Experimental Station, which presented adaptations of the P.V.5 and

P.V.5a types, and Parnall which entered its second design for the Admiralty, the N.2A, which was to be later named the Panther.

The N.2A was the first design for the Parnall company from the drawing board of Admiralty designer Harold Bolas. To comply with the specification's requirements, Bolas introduced something of an innovation in the structural design of his N.2A. The fuselage featured a wooden monocoque construction, a reflection of Harold Bolas's earlier experiences with the A.D. Flying-Boat and Navyplane, while another novelty was the unorthodox method employed to facilitate stowage aboard an aircraft carrier. In this instance the rear fuselage section was hinged just aft of the observer's cockpit, and could be swung to lie parallel to the starboard mainplanes. To obviate chafing, the tail unit control cables were located in a special channel on the starboard side of the fuselage.

The fuselage was built as two sections, each consisting of plywood formers to which was screwed and glued an outer skin, also formed of plywood and having fabric covering. The whole was based on a frame of four longerons, which carried the plywood formers as well as providing 'hard spots' at the fuselage folding points.

Air bags were installed in the rear fuselage section to provide buoyancy in the event of the aircraft being ditched. The instrument panel was hinged in order to provide easy access for maintenance from the rear. The pilot's cockpit was beneath the upper centre section and immediately above the main fuel tank, which had a maximum capacity of 48 gal, while two

The novel way in which the fuselage of the Panther was hinged to allow for stowage of the type aboard ship can be clearly seen in this photograph of the sixth and last prototype N.96 (Parnall c/n P.707). The flotation bag in the rear of the fuselage is just visible. (*K E Wixey Parnall collection*)

When the fuselage of the Panther was completely disconnected, it could be transported by lorry as shown here. (*J M Bruce/G S Leslie collection*)

gravity tanks, installed within the upper centre-section, contained a further ten gallons. The fuel was pumped up to these tanks by means of a small wind-operated pump attacked to a short strut on the fuselage. The N.2A incorporated single-bag biplane wings of equal span and conventional construction, although the ailerons were positioned well inboard from the detachable wingtips, a combination that allowed for easier stowage. An opening in the upper centre-section provided the pilot with a rather laborious means of entry to the cockpit, a feat which also required the lowering of a centre-section trailing-edge, which was hinged to the rear spar. This aperture did have one advantage, however, in that it presented the pilot with a clear view immediately overhead. This rather cumbersome means of ingress to the pilot's cockpit, necessitated by the unusually high positioning of the two crew members (the observer entered by a more orthodox method), was compensated for when airborne by an excellent all-round view. Another great advantage for the pilot, especially in a naval aeroplane, was the exceptionally good forward view when making carrier deck landings.

The Parnall N.2A (the name Panther was applied to the sixth prototype) was powered by a 230 hp Bentley B.R.2 nine-cylinder rotary air-cooled engine, one of the most powerful rotary aero-engines ever built in quantity. This powerplant was encased in a shapely convex cowling divided radially and open at the bottom for cooling, a feature which served to improve the airflow and reduce drag.

The engine and its auxiliary components were mounted on projecting spars, and could be fitted or removed from the aircraft as a complete unit;

A production Panther. (*K E Wixey Parnall collection*)

The prototype Panther, N.91. On this machine the pilot's forward-firing Vickers machine-gun is fitted in the original port side position; this gun was removed later, and did not appear on subsequent models. Note the absence of a hydrovane, and the .303-in Lewis machine-gun in rear cockpit. The Parnall trade insignia appears on rear of the fuselage. (*Parnall & Sons*)

the N.2A was one of the first aeroplanes to incorporate this feature. Large slots situated behind the engine and contained within the aircraft's fuselage profile allowed for the outlet of air and exhaust gases. The empennage was of conventional construction, but even that had a novel element in the actual layout, for the elevators and the rudder hinge lines were inclined forward in plan view.

91

The first N.2A prototype, N91, was ready for its initial trials in April 1918, and it appeared with an undercarriage of the cross-axle type having two V struts with widened apexes. The tailskid was attached to a strengthened former, and differed from normal practice by virtue of a special ball-type fitting designed to assist take-off procedure aboard ship. Another feature was the jettisonable wheels. These could be released by a cable and spring mechanism operated from the cockpit if a forced alighting at sea became imminent.

The prototype N.2A was armed with a fixed forward-firing .303-in Vickers machine-gun mounted on the port side of the pilot's cockpit, while the observer/gunner in the rear cockpit was provided with a .303-in Lewis gun mounted on a pillar. The pilot's gun was later dispensed with, however, and all subsequent prototype and production Panthers were armed with just the observer's Lewis gun.

On undergoing manufacturer's trials the prototype N.2A was found to be nose-heavy, and before leaving Bristol for its official trials at the A & AEE, Martlesham Heath, in May 1918, the aircraft was modified to include horn-balanced elevators with a pronounced increase in the forward slope of the hinge lines.

The Martlesham trials proved disappointing; the N.2A's maximum speed of 108.5 mph at 2,000 ft, and climb to that altitude in 2 min 20 sec was little improvement over earlier RNAS aircraft types possessing much less power. Nevertheless it was decided to proceed with development of the Parnall machine, and the prototype was returned to the Bristol works for the installation of flotation gear. That was in June 1918, but in the following October the prototype was reported as still being at Parnall's works.

A Panther with the modified undercarriage struts and deck-landing hooks beneath the axle. Just visible is the lowered trailing-edge section in the upper centre-section to allow the pilot entry into the cockpit. (*J M Bruce/G S Leslie collection*)

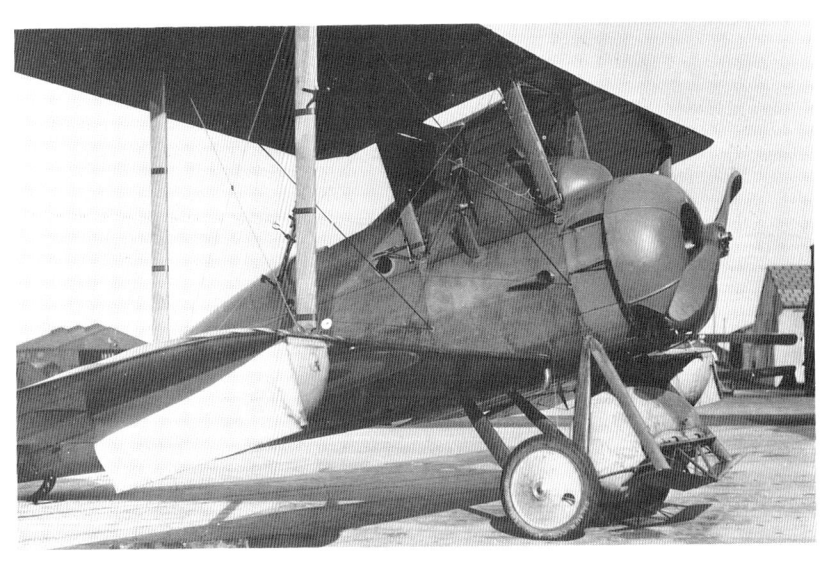

One of the first three prototype Panthers is seen here at the Isle of Grain RNAS. The Parnall-type flotation bags are inflated, one under each lower wing, plus one between the undercarriage legs. (*J M Bruce/G S Leslie collection*)

A further five N.2As were produced by Parnall, all classed as prototypes. The second machine, N92, was fitted with an identical undercarriage to the first prototype, but the third prototype, N93, was equipped with a hydrovane attachment designed to prevent the aeroplane from nosing over in the event of a forced alighting. This hydrovane was constructed of wood and steel and was adopted as standard equipment on subsequent N.2A prototypes and production machines.

By the summer of 1918 the first three prototype N.2As had been completed and were subjected to tests involving Parnall's own design flotation gear. Deemed necessary in an aeroplane expected to operate mainly over water, this gear consisted of air bags fixed beneath the lower wings, these being additional to the air bags contained in the N.2A's rear fuselage.

On 22 June, 1918, the second prototype N.2A was sent to Turnhouse (Edinburgh) for trials with the Fleet, and was eventually taken on board the battle-cruiser HMS *Repulse*. This was presumably for the purpose of trying out the Parnall machine in take-offs from a small platform attached to one of the ship's gun turrets, a practice then in vogue for launching naval scouting aircraft from the larger warships.

The third prototype N.2A was completed in July 1918, and after being equipped with the Parnall flotation gear was flown to the Isle of Grain Naval Experimental Station for ditching trials. While there the Parnall flotation gear was removed to be supplanted by the Isle of Grain's own system. This consisted of three inflatable air bags, one in the rear fuselage compartment, and one each stowed in tubular steel containers attached to the top of the undercarriage V-struts. These bags were inflated by means of an air bottle charged at a pressure of 1,800 psi. After undergoing successful trials, this gear was adopted as standard equipment for all production Panthers.

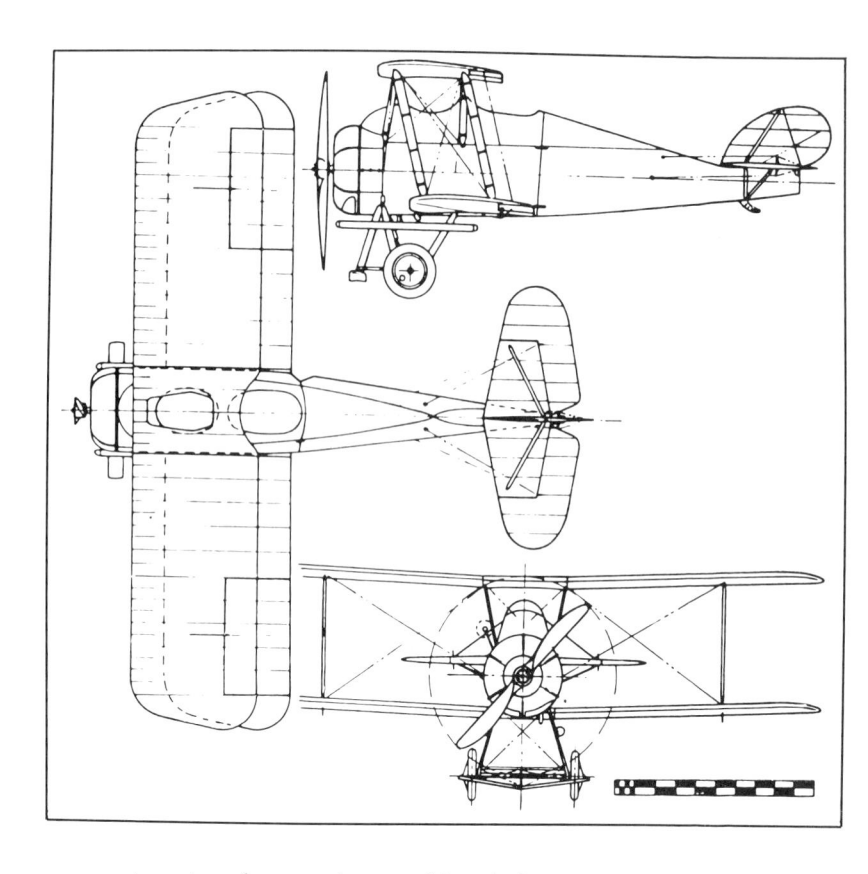

In general the flotation bags were constructed with several layers of rubberized fabric, and most were provided with flaps with which they could be attached to the aircraft's structure. It was normal practice for the bags to be installed relative to the aeroplane's greatest concentration of weight, but the location of bracing wires and the aircraft's centre of gravity had also to be considered. The simultaneous release of all bags was usually accomplished by means of a T-shaped handle positioned either in the upper right-hand side of the instrument panel, or in the upper wing centre-section. A hand-operated pump was also often provided to top up the bags after inflation, or to replace lost air should a slow leak have occurred. The bags were capable of keeping an aeroplane afloat for about ten hours in a calm sea, but rough waters could result in the waves chafing the bags and subsequent loss of buoyancy.

Although contracted to the Bristol Aeroplane Co, this production Panther, N7406, (Parnall c/n P.1/10650) is under construction at the Coliseum works of Parnall & Sons, Park Row, Bristol. (*Parnall & Sons*)

The tests at the Isle of Grain were undertaken by Maj W G Moore, DSC, and after the buoyancy trials and wheel jettisoning tests, the third prototype N.2A was subjected to alighting experiments using the hydrovane. These proved satisfactory, with the aircraft alighting at a very low speed, planing along on the hydrovane and settling down on the water undamaged.

Once recovered from the water the N.2A was ready for flying again immediately. At about the time these trials were taking place, a new official system of nomenclature was introduced for British military aeroplanes, and Parnall's N.2A was named Panther, coming officially within the class known as the RAF Type 21, which applied to Fleet Reconnaissance shipborne aircraft.

Meanwhile the fourth prototype N.2A (N94) flew to the Royal Aircraft Establishment at Farnborough to undergo proof-loading tests, the fifth machine (N95) going to Turnhouse, where it flew on trials with the Fleet, at the same time participating in experiments with the Grain Flotation Gear. The sixth and final N.2A prototype (N96) was equipped with Grain Flotation Gear, a hydrovane and two extra handling positions which were embodied in the fuselage. It was this sixth machine that was officially named Panther, and which was considered equivalent to a production aircraft.

Parnall was awarded two contracts for the construction of 312 production Panthers (N7400–N7549 and N7680–N7841), but with the signing of the Armistice in November 1918, the second contract was cancelled. This annulment created friction between Avery (Parnall's

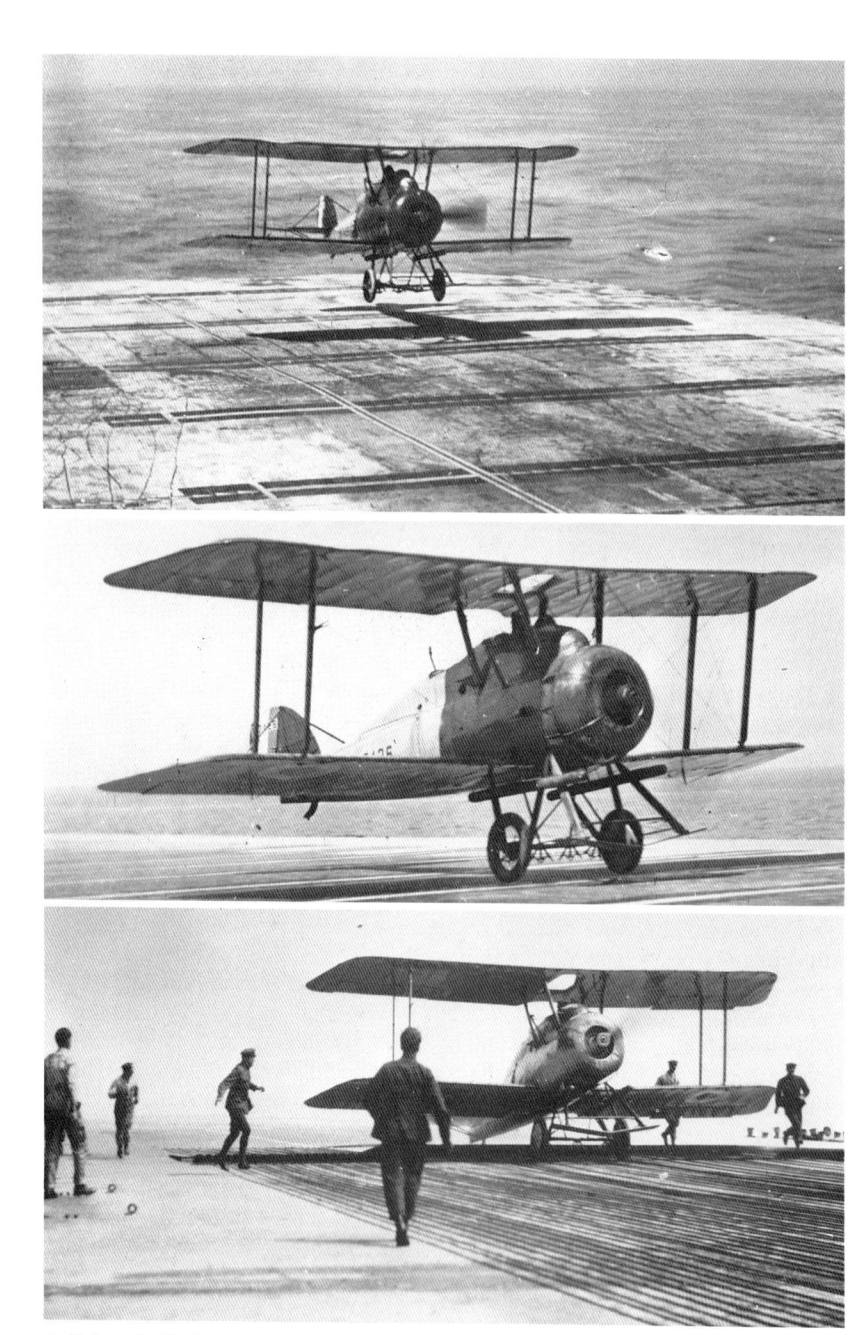

A Bristol-built Panther about to touch down on HMS *Argus* (top) and two views of Bristol-built Panther N7425 on HMS *Argus*. The longitudinal wires were the cause of many damaged aircraft. (*J M Bruce/G S Leslie collection*)

controlling group) and the Air Ministry, and as a consequence both the Panther contracts were cancelled. The first order was later revised and offered to The British & Colonial Aeroplane Company at Filton, which readily accepted the Panther contract and thus helped to alleviate the rising unemployment figures in the area.

It is apparent, however, that Parnall did produce a small number of production Panthers in its Bristol works, a fact proved by a surviving photograph showing Panther N7406 in the Coliseum works, and bearing the unmistakable Parnall factory number P.877.

How many Panthers were actually completed by Parnall from the Air Ministry contract to The British & Colonial Aeroplane Company is uncertain, but fuselages for machines up to N7426 are believed to have been built in the Coliseum works by Parnall on behalf of British & Colonial before Panther production began at Filton.

The second Panther contract remained void, and work on the 162 machines (N7680–N7841) was never started. The original Air Ministry order for 150 Panthers was complied with during 1919 and 1920 at Filton, and the type entered service with the British Fleet aboard the aircraft carriers HMS *Argus* and *Hermes* whence the Panthers participated in the early development of carrier deck flying. For this purpose they were equipped with special fasteners attached to the undercarriage axle, these fasteners, or clips, engaging longitudinal wires running fore and aft along the carrier's deck. The wires themselves acted not only as guide lines and assisted in friction braking, but were also directed over a number of transverse, hinged, wooden barriers, which helped to brake the aircraft as it pushed them down during its landing roll. Under these conditions it was inevitable that a number of aircraft sustained varying amounts of damage while in the process of landing on the carrier deck. Indeed during one set training period aboard HMS *Argus* in 1924, it was recorded that only five landings in six escaped mishaps. This system of carrier deck landing proved so costly in damage to Fleet Air Arm aircraft that it was abandoned in favour of the old rope and weights method until a more satisfactory system was available.

Production Panthers were later modified to include large horn-balanced rudders, oleo-type undercarriage legs, a wider-track undercarriage, and improved deck-landing cable hooks.

A number of Panthers were rebuilt under contract including eighteen sent to Gloucestershire Aircraft at Cheltenham in 1923 and, although unconfirmed, it is believed a small number of Panthers were renovated by the newly formed George Parnall company at the Coliseum works, Park Row, Bristol.

Service pilots reported the Panther as pleasant to fly with few vices, the most noticeable being an adverse effect on rudder control when the aircraft was flying at low speed. It was also agreed that the Panther's Bentley engine required frequent coaxing and could become very irksome during flight. The well-known test pilot Capt Norman Macmillan spoke highly of the Panther in regard to his personal experience with the type.

In addition to serving with the carriers HMS *Argus* and *Hermes*, Panthers operated with shore-based units including, No.421 Fleet Spotter Reconnaissance Flight at Gosport, Nos.441 and 442 Fleet Spotter Reconnaissance Flights at Leuchars and, also at Leuchars, with No.406 Fleet Fighter Flight. Panthers continued to serve with the Fleet Air Arm until 1926, when those machines still serving with No.442 Flight were finally replaced by Fairey IIIDs.

Due to the rate of attrition caused mainly by carrier deck landing damage, and despite the availability of sixteen spare Panther airframes produced at Filton, relatively few of the type survived to be offered on the civil market. Any that did were sold privately by the Aircraft Disposal Company. One such machine, G-EBCM, was converted purely to take part in the Royal Aero Club race meeting held at Croydon on 17 April, 1922. This particular Panther (ex-N7530) had first been completed at Filton on 23 June, 1920 and first flew in its civil guise on 13 April, 1922. Four days later it flew in the Royal Aero Club race piloted by A F Muir.

The Panther did arouse the interest of some foreign observers, among them representatives of the United States Navy and the Imperial Japanese Navy. The US Navy placed an order for two Panthers which were allotted the US Naval Flying Corps serial numbers A.5751 and A.5752. Both machines were shipped to the United States during 1920, and were fitted with the 230 hp Bentley B.R.2 rotary engine, hydrovanes and the Isle of Grain flotation gear. In view of the subsequent trials that both of these aircraft underwent in the United States, the Parnall Panther can justifiably

This updated Panther has a modified horn-balanced rudder and oleo undercarriage legs. A Blackburn Dart is in the background. (*J M Bruce/G S Leslie collection*)

be regarded as one of the founder types of aeroplane that helped to develop naval aviation in the USA.

Meanwhile the Imperial Japanese Navy was keen to build up its naval aviation potential. During 1921 a British Air Mission, headed by Col The Master of Sempill, arrived in Japan. Their purpose was to advise on the most suitable and best equipment with which the Imperial Japanese Navy could establish its new air arm. The result was a number of British aircraft types being ordered for service with the Japanese Navy. Among these were twelve Parnall Panthers, all of which were fitted with horn-balanced rudders, and these machines served for some time with the Japanese Fleet from a base at Yokosuka.

Despite any shortcomings it possessed, there is little doubt the Parnall Panther played an important part in the development of carrier deck flying techniques, and it was an early factor in the evolution of the carrier-borne strike aircraft which were to participate so vitally in the war at sea two decades later.

Parnall N.2A Panther

Two-seat carrier-borne Fleet Spotter and reconnaissance biplane. 230 hp Bentley B.R.2 nine-cylinder air-cooled rotary engine.

Span 29 ft 6 in; length 24 ft 11 in; length folded 14 ft 6 in; height 10 ft 6 in; chord 6 ft 3 in; maximum gap 6 ft 3 in; minimum gap 6 ft 2½ in; wing area 336 sq ft; aileron area (each of four) 11.3 sq ft; tailplane span 12 ft; tailplane area 18.4 sq ft; total elevator area 19.3 sq ft; fin area 6.85 sq ft; rudder area 4.4 sq ft.

Empty weight 1,328 lb; loaded weight 2,595 lb. Gross weight of civil Panther 2,369 lb.

Maximum speed 108.5 mph at 6,500 ft, 103 mph at 10,000 ft; climb to 2,000 ft, 2 min 20 sec; to 6,500 ft 9 min 20 sec, to 10,000 ft 17 min 5 sec; service ceiling 14,500 ft, endurance 4½ hr.

One .303-in pillar-mounted Lewis machine-gun in rear cockpit. First prototype had one fixed forward-firing .303-in Vickers machine-gun on port side of pilot's cockpit.

Production

Six prototypes. Full production details in Appendix A.

George Parnall and Company 1920–1935

Parnall Puffin

Not the kind of man to rest on his laurels, George Parnall, after resigning as managing director of Parnall & Sons in 1919, soon established his own business in the Coliseum works at Park Row, Bristol. Under the trading name of George Parnall & Co, newer, larger types of shopfittings and display cabinets were offered to British traders. In addition to this it was not long before the first aeroplane designed and built by George Parnall's new company was being constructed alongside the other creations in wood. The aircraft was a two-seat naval amphibian named the Puffin.

Designer Harold Bolas, responsible for the earlier Panther built for Parnall & Sons, had remained at the Brislington factory after the cessation of hostilities, but at the invitation of George Parnall he joined the new George Parnall company in 1920 as its chief designer of aircraft. The Puffin was Bolas's first design for George Parnall and was described in the

The first prototype Parnall Puffin, N.136, seen here after its first modification involving the redesigned central float with an upward curve to the bow. There are additional support struts inserted between the top of the float and the Napier Lion engine cowling. (*Imperial War Museum*)

firm's sales brochure as a 'Two-seater Amphibian for fighting and reconnaissance work with the Fleet as supplied to the British Air Ministry'.

The Puffin was designed in response to the Air Ministry's RAF Type 21 Specification of 1920, calling for an experimental aeroplane suitable for operating from an aircraft carrier as an amphibian.

The only other competitor for the contract was Fairey Aviation with its Pintail which, although powered by the same engine as the Puffin, and incorporating a similar layout for the fin and rudder, proved to possess very different flying characteristics from Parnall's machine.

The Parnall Puffin was of two-bay biplane configuration, strut and wire-braced in the conventional manner, while the mainplanes, which folded back alongside the fuselage for ease of stowage, were staggered and of parallel chord. A more unusual feature was the location of the fin and rudder below the rear fuselage, designed to allow an unobstructed view and field of fire for the observer/gunner in the rear cockpit. The layout was reminiscent of the German Hansa-Brandenburg W 12, 19, 29 and 33 series of seaplanes which became quite familiar during the First World War.

The Puffin was equipped with a two-position adjustable seat for the pilot, but those who flew the type reported the all-round view as excellent with the lower seat position sufficing. Stick and rudder bar controls were fitted, and the elevators, rudder and ailerons were all provided with a selectable two-speed gear system operable by the pilot at all times, which afforded positive control at low speed, and light control at high speed.

Power for the Puffin was provided by a 450 hp Napier Lion II driving a two-blade wooden propeller with reinforced metal leading-edges, the reduction gearing from the engine to the propeller being 44:29. A battery starter was provided for the Lion engine, an arrangement that was not as satisfactory as might first appear. This Napier starting system relied on a low capacity type of battery, and as electric starter trolleys did not then exist, there was no plug-in to an external power source, reliance being centred wholly on the aircraft's internal battery. There was no dynamo fitted into the system either, so the battery had to be removed from the aeroplane for recharging.

The Napier Lion did, however, possess a novel priming device designed to conserve battery current. Each cylinder head was fitted with a sliding rod connected to the pilot's cockpit by a linkage. When the pilot pulled on this mechanism it actuated four levers, each of which opened the front inlet valve and exhaust valve in one cylinder. This action compressed the engine, which then turned over easily. Nevertheless the electric starter did fail at times, and because of the Puffin's central float, it was not possible to start the engine in the usual way by swinging the propeller. The method was to prime the engine as for an electric start, and when everything was ready, the Parnall staff in attendance would pull on a rope attached to the propeller tip! This action hauled the pistons over compression while the pilot operated the starter magneto and, providing the Lion engine fired, the rope fell clear of the propeller and float.

The second Puffin (N.137), with a further improved main float, displayed in 1920, probably at Hendon. (*Real Photographs/MAP*)

Another problem with the Puffin's powerplant involved the system of carburation. A double carburettor was located on the port side of the engine, while a single carburettor was attached to the starboard side, and to balance this method of carburation was an art in itself. An atomiser, worked by an air pump, operated in conjunction with a needle valve controlled by the pilot, the end product often ending in an emission of smoke from unburnt fuel as well as a frequent loss of rpm which could be as much as 1,200 dropping from 1,800. This problem was eventually overcome in the Puffin by changing the main jets in the carburettor from 660 mm to 700 mm, which resulted in improved engine output figures of 1,900 rpm static, 2,060 rpm full throttle at sea level, and 1,980 rpm at 10,000 ft.

The Puffin was mounted on a single large central float of wooden construction, broad in the beam and attached to the lower fuselage by means of sturdy struts. It was in fact the first British seaplane to feature such a float, and was considered among its contemporaries as an intermediary between the twin-float seaplane and the flying-boat with its full length hull.

This lengthy float was intended to give the aircraft longitudinal stability, and was hinged at the rear to form a tailskid, which was supported by a shock absorber strut. A water rudder was fitted behind the float. The wheels were mounted either side of the float, and retracted manually upwards on their axle by means of a worm and nut gear operating through a vertical slot in the float. Lateral stability was provided by two deeply-

Third Parnall Puffin (N.138), with revised central float having an artificial chine and flat top to the forward end. Note, method of applying rudder serial number, also large outboard stabilising floats. (*Mark Parnall*)

profiled wingtip floats attached directly to the underside of the outer lower mainplanes.

The Air Ministry instructed George Parnall & Co to produce three prototype Puffins (N136–N138), and likewise Fairey Aviation was issued a contract to build three Pintails (N133–N135).

The first Puffin made its initial flight on 19 November, 1920, from the Isle of Grain Naval Air Station, piloted by Capt Norman Macmillan. It had been considered necessary to take off on the first flight from Grain's rough aerodrome after starting difficulties with the Lion engine made water launching too hazardous. The large wingtip floats were also removed for this flight as a precautionary measure, but the following day the first Puffin was launched as a seaplane from the Isle of Grain slipway.

During test flights the Puffin was found to be tail heavy in flight and several unsuccessful attempts to remedy this defect were tried out. These included increasing the tailplane incidence from 4 deg (maximum) to 6 deg by means of links, the injection of first ink and then milk into the slipstream between the fuselage and lower centre-section to indicate visibly the airflow, the fitting of a special pitot head to take in-flight readings (unsatisfactory when the rubber tubing kinked) and the stripping of all fabric from the lower centre-section.

This latter, rather drastic, step did slightly reduce the Puffin's tail heaviness, but the real cause of the trouble remained unknown, although it was suggested that downwash from the upper mainplane could have been the culprit.

When first tested as a seaplane the Puffin's central float proved extremely troublesome, due mainly to the float's short front section and

The third Puffin (N.138), with water rudder at the tail of the revised main float and ring mounting for the rear machine-gun. The unorthodox tail unit is clearly seen in this view. (*Parnall & Sons*)

straight top decking, a combination which rode badly in rough water. Indeed the water thrown back from the float smashed the propeller, damaged the radiator and strained the engine mountings! The damaged components were returned to George Parnall's works and the main float subjected to water tank tests. A number of modifications were made to the float including an extended upward-curving front section. This resulted in an extra pair of supporting struts being required, and these were fitted between the underside of the engine compartment and the forward part of the lengthened float.

A six-foot scale model of the Puffin was built by George Parnall, and tested on Bristol's Henleaze Lake, which in those days was quite large. The model was launched and trials of the central float undertaken by means of a winch attached to a motor-cycle engine, which hauled the model by means of a fisherman's greased line.

Further tests with the full-size Puffin prototype still proved unsatisfactory in rough water however, despite the tank and lake tests (in those days the testing of models in simulated scale conditions did not include rough water scale testing). Even after the new curved front extension was added, the Puffin's central float still flung back spray, enough to cut the full throttle rpm down to 1,700. Harold Bolas himself flew in the Puffin with Macmillan to see for himself the behaviour of the float, and as a result further modifications were introduced.

This time an artificial chine containing an outward and downward sweep was incorporated, and after this improvement the Puffin performed much more sedately on rough water both during take-off and when alighting. The third prototype Puffin was fitted with a further improved float which possessed a straight-topped front section.

Despite its promise as a successful naval amphibian, and the use of a very satisfactory amphibious gear in its make-up, the Puffin failed to reach production status. The type appeared at a very austere time; the RAF had already been greatly reduced in numbers as the Treasury imposed stringent restrictions on Government spending. No justification could, at the time, be found for the production of new military aircraft, certainly not in a category of the Puffin (or Fairey Pintail) amphibious types.

The three Puffins were eventually passed to the RAF for experimental purposes, a capacity in which the first machine (N136) was employed for some considerable time at the Isle of Grain Naval Air Station.

Parnall Puffin

Two-seat fighter and reconnaissance amphibian for carrier service. 450 hp Napier Lion II twelve-cylinder broad-arrow water-cooled engine.

Span 40 ft; length (approx) 30 ft; height 11 ft 6 in.

Approx loaded weight 5,000 lb.

Maximum speed 110 mph at sea level.

One fixed forward-firing .303-in Vickers machine-gun, one .303-in Lewis machine-gun on Scarff ring mounting in rear cockpit.

Production

Three prototypes only, N136–N138. See Appendix A.

Parnall Plover

Following the 1918 armistice the British Government's financial stringency tightened to a stranglehold on the development of military aviation, naval flying in particular being very badly hit. Indeed by 1920 British naval air units had been reduced to a token force of one Fleet spotter reconnaissance squadron, half-a-squadron of torpedo-bombers, one fighter flight, one seaplane flight and one flying-boat flight. Between 1919 and 1922 the only British aircraft-carrier in commission was HMS *Argus*, from which flew an ageing collection of Nieuport (Gloster) Nightjar, Parnall Panther, Sopwith Cuckoo and Westland Walrus biplanes.

It was not before time, therefore, when in 1922 the Air Ministry issued Specification 6/22 calling for a single-seat carrier-borne naval fighter capable of operating in the amphibious role. It was also stipulated that the resulting aeroplane should be able to use both the Bristol Jupiter and Armstrong Siddeley Jaguar radial engines.

Response to the specification came from two manufacturers, Fairey Aviation and George Parnall. In the event Fairey's design, the Flycatcher, proved the more successful, but a number of Parnall's type, the Plover, did serve with the Fleet for a year or so in 1923 and 1924.

The Parnall Plover was one of the first generation of purpose-built British fighters intended for aircraft carrier operations, and in fact was

Powered by a 385 hp Armstrong Siddeley Jaguar engine, this was the third prototype Parnall Plover (N162), which was built in landplane form. (*MoD*)

similar in some respects to its rival the Flycatcher. Dimensions, plan view and performance were quite comparable, but whereas Fairey's employed a composite fuselage structure of wood and metal, Harold Bolas for George Parnall designed the Plover to be constructed entirely from wood.

One of seven production Plovers (N9702–N9708), N9702 looks sturdy enough, but a weakness occurring spasmodically in the centre-section of Plovers was mainly responsible for their short service careers. (*MoD*)

The first production Plover (N9608) at Yate aerodrome in 1923, with Norman Macmillan in the cockpit. (*Mark Parnall*)

Another factor in the Flycatcher's favour was the use of the Fairey Patent Camber Gear, which with its high-lift capabilities proved an asset for carrier deck landings.

The Parnall Plover was equipped with full-span ailerons on both upper and lower mainplanes, but in other respects it was of conventional biplane layout with staggered equal-span single-bay wings with N interplane struts. The empennage had a well-rounded fin and rudder, the tailplane was strut- and wire-braced to the lower sides of the rear fuselage, and the fin was braced to the tailplane. The Plover's airframe was fabric-covered.

For use as a landplane the Plover was fitted with an orthodox cross-axle type of undercarriage incorporating oleo legs, but a pair of floats were interchangeable for employment as an amphibian. These floats were flat-topped, curved and broad of beam at the bottom, and featured a single step near their mid-point. A set of wheels projected from beneath the floats, the main pair located at the steps, and a smaller pair at the rear of the floats. Water rudders were fitted to the floats, and the whole unit was attached to the Plover's fuselage by four main struts and two oleo legs. A tailskid was fixed beneath the rear fuselage, this being retained on the amphibious version.

The first Plover (N160) appeared early in 1923 as the prototype landplane powered by a 436 hp Bristol Jupiter IV radial engine. The second machine (N161), also powered by a Jupiter IV, emerged as the amphibian prototype, while the third prototype (N162) was in land-plane configuration, but was powered by a 385 hp Armstrong Siddeley Jaguar.

Parnall Plovers were intended as replacements for the Nieuport Nightjar, and after prototype trials the Air Ministry ordered ten

The second prototype Plover (N161), powered by a Bristol Jupiter IV, is seen here at the MAEE, Felixstowe, in amphibious configuration. (*Imperial War Museum*)

The second prototype Plover at Felixstowe as an amphibian. (*Imperial War Museum*)

production Plovers from George Parnall (N9608–N9610 and N9702–N9708).
 The first two production machines were completed as landplanes, the third as an amphibian, and the remaining seven aircraft as landplanes. By the end of 1923 all production of Plovers had been delivered.

Production Plover, N9702, one of a small batch of ten built for naval service. (*MAP*)

The third prototype Plover, N162, powered by a 385 hp Armstrong Siddeley Jaguar. (*Imperial War Museum*)

Six Plovers entered service during 1923 with Nos. 403 and 404 Fleet Fighter Flights, where they flew as contemporaries of the Nightjars and Flycatchers of 401 and 402 Flights respectively. Despite its cleaner lines and higher maximum speed than the Fairey Flycatcher, however, the Plover had a limited Service career and did not enjoy the Flycatcher's popularity. This was attributed to a tendency on the part of the Plover towards

The second Plover prototype (N161), powered by a 436 hp Bristol Jupiter IV, in amphibious configuration on Yate aerodrome, circa, 1923. (*Mark Parnall*)

structural weakness occurring at times in the area of the centre-section. On one occasion a pilot flying a Plover on a routine test flight from Leuchars in 1924, was lucky to escape with his life; after performing a series of aerobatics the Plover's centre-section suddenly collapsed; the pilot fortunately managed to make a forced landing on moorland.

During 1924 an increasing number of Flycatchers entered service with the Fleet Air Arm and demonstrated their superiority. As a consequence those Parnall Plovers still remaining in Fleet units were quickly replaced, and by the end of 1924, all Plover fighters still in first line service had been withdrawn from the fleet.

Some Plovers were used for test purposes later, as the following extracts from the personal flight log of Capt Frank T Courtney, the well-known free-lance test pilot of the 1920s, testify:

18.2.25	Plover	N9708 35 minute test flight from RAE, Farnborough. Vibration tests.
16.3.25	Plover	N9608 30 minute test flight at Filton. Engine cowling/height tests.
16.3.25	Plover	N9608 Second test flight of 25 minutes' duration (N9608) same day. Engine/level tests.
17.3.25	Plover	N9707 15 minutes' delivery flight Filton to Yate. Second delivery flight of 10 minutes' duration Filton to Yate with Plover N9706. Third delivery flight of 10 minutes' duration Filton to Yate with Plover N9608.
25.3.25	Plover	N9706 40 minute delivery flight from Yate to RAE Farnborough.
22.5.25	Plover	N9708 15 minute delivery flight Yate to Filton

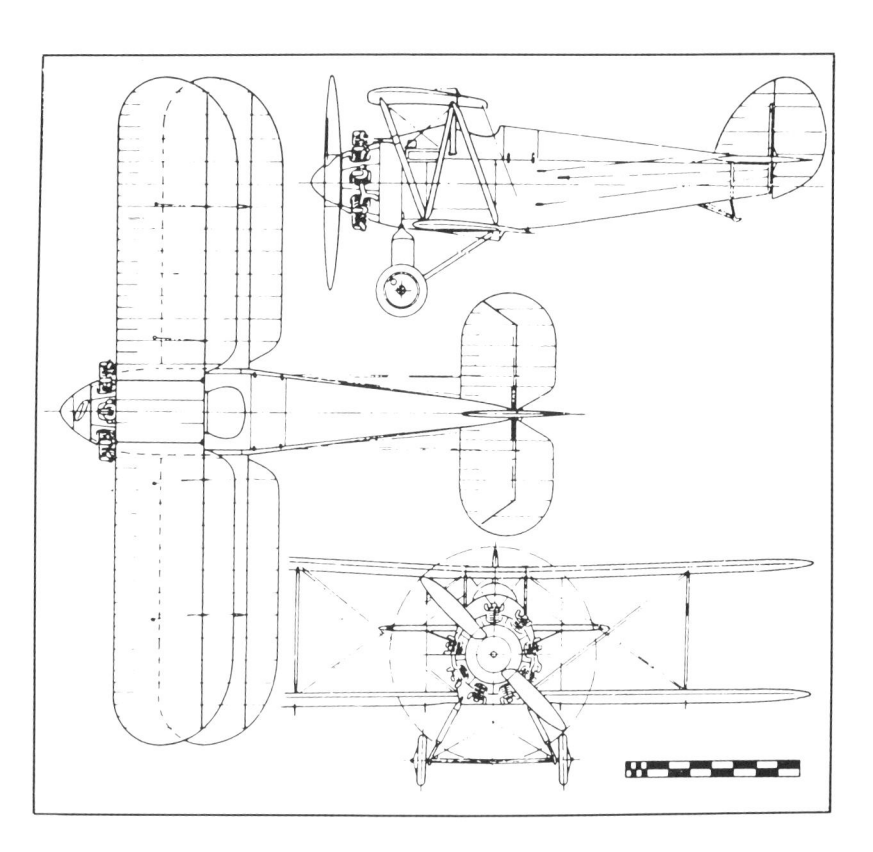

The civil Plover, G-EBON (ex-N9705), which flew in the 1926 King's Cup Race, piloted by Sir C J Quintin Brand. (*Real Photographs via MAP*)

On one occasion Roy Fedden, enthused by the successful results achieved in France whereby Gnome-Rhône Jupiter engines had been tested with separate helmet fairings for each cylinder, tried the same experiments at Filton on a Jupiter engine installed in a Plover flying test-bed.

One Plover was civilianised to be entered on the British civil register as G-EBON, this machine (ex-N9705) receiving a C of A on 7 July, 1926. This Plover was entered in the 1926 King's Cup Air Race, which took place on 9 and 10 July, but piloted by Sqn Ldr Sir C J Quintin Brand. G-EBON was forced to retire from the race with fuel feed trouble. It was written off after a crash in January 1929.

Parnall Plover

Single-seat carrier-borne fighter. 436 hp Bristol Jupiter IV nine-cylinder or 385 hp Armstrong Siddeley Jaguar two-row fourteen cylinder air-cooled radial engine.

Span 29 ft; length 23 ft; height 12 ft; wing area 306 sq ft.

Empty weight 2,035 lb; loaded weight 2,984 lb.

Maximum speed 142 mph at sea level; climb to 20,000 ft, 25 min 13 sec; service ceiling 23,000 ft; approximate range 300 miles.

Two fixed forward-firing .303-in Vickers machine-guns

Weights and performance with Jupiter engine

Production

Three prototypes, one amphibious and two landplanes, and ten production aircraft, one amphibian and nine landplanes. See Appendix A.

Parnall Possum

After the Armistice of 1918, efforts were made to divert the energies of war to the advancement of technology for peaceful means and to improve public transport and communications. One move in this direction was ventured by the British Air Ministry, whose Directorate of Technical Development put forward proposals for the introduction of special cargo-carrying aeroplanes. These machines would be given the primary role of carrying mail in an endeavour to speed up the postal services.

At least four types of 'postal' aircraft were designed and built in response to the proposal: the Bristol Type 37 Tramp (J6912), Boulton & Paul Bodmin (J6910–J6911), Westland Dreadnought monoplane (J6986) and the Parnall Possum (J6862–J6863).

The Westland Dreadnought postal was based on the principles of the Russian designer M Voevodskii, and followed similar lines to those applied by Harold Bolas in his own 'bodyless' ideas. The other three types,

Parnall Possum J6862 at Yate in 1923. (*Parnall & Sons*)

however, although intended as mailplanes, were in the event used to test outboard propellers driven by geared shafts connected to a mid-fuselage-mounted powerplant. Bristol's Type 37 Tramp was powered by four 240 hp Siddeley Puma water-cooled engines mounted in the fuselage, whence two outboard propellers were driven by a system of extension shafts. Boulton & Paul's Bodmin design employed the same principle, but was powered by only two engines in the fuselage.

George Parnall's Possum, of which two were built during 1923 and 1925 respectively, as a medium-range postal and military conversion of the same, was of triplane configuration, and was powered by only one engine, a 450 hp Napier Lion.

This was mounted longitudinally inside the aircraft's flat-sided ply-covered fuselage and located at the Possum's centre of gravity. The three cylinder blocks of the Lion engine were left exposed, while power to the two outboard wooden propellers, which had a diameter of 9ft 6in each, was transmitted through a bevel-gear drive to shafts in the leading-edge of the centre-wing of the triplane layout.

The unusual layout of the Possum triplane allowed the two propellers to be driven from a single, centrally-located, Napier Lion engine via extension shafts buried in the centre wing. (*Mark Parnall*)

In this view of Possum J6862, its Napier Lion engine can be seen located between the front cockpit and the rear gunner's position. The starboard external radiator is on the side of the fuselage. The number 10 on its fuselage was its exhibition number for the RAF Hendon Air Pageant held on 28 June, 1923. (*Parnall & Sons*)

The use of a triplane configuration by Harold Bolas was to allow the drives from the fuselage to the two airscrews to be housed in the central wing. The shafts themselves were completely enclosed in a casing and ran between the leading-edge and the front spar. The propellers contra-rotated, and at the Possum's cruising speed their rpm was so low, due to the reduction gearing, that it was possible to discern individual blades in motion.

The shafts and reduction gears were manufactured by D Napier and Sons, producers of the Lion engine which, in the case of the Possum, featured an unusual cooling arrangement. The radiators were fixed externally, one being attached to each side of the rectangular section fuselage, and were hinged to allow the radiating surface to be turned in variance with the airflow. The radiators could be worked by the pilot from the cockpit thus enabling him to regulate the engine cooling rate. The water header tank was located in the centre-section of the top wing, and beneath it there was a large gravity-feed fuel tank.

A novel introduction on the Possum was its swivelling tailwheel which was fitted with an automatic brake. Most contemporary aircraft employed tailskids to support the rear end of the fuselage, but the Possum's pivoting tailwheel with its automatic brake proved far more effective.

The brake friction increased progressively as the load on the tailwheel increased, but if required, the pilot could release the tail brake completely by operating a lever in the cockpit. This arrangement, combined with the large diameter slow-speed propellers, made the Possum an exceptionally easy type to handle on the ground.

The Possum's triplane wings were unstaggered, and all three mainplanes incorporated symmetrically balanced, long-span, cable-controlled ailerons. Even so, pilots reported that in flight the aircraft's aileron control was heavy, rudder control rather light and elevator control extremely sensitive.

The forward gun position and gravity-feed fuel tank can be clearly seen in this view of Possum, J6862. (*Parnall & Sons*)

Of all-wooden construction with fabric-covered wings and tail surfaces, the Possum's fuselage was covered by plywood panelling. The triplane wings were of equal span, strut- and wire-braced. The empennage was a conventional style layout with a rounded fin and rudder, the tailplane being in the mid-position. An early type of oleo undercarriage with oil dashpots and rubber buffers was incorporated, the mainwheels being located on a fairly wide-track cross-axle.

Despite its intended purpose as a civil mailplane the Possum inevitably appeared in military guise, the front and rear cockpits being fitted with Scarff gun mountings. The forward gunner's position was installed a short way back from the aircraft's nose, while the rear gunner sat in line with the trailing-edge of the centre wing. A parachute compartment was within easy reach of the crew, and equipment on board the Possum included wireless, photographic apparatus and, at one time, a rocket firing device. The aircraft was also tested for bombing and reconnaissance duties.

The first prototype Possum, J6862, built to Air Ministry Specification 9/20, made two preliminary ground hops, the first on 13 May, 1923, and the second on 10 June.

These short hops were made after the aircraft's rudder had twice been enlarged, and were made with Wing Cdr Norman Macmillan at the controls. On 19 June Macmillan took the Possum up on its first official test flight, from Filton, with Harold Bolas as passenger; the designer wanted to observe for himself the in-flight behaviour of the machine's unorthodox drive system to the propellers. As a matter of interest, the person carried as an observer on the Possum's original ground hops was a Mr Bryant whose sister later married Harold Bolas.

Considering it was powered by only one 450 hp Napier Lion engine, the Possum was quite a large aeroplane. Its large-diameter propellers and unstaggered triplane wings are well shown in this view of the first example built, J6862. (*Parnall & Sons*)

On 15 April, 1924, the Possum was flown to the RAE at Farnborough and on 28 June appeared in an all-silver finish at the RAF Hendon Air Pageant, where it received its first public showing. On 13 December that year this Possum was flown at the A & AEE by R Ivelaw-Chapman.

Plans to construct a second Possum at George Parnall's Coliseum works did not immediately materialise, and the Napier Lion engine intended for the second prototype was left gathering dust for several months. Indeed hopes for the building of a second Possum had almost been given up when, suddenly, it was decided to go ahead and complete the second machine. By

In this view of the second Possum, J6863, taken at Martlesham Heath, circa, 1925–26, the hinged radiator can be seen swung out on the starboard side of the fuselage. Close scrutiny also reveals the three ailerons in a slightly lowered position on the starboard side. (*Parnall & Sons*)

then the Lion engine was so dirty it had to be stripped down, cleaned and re-assembled as the second Possum, J6863, took shape on the factory floor. This second machine made its first flight from Yate aerodrome on 27 April, 1925, and later appeared in that year's RAF Hendon Air Display, again like the first prototype in an all-silver finish with standard RAF markings.

By the time this second Possum prototype had made its appearance at Yate, Norman Macmillan had ceased being a free-lance test-pilot (prototypes from various aircraft firms were test flown on a contract basis) and had joined Fairey Aviation as chief test pilot.

As a result Frank Courtney became responsible for flight testing the second Possum prototype. The following extracts from Courtney's flying log indicate to some extent the early flights taken with this aeroplane.

27.4.25	Possum J6863	10 minute first flight at Yate aerodrome.
28.4.25	Possum J6863	15 minute routine test flight at Yate (Napier Lion engine).
29.4.25	Possum J6863	15 minute test flight at Yate (Mr Copley on board). Second flight of 30 minutes.
30.4.25	Possum J6863	1hr 35min duration test flight (Mr Healey on board).
15.7.25	Possum J6863	1hr 20min flight from Yate on finishing contract this aircraft.

The second Possum was flown by Sqn Ldr T H England at the A & AEE on 17 August, 1925, and again in February 1926. Both Possums were in fact flown in an experimental capacity at Martlesham for some time, but their ultimate fate is unknown.

Parnall Possum

Three-seat experimental mail and military triplane. 450 hp Napier Lion twelve-cylinder broad-arrow water-cooled engine driving two outboard airscrews through bevel-gear and extension shafts.

Span 46 ft; length 39 ft; height 13 ft 9 in; wing area 777 sq ft.
Loaded weight 6,300 lb.
Approximate maximum and cruising speeds believed to be 105 mph and 80 mph.
Provision for fore and aft .303-in Lewis machine-guns on Scarff ring mountings.

Production

Two prototypes built under contract No.305924/20 of 7 April, 1921. See Appendix A.

The Parnall Pixie in its original form as built for the 1923 'Motor Glider' or Light Aeroplane trials at Lympne. Here the Pixie is powered by a 3½ hp (500 cc) two-cylinder Douglas engine, and is in its Mk.I configuration by having the large wings fitted for the fuel consumption tests. (*George Jenks*)

Parnall Pixie Series

In 1923 the *Daily Mail* offered a prize of £1,000 in a 'motor glider' competition, while at the same time the Duke of Sutherland promised £500 to the pilot of the aeroplane making the lor ?est flight on one gallon of petrol. The duke stipulated that the aeroplane concerned must be fitted with an engine of not more than 750 cc capacity. This combined challenge resulted in the setting up of a Light Aeroplane Competition by the Royal Aero Club. The contest was to be at Lympne aerodrome in Kent, where the events were scheduled to take place during October 1923.

A number of interesting machines were entered for this, the first of several light aeroplane trials to be held annually. Among those aircraft at the first meeting was the Gloster Gannet, English Electric Wren, the ANEC, a de Havilland D.H.53 Humming Bird, and the Parnall Pixie I/II, unregistered but entering the Lympne trials as No.9.

In designing the Pixie for George Parnall, Harold Bolas realised that no one aeroplane could possibly win all the prizes eventually offered for the competition, so he decided to produce an aeroplane with interchangeable components.

This involved employing one type of fuselage, tail unit and undercarriage, but using a design in which alternative sets of mainplanes could be used. In addition provision had to be made for the interchangeability of a small or large capacity powerplant which included alternative propeller requirements. After much sketching, rejection of ideas and a lot of replanning, Harold Bolas finally produced what he believed were the answers in the shape of the designs for the Pixie Marks I and II.

A combination of wing and engine variations resulted in the Pixie I monoplane, which had large wings and a small motor for the fuel consumption tests, or alternatively large wings and a more powerful motor for the height tests. When fitted with small wings and a high capacity engine for the speed trials, the Pixie became the Mark II.

The Pixie I was powered by a $3\frac{1}{2}$ hp (500 cc) twin-cylinder Douglas motor-cycle engine for the fuel consumption tests, and for the altitude and speed trials a 6 hp Douglas was installed. These Douglas engines were air-cooled flat twins with external flywheel and chain drive to an overhead shaft which carried the wooden propeller. When undergoing tests at the Douglas works in Kingswood, Bristol, the second engine of 6 hp (736 cc) developed 36 bhp at 6,000 rpm, and it is interesting to observe that the longest full-throttle flight with this engine lasted for twenty-one minutes.

The Pixie possessed an external air intake located below the cowling, while the throttle, air and ignition were controlled by Bowden cable from the cockpit. The capacity of the fuel tank was 3 Imp gal, and the oil tank contained three-quarters of a gallon of oil.

Fuselage width between the Pixie's wing roots was two feet, the large wings, when fitted, having a span of 29 ft and the smaller wings 18 ft. A pilot weight of 168 lb was allowed for, and when in small wing configuration the Pixie II had a total loaded weight of 460 lb with a wing loading of $7\frac{1}{2}$ lb/sq ft. The landing speeds with alternative wing fittings were 33 mph (large wings) and 45 mph (small wings).

The Pixie's fuselage was constructed of spruce longerons, while diagonal struts, fixed together with three-ply gussets, were well glued, through fastened and roved. No wire bracing was employed, and no further trueing-up was required after completion of the fuselage structure. The

For ease of both stowage and ground transport, the Pixie's wings could be removed and attached along the fuselage sides as shown here. (*T I Jackson Ltd*)

Here the Pixie is in Mk.II form, with smaller wings and a 6 hp (736 cc) Douglas engine, in readiness for the 1923 speed trials at Lympne. (*Mark Parnall*)

front end was covered with a metal plate providing a shield between the engine and the cockpit. A fairly large pilot could be accommodated within the confines of the cockpit, which contained the necessary instrumentation including air speed indicator, cross level, aneroid, engine revolution counter, fuel gauge, oil sight feed and engine switch.

When seated in the cockpit the pilot was provided with a canvas cockpit cover which fitted up to his neck by means of a zip-fastener. This sealed off the cockpit from severe draughts and enhanced the streamlining of the fuselage. No windscreen was fitted to the single cockpit.

The wings were of mixed wood and steel construction, steel fittings being employed at fuselage attachment points, while the internal wing bracing consisted of grooved steel rods. The design of the wing was rather unusual; from the fuselage to just beyond the bracing strut attachment the chord was constant and the spars parallel, but past this point the front spar continued straight, while the rear spar raked sharply forward to meet the front spar at the wingtip.

The aileron spar was hinged to the outer portion of the rear spar giving the aileron a forward sweep. This arrangement resulted in extremely stiff wing torsion and more effective aileron control. Wing attachment points and bracing struts were easily removable to facilitate rapid stowage, and after removal the wings could be attached, one each side of the fuselage lengthwise, for transport. Hinged inspection doors were incorporated in the wing surfaces of the Pixie allowing for ready inspection of control cables and levers.

The tail unit was constructed entirely of fabric-covered steel framing, a combination ensuring robustness and stiffness. The tailplane was of triangular form. The rear spar, which was arranged to hinge about the fuselage transom, was fixed at the front, and permitted the use of several angles of incidence. The divided elevators extended across the whole span of the fixed tailplane, and incorporated a central lever operated by a

An extremely rare shot of the 'high-speed' Pixie, the type's diminutive size being emphasized here by the men in attendance. (*J M Bruce/G S Leslie collection*)

tubular member passing through a slot in the transom. The fin and rudder were of similar construction.

The Pixie's undercarriage consisted of two chrome nickel-steel tubes. These were attached to the top of the cross fuselage member in the rear of the cockpit, and diverged from there downwards and forward through sockets in the bottom of the fuselage to the axle, which was pin-jointed to forks in their lower ends. The axle itself was wide-based and had considerable overhang on each side of the tube attachment points. The advantage of this design of undercarriage was that rubber shock-absorbers could be dispensed with, thus eliminating the possibility of the rubber cord perishing.

In addition there was no necessity for cable cross bracing, thus doing away with the usual tightening up process required, and ground taxi-ing was much steadier due to the wide wheel track.

Contemporary aeronautical experts remarked on the excellence of Harold Bolas's undercarriage design for the Pixie. The tailskid had its upper end hinged to the fuselage top member, the skid itself being reinforced with a steel sleeve which helped prevent damage caused by hammering action. The mainwheels were wire-spoked with fabric disc covering.

To facilitate the installation of various powerplants in the Pixie, the engine mounting was a separate section to the fuselage and was constructed of tubular steel with swaged-rod cross-bracing. Special attention was given to render the mounting sufficiently rigid to withstand the shocks of persistent misfiring.

Normal controls were employed, but levers were used in place of pulleys for cable runs to reduce fraying. Yawing tendency and consequent undue use of the rudder were minimized by the provision of differential aileron control. For a given movement of the control column the angular motion of the upward moving aileron was considerably greater than that of the downward moving one. This arrangement, combined with the particular design of wing applied to the Pixie, enabled the aeroplane to be controlled by a much smaller rudder surface than would otherwise have been necessary. Indeed this was a feature of the Pixie which was believed to have accounted for the large degree of effectiveness of its controls, and especially the fact that what appeared to be an utterly inadequate rudder was in fact entirely satisfactory.

The fuel tank was located in front of the instrument panel, while the carburettor was gravity-fed and a petrol filter and shut-off cock, close to the tank, could be conveniently operated by the pilot from the cockpit. The external air intake eliminated the possibility of a back-fire through the carburettor which could ignite petrol fumes inside the cowling. The cowling was attached to the engine compartment by special Parnall-designed toggle clips, which ensured that the cowling was held rigidly in place and could not shake loose in the air. The engine section could be completely opened up for inspection within a few seconds.

In addition to the Douglas engines fitted to the Pixie, Parnall envisaged the type as being suitable for the 698 cc or 1,000 cc Blackburne, and the 1,070 cc flat-twin Bristol Cherub, all of which had direct drive to the propeller. The company recommended in their contemporary brochure that the Blackburne 1,000 cc or Bristol Cherub be installed: 'since such a power will enable the machine to be flown with the engine well throttled back with consequent increase in reliability and life of the engine'. It was also pointed out that the adoption of a direct-drive saved weight and reduced the risk of possible transmission troubles.

The final covering and finish of the Pixie comprised a specially light and strong linen fabric possessing excellent tensile strength in both directions, and which could be dope-finished in any colour scheme desired.

The Parnall Pixie I made its first flight from Filton aerodrome on 13 September, 1923, piloted by Norman Macmillan. In its Mk.II form the Pixie made its initial flight from Filton on 4 October the same year, and

The Pixie Mk.II, powered by the 6 hp Douglas engine, with early style fin and rudder.
(*J M Bruce/G S Leslie collection*)

was reported to be a joy to handle. It was said to have exceptional stability in all but the very roughest of weather.

The 1923 Light Aeroplane Trials were scheduled to take place at Lympne from 8 to 13 October, prizes being offered for the greatest mileage flown on one gallon of petrol, the fastest laps in two consecutive runs over a 12½ mile course, the greatest altitude reached, and the maximum duration achieved – allowing stops for refuelling.

After arriving at Lympne with the Pixie, Norman Macmillan found that in its Mk.I configuration, with 29 ft span wings and the 500 cc Douglas engine, the machine could not approach the economical consumption figures of the English Electric Wren (2½ hp ABC) or the ANEC (3½ hp Blackburne). Nevertheless the Pixie I managed to fly a distance of 53.4 miles on one gallon of petrol and covered ten laps of the 12½ mile course.

On 10 October the Pixie was flown to Croydon, where a number of aircraft were being demonstrated to a group of Dominion Prime Ministers. Norman Macmillan was flying the Pixie, which was on that occasion in its Mk.II form, when just after taking off one cylinder cut out. Macmillan, brilliant airman that he was, carried on to make a brief flight at tree-top height, rounding the Croydon hangars at only ten feet! The Pixie scraped over the boundary fence and landed safely, a truly remarkable piece of flying on just one cylinder!

The following day the Pixie was back at Lympne and, still in its Mk.II configuration – 18 ft span wings and 736 cc Douglas – Macmillan entered the machine in the Abdulla Tobacco Company's £500 speed contest. Despite gusty conditions the little Pixie won at a speed of 76.1 mph. On 13 October, again in its Mk.II form, the Pixie attained a speed of 81.2 mph during one lap.

On 27 October the Pixie II was entered for the Wakefield Prize at RAF, Hendon, where the course comprised a number of pylons erected inside the aerodrome boundary. Again in the very capable hands of Norman Macmillan, the Pixie II romped home to win the speed competition at an average speed of 81 mph.

Seen here on Yate aerodrome in 1924, the Pixie III, with its 32 hp Bristol Cherub series III flat-twin air-cooled engine, also has improved undercarriage supports. (*Rolls-Royce, Bristol*)

The rivalry at Lympne during the October events encouraged aircraft manufacturers to set their sights on further prizes, and of course the resulting prestige which would be gained from another series of trials, scheduled to be held again at Lympne in 1924. This competition was intended for the benefit of the Air Ministry which was seeking a suitable training aeroplane for the use of the numerous civil flying clubs which were beginning to be formed around the country.

Noticeable by its absence in the 1924 Lympne events was a de Havilland product, but other types appearing included the Bristol Type 91 Brownie, Westland Woodpigeon, Gloster Gannet, Hawker Cygnet, Beardmore Wee Bee and the Parnall Pixie Mk.III.

In the Pixie Mk.III Harold Bolas had revised the original Pixie design and converted it into the required two-seat arrangement demanded for the trials, a standard windscreen being fitted to the rear cockpit. In addition facilities were provided for the fitting of a removable upper wing, which enabled the aircraft to be converted into a biplane, an extra feature giving further benefits in performance both during landing and taking off. The upper wing was strut-braced and, in addition to being detachable, was over six feet shorter in span than the lower wing. The Pixie III had a strange appearance when airborne in biplane form.

Other than the two-seater arrangement and detachable upper wing, the 1924 version of the Pixie was fundamentally similar in most respects to the previous year's model.

Like the Pixie I and II, the revised version was fitted with a semi-cantilever monoplane wing in which the mainplanes were attached to the bottom of the fuselage and braced to the top decking by means of adjustable streamlined struts. In the Pixie III the wing spars were of box section, and narrow strips were screwed to the flanges externally on which rested the three-ply webs of the ribs. This relieved the flanges of their shear load. Tie-rod bracing was employed, and it is interesting to note that the lift struts were attached to the tubular drag struts and not to the spar

Pixie III, G-EBJG, piloted by Frank Courtney, about to take off at Yate. (*Eric Harlin*)

flanges direct as was the usual practice. This type of attachment avoided twisting stress on the spars, and as the strut fittings were placed close to the spar walls, the tubular drag struts were not subjected to bending loads.

The pin joints of the wing roots to the fuselage were not placed on the neutral axis, but on the lower flange, the front hinge being a universal joint about which the wing could swing when the rear spar pin and the strut attachments were unfastened. The wing could then be tilted with its trailing-edge upwards and pushed back to lie along the sides of the fuselage. An improvement in the design of the undercarriage fitted to the Pixie III comprised two steel tube legs running through the fuselage floor to the top longerons. This revised undercarriage was of the cantilever type there being no fore and aft bracing employed. The legs were fitted with oleo-pneumatic shock-absorbers giving a fair amount of travel, movement of the telescopic tubes in conjunction with the deflection of the axle resulting in excellent springing.

George Parnall's company produced two Pixie IIIs for the 1924 Lympne trials; G-EBJG, the first machine, was powered by a 32 hp Bristol Cherub III flat twin, while the second Pixie III (G-EBKK) was fitted with a 35 hp Blackburne Thrush three-cylinder radial engine.

The first flight of G-EBJG took place at Yate aerodrome on 5 September, 1924 (George Parnall had by then acquired the Yate site although transfer of the company from Bristol was not wholly completed until the following year), after which it was found modifications were necessary to the rudder and elevator. Once these alterations had been made both Pixie IIIs were flown to Lympne ready for the trials.

As the Pixie IIIs could be flown in both monoplane and biplane configuration the racing numbers 17 and 18 were at first allotted to G-EBJG, and number 19 to G-EBKK. However, in the qualifying trials a misunderstanding arose in which number 17 was withdrawn on the order of the judges; it was required that all aeroplanes competing must be present simultaneously. This of course was impossible in the case of G-EBJG

With its front cockpit faired over, Pixie III No.18 (G-EBJG) at the Lympne for the 1924 Light Aeroplane Trials. The engine was a 32 hp Bristol Cherub III. (*Parnall via T I Jackson Ltd*)

The Pixie III G-EBJG was flown officially in monoplane configuration for the 1924 Lympne Light Aeroplane Trials. It carried the number 18 as here, but was not flown officially at the trials in its biplane form. (*Parnall via T I Jackson Ltd*)

which, as number 17 and 18 was the same machine. In the event G-EBJG flew as number 18, while G-EBKK, flying in only its biplane form, was given the designation Pixie IIIA and remained as number 19.

During the 1924 Lympne competitions G-EBJG (18) was flown by Flt Lieut 'Rollo' A de Haga Haig, and G-EBKK (19) was in the very capable hands of Sqn Ldr W Sholto Douglas. Throughout the events both Pixies suffered from mechanical troubles. On 27 September number 18 managed one circuit only before a loss of oil pressure forced it to land. The following day number 19 was obliged to land with engine trouble, although on the 29th this aircraft did manage to complete a number of laps. Tuesday, 30 September, proved to be no better with de Haga Haig having to force-land with a broken conrod, and Sholto Douglas being forced down with a seized-up Thrush engine. By 1 October a spare ungeared Bristol Cherub engine had been installed in number 18, and de Haga Haig flew it in Mk.III monoplane form in readiness for the forthcoming Grosvenor Cup Race.

A very polished performance of aerobatics including, loops and rolls, believed to have been the first time such manoeuvres had been made in an aeroplane of that class, was given by de Haga Haig, a display he repeated the following day. Number 19 as the biplane Pixie IIIA took part in the slow speed trials, despite the fact it was still plagued with engine troubles.

The Grosvenor Cup Race was to take place on 4 October, and on the previous day, G-EBJG and G-EBKK were joined in the air by one of the earlier Pixie monoplanes (G-EBKM). This machine was a Mk.II and had been re-engined with a 1,000 cc Blackburne vee twin, having apparently been kept clandestinely in a hangar all week. The sudden appearance of this third Parnall Pixie made it favourite for the race, but unfortunately the aircraft lost its propeller on a landing approach, and the substitute airscrew fitted somewhat retarded the Pixie II's top speed. The race ended

Pixie II G-EBKM, which was originally an experimental military trainer J7324. In this view it is powered by a 696 cc Blackburne Tomtit engine. For the Lympne trials it was fitted with a more powerful Blackburne vee twin. (*MAP*)

with G-EBJG (18) coming in fifth, the severely handicapped G-EBKM finishing in sixth place and G-EBKK (19) being withdrawn with engine trouble.

In spite of its apparent faults the Pixie was considered by George Parnall to be basically a fine aeroplane in which the major problems could be solved by installing a more suitable powerplant. Encouragement came too in the form of an Air Ministry contract, number 487254/24, for the construction of two Pixie trainers to Specification 44/23. These machines, J7323 and J7324, were each powered by the 696 cc Blackburne Tomtit engine, and one of them appeared at the 1924 RAF Air Pageant at Hendon.

The two military Pixies were sent to the A & AEE, Martlesham, and while there, J7323 was flown by H F U Battle on 3 July and on 3 October by R Ivelaw-Chapman, who also flew J7324 at the establishment on 1 December the same year. T H England also flew J7323 on 8 April, 1925, at the A & AEE, and again in May 1926.

In the meantime the civil Pixie III, G-EBJG, was also sent to the A & AEE for testing by Service pilots. They reported the type as excellent for its intended purpose as a two-seat trainer, although there were some reservations about the downwards view over the wing.

On 25 August, 1925, G-EBJG was returned to Yate, where G-EBKK was already in use as an engine test-bed, having had its Blackburne Thrush discarded in favour of a 1,000 cc Anzani. However, this engine too was in turn replaced by a Bristol Cherub III, the powerplant with which G-EBKM was fitted for its entry in the 1925 Bank Holiday races held at Lympne aerodrome where it was flown by Frank Courtney.

During 1926 the two Pixie IIIs were permanently converted into monoplane configuration, each powered by the 32 hp Bristol Cherub III. In September that year G-EBJG was entered again for the Air Ministry

The Parnall Pixie III

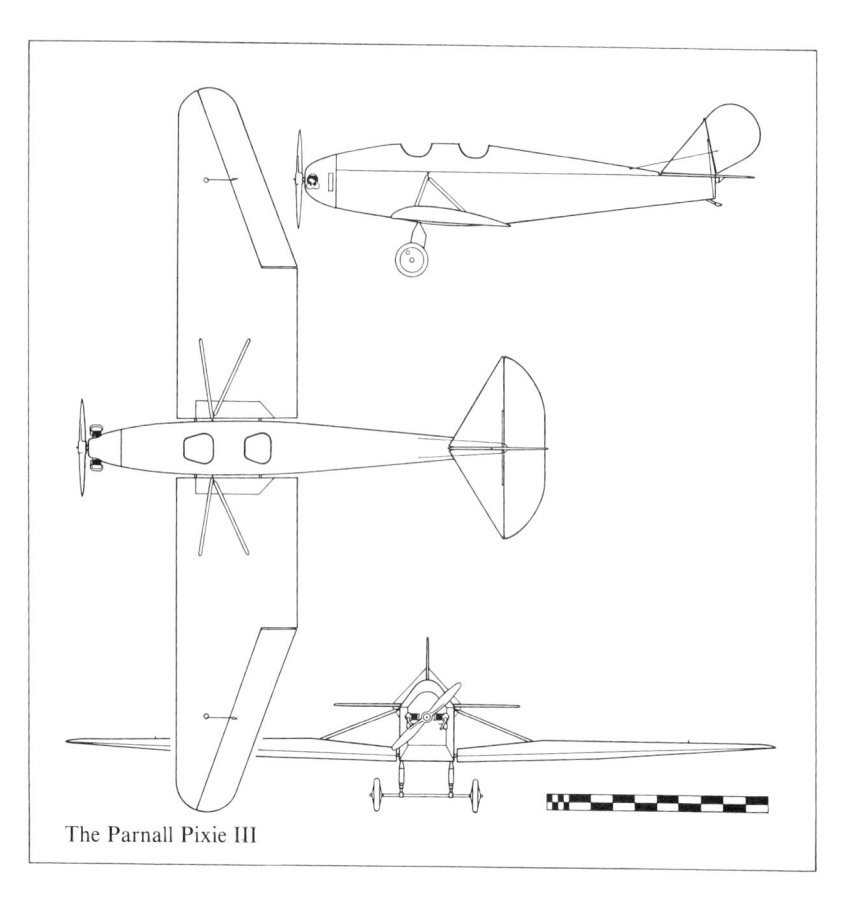

trials to be held at Lympne. Piloted by Frank Courtney and displaying the racing number 14, the first Pixie III ended up in fourth place in the week-long event. The overall winner was the Hawker Cygnet G-EBMB which now resides in the Camm Memorial Hall at the RAF Museum, Hendon. Pixie III G-EBKK, was eventually sold to the Bristol and Wessex Aero Club, but this machine was destroyed in a crash during September 1930.

After returning from Lympne to Yate in 1926, G-EBJG went to the Bristol Flying School which owned it until 1933. It was sold that March to C B Thompson of Rugby. In April 1935 this aeroplane was purchased by S L Dodwell of Hinckley and stored at Hanworth in 1936. After passing to R G Carr of Kirklinton, the aircraft was stored for the duration of the war. Later, G-EBJG went to D I Taylor and R H Grant and, in 1957, K C D St Cyrien at Reigate.

Eventually passing to a Mr Thorpe from Cropthorne, Sussex, this by then quite rare aeroplane might have ended its days on a bonfire, but for

The Parnall Pixie IIIA

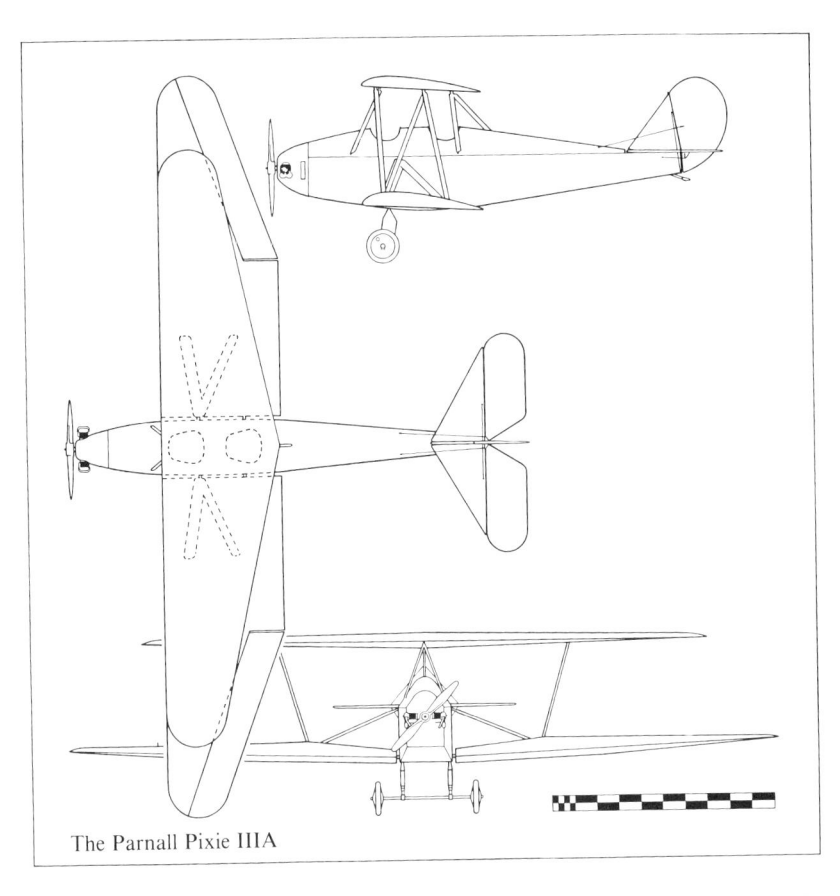

the timely intervention of James Rowe of Stratford-upon-Avon. He retrieved the remains of G-EBJG, and later presented them to the Midland Aircraft Preservation Society at Coventry.

Of the earlier Parnall Pixies, the prototype as already mentioned was converted to Mk.III configuration, while the two military machines ended their days in civil guise. The first (J7323) appeared at the 1924 RAF Hendon Air Pageant, where it bore the number 13 on its fuselage sides. This aircraft later served at RAF Wittering before being sold and passing into the hands of the Linnell brothers. They later sold the Pixie to the Bedford Flying Club, after which it went to C P B Ogilvie in whose hands it was last heard of in 1936.

The other military Pixie (J7324) was designated the single-seat Mk.II and, after its RAF service was completed, returned to Parnall at Yate. Registered G-EBKM, this was the third Pixie which made the dramatic appearance at the Lympne trials mentioned earlier, and it was afterwards flown regularly by Frank Courtney. He flew it in the air races held at

Lympne in August 1925, an event for which it was fitted with a large rudder. After flying at a number of air meetings in Britain, G-EBKM was eventually purchased by F J Cleare of Maylands, Romford, Essex, on 17 April, 1936. On 7 August, 1937, a C of A was issued for this aircraft and it was sold to Ray Bullock of Fraddon in Cornwall in January 1939. On 19 April G-EBKM crashed at Colan and was written off.

The personal flying log of Frank Courtney once again reveals some interesting reflections on the Pixie's flying career during 1925 and 1926:

7.2.25	Pixie III G-EBKK	10 minute test flight from Filton. Propeller came off!
26.3.25	Pixie II G-EBKM	15 minute test flight at Yate (1,000 cc Blackburne engine). Second test flight of 15 minutes' duration in Pixie III G-EBKK (geared Bristol Cherub engine).
4.6.25	Pixie III G-EBKK	Taken on 10 minute test flight from Yate.
15.7.25	Pixie III G-EBKK	15 minute test flight at Yate. Later same day at Yate, Pixie II G-EBKM taken on 15 minute test flight on propeller test.
1.8.25	Pixie II G-EBKM	10 minute test flight (propeller test) at Lympne. Second flight, 40 minutes in 2nd heat of Holiday Handicap Race (2nd). Third flight at Lympne, again in Pixie II G-EBKM, final race. Propeller broke in heavy rain! Later same day Pixie II G-EBKM, Scratch Race (speed) of 40 minutes at Lympne.
2.8.25	Pixie II G-EBKM	Five minute test flight (propeller test). Second flight Pixie II (G-EBKM, 15 minute 3 km speed test at Lympne. Third flight Pixie II G-EBKM, 25 minute 50 km speed test at Lympne.
3.8.25	Pixie II G-EBKM	Five minute propeller test flight. Later same day flew Pixie II G-EBKM in Lympne International Handicap Race 2nd heat. Time 1 hr 20 min. Third flight same day Pixie II G-EBKM 1 hr 20 min at Lympne in Grosvenor Cup Race.
6.10.25	Pixie II G-EBKM	Flown for 30 minutes at Stag Lane for cinema!

28.8.26	Pixie III G-EBJG	30 minute test flight at Yate in preparation for Lympne trials.
29.8.26	Pixie III G-EBJG	1 hr 30 min test flight at Yate for Lympne trials.
30.8.26	Pixie III G-EBJG	45 minute test flight at Yate in preparation for Lympne trials. Later same day 15 flight to Filton looking for suitable propellers! Later again same day 30 minute flight undertaken in Pixie III G-EBJG at Yate on take-off and landing tests.
9.9.26	Pixie III G-EBJG (No.14)	15 minute test flight at Lympne.
10.9.26	Pixie III (No.14)	20 minute flight in eliminating trials at Lympne in preparation for *Daily Mail* Light Aeroplane Competition.
11.9.26	Pixie G-EBJG (No.14)	15 minute flight in further eliminating trials at Lympne in *Daily Mail* Light Aeroplane Competition.
12.9.26	Pixie III G-EBJG (No.14)	Flight of 5 hr 30 min duration from Lympne to Brighton in *Daily Mail* Light Aeroplane Competition. Made forced landing at Brighton.
13.9.26	Pixie III G-EBJG (No.14)	Flight of 6 hr 15 min duration, Lympne–Eastbourne–Hastings, in *Daily Mail* Light Aeroplane Competition.
14.9.26	Pixie III G-EBJG (No.14)	Flight of 6 hr 15 min duration from Lympne to Thanet in *Daily Mail* Light Aeroplane Competition.
15.9.26	Pixie III G-EBJG (No.14)	Flight of 6 hr 15 min duration from Lympne to Brighton in *Daily Mail* Light Aeroplane Competition.
16.9.26	Pixie III G-EBJG (No.14)	Flight of 6 hr 15 min duration from Lympne to Thanet in *Daily Mail* Light Aeroplane Competition.
17.9.26	Pixie III G-EBJG (No.14)	Flight of 3 hr 25 min duration from Lympne to Croydon in *Daily Mail* Light Aeroplane Competition.
18.9.26	Pixie III G-EBJG (No.14)	Routine test flight of 15 minutes at Lympne. This aircraft flown same day in three races at Lympne. 1 hr 10 min in the MMT; 1 hr 10 min in the Grosvenor Cup and 45 minutes in Lympne Handicap.

19.9.26   Pixie III G-EBJG   Flew sundry flights and joy-rides for
                                    45 minutes at Lympne.

In his book *Flight Path* Frank Courtney has this to say about Parnall's diminutive aeroplane: 'The Parnall Pixie II, my special mount in the 1925 Light Aeroplane Trials at Lympne, was a midget single-seat, low-wing monoplane of ingenious design with sharply tapered wings of 18 ft span, powered by a motor-cycle engine geared down to a matchstick of a propeller. Flying it was rather like flitting through the air on a noisy postcard. The pilot's goggles were the only windshield. Wide open it would do somewhere around 70 mph. The Pixie's engine did not like too much full throttle, and was prone to failure, usually at the most inconvenient time in a race. When racing took place in raining weather, the Pixie's tiny propeller has been known to be chewed down to a useless club when confronted with a heavy shower of rain.'

On one particular occasion Courtney had the experience of seeing his propeller come adrift, race on ahead of the aircraft and then shoot back towards him as the Pixie overtook its own propeller! It appears the friction of torque reaction on what was probably a loose propeller boss, burned through the wood around the boltholes until the propeller was loose enough to take off on its own.

There was a rather comic ending to that particular flight; after Courtney had managed to get the Pixie down safely on a vegetable patch, he climbed from the aircraft to find a small boy running up to him clutching the rogue propeller. He said something had fallen off the aeroplane, and was the propeller it. Courtney replied: 'thank you, yes it was'.

Parnall Pixie I and II

Single-seat sports or Service trainer monoplane. 3½ hp (500 cc) Douglas two-cylinder flat-twin air-cooled engine or 6 hp (736 cc) Douglas.

Span 29 ft; length 18 ft; height 6 ft (Pixie I). The Pixie II had a span of 18 ft.

Empty weight 279 lb, loaded weight 457 lb (500 cc Douglas); loaded weight 460 lb (736 cc Douglas).

Maximum speed (736 cc Douglas) 81.2 mph timed against 35 mph wind. Constructor's estimates – maximum speed over a straight course in calm conditions 95–100 mph; maximum speed (1,000 cc Blackburne and 29 ft span) 90 mph; landing speed 33 mph; ceiling 18,000 ft; maximum speed (1,000 cc Blackburne and 18 ft span high-speed wing) 105 mph; landing speed 45 mph; ceiling 14,500 ft.

Production

One originally built with alternative wings. Two Pixie II trainers for Air Ministry, one later transferred to Parnall for civil use.

Parnall Pixie III and IIIA

Two-seat sports or Service trainer monoplane (Mk.III) or biplane (Mk.IIIA). 32 hp Bristol

Cherub III flat-twin air-cooled engine or 35 hp Blackburne Thrush three-cylinder air-cooled radial. 1,100 cc Anzani experimental installation in 1925.
 Pixie III: Span 32 ft 5 in; length 21 ft 2 in; height 6 ft 1 in, wings folded 7 ft 5 in; wing area 137 sq ft.
 Pixie IIIA: Upper wing span 25 ft 8 in; length 21 ft 2 in, height 8 ft 6 in; wing area 238 sq ft.
 Pixie III: Empty weight 522 lb; loaded weight 925 lb.
 Pixie IIIA: Empty weight 540 lb; loaded weight 891 lb.
 Maximum speed (Cherub III) 75 mph.

Production

Two built. See Appendix A.

Third contender for Specification 5/24 came from Parnall as the Perch (N217), which is seen here in landplane form at the A & AEE, Martlesham, in April 1927. (*Parnall & Sons*)

Parnall Perch

When the Air Ministry issued Specification 5/24 calling for a two-seat naval training aeroplane, which was to be capable of operating with either a landplane or twin float undercarriage, it was also stipulated that the resulting design should be suitable for carrier deck landing training.

At least three aircraft manufacturers responded, Blackburn with the Sprat, Vickers with its Type 133 Vendace, and Parnall who offered the Perch.

When he designed the Perch, Harold Bolas decided to incorporate side-by-side seating to facilitate the training requirements of both the pilot instructor and his pupil. In compliance with the other stipulations of

Taken in 1927, this photograph shows the installation of the 220 hp Rolls-Royce Falcon III engine in the Perch naval trainer. (*Parnall & Sons*)

Specification 5/24 the Perch could be flown as a twin-float seaplane or, when fitted with wheels, as a shore-based or carrier-borne aircraft.

Power was provided by a 270 hp Rolls-Royce Falcon III driving either a two- or four-blade wooden propeller. The engine was enclosed in a neat metal cowling which had a steep downward slope on its upper surface, this incline continuing from the rear of the engine-bay up to the cockpit. This resulted in the upper fuselage profile having a pronounced hump effect, which was of great advantage to the crew because of the excellent forward view, an asset when landing on the flight deck of an aircraft carrier.

Constructed mainly of wood the Perch possessed slightly staggered

The Perch on twin floats, at Felixstowe. (*Parnall & Sons*)

wings of equal span which were fitted with conventional wire-braced interplane struts. Horn-balanced ailerons were incorporated into both upper and lower mainplanes of the two-bay layout.

The upper centre-section had a cut-out that was level with the crew's line of sight, the centre-section itself being braced by deep outward slanting struts which joined, at a mid-fuselage position, a pair of lower bracing struts sloping outwards to attachment points on the upper surface of the lower wings each side of the fuselage. The first pair of interplane struts were located quite close to this system of centre-section struts, while interplane movable linkage struts operated the four ailerons.

The Perch's empennage was of conventional layout and included a well rounded fin and rudder, a wide-chord tailplane located on top of the rear fuselage, and ample elevator surface. Elevators and rudder were horn-balanced.

A cross-axle type of landplane undercarriage was fitted which had oleo front legs braced at the rear. A conventional tailskid was fitted beneath the rear fuselage. When converted into a seaplane the Perch was equipped with twin floats which were fitted to the land-type undercarriage oleos and bracing struts. Also on the seaplane version, additional support struts ran from a point approximately three-quarters of the way back on top of the floats, and angled back to attachment points on the fuselage bottom well aft of the lower wing trailing-edge.

Lengthy exhaust pipes extended each side of the fuselage to a point aft of the trailing-edges. A large radiator was situated between the undercarriage legs, but as this was not always apparent, it has been assumed that other cooling methods were experimented with on this aircraft.

Making its first flight from Yate aerodrome on 10 December, 1926, flown by Frank Courtney, the Perch underwent a series of tests at Yate before going to the A & AEE at Martlesham in April 1927.

After its contractor's trials the Perch was sent to the Marine Aircraft Experimental Establishment (MAEE) at Felixstowe, where sea-going trials were undertaken.

Unfortunately for Parnall no production orders were forthcoming for their Perch trainer, and only one was built. Some details of the early flight testing undertaken with this aeroplane are related in the following summary from Frank Courtney's log for 1926 and 1927.

22.12.26	15 minute test flight at Yate.
6.1.27	20 minute test flight at Yate testing radiator.
14.3.27	30 minute test flight on light load tests. Similar flight in Perch N217 later same day under full load conditions.
15.3.27	Two hour duration flight from Yate with full load.
29.3.27	20 minute test flight at Yate, followed by second 25 minute test flight same aircraft.
30.3.27	10 minute test flight from Yate aerodrome.

The main features of the Perch are well shown in these views taken at Felixstowe. (*Parnall & Sons*)

5.4.27	Flown on 1 hr 35 min delivery flight from Yate aerodrome to Martlesham Heath. Harold Bolas on board.
27.4.27	Perch N217 At Felixstowe, two flights of 1 hr 30 min and 45 min on contractor's trials.
28.4.27	Perch N217 1 hr 45 min flight on contractor's trials at Felixstowe.

Parnall Perch

Two-seat naval biplane for frontplane or deck-landing training. 270 hp Rolls-Royce Falcon III twelve-cylinder vee water-cooled engine.

Span 40 ft; length 29 ft 6 in; height 13 ft.
Empty weight 2,800 lb; loaded weight 4,500 lb.
Maximum speed 115 mph; cruising speed 98 mph; climb to 5,000 ft, 11 min; service ceiling 12,000 ft; range 500 miles.
Approximate figures.

Production

One built, N217, in 1926. See Appendix A.

Parnall-built Cierva C.10 military Autogiro J9038 on Yate aerodrome, circa, 1927.
(*George Jenks*)

Autogiros

The Cierva Autogiro Company was formed in Britain in 1926 and, although the main contract for production was allocated to the Hamble works of Avro, two machines, the C.10 and C.11, were built by Parnall at Yate.

These two Autogiros were both completed during 1927, the C.10 being a military machine intended for experimental purposes only. This aircraft, J9038, had a 30 ft diameter rotor with four paddle-shaped rotor blades, the

The C.10 J9038 nearing completion at the Yate works of Parnall. The mountings for the 90 hp Armstrong Siddeley Genet engine, the stub wings and horn-balanced elevators can all be seen. (*Parnall & Sons*)

outer portions of which were built up on a ribbed aerofoil section. The fixed rotor head, supported by struts, was positioned above the forward fuselage and immediately in front of the single open cockpit, which was without a windscreen. Four bracing wires stretched from the top of the rotor head, one to each rotor blade.

A stub wing, of about 17 ft span, was located each side of the lower fuselage and bracing struts ran from the upper surface of each of these 'wings' to the fuselage top longerons.

The empennage comprised a rectangular tailplane, well-rounded fin and rudder, and horn-balanced elevators.

A conventional cross-axle type undercarriage was fitted to the C.10 and there was a fairly tall tailskid located beneath the rear of the fuselage.

Power for this autogiro was provided by a 70 hp Armstrong Siddeley Genet I radial engine driving a two-blade wooden propeller.

During April 1928, the C.10 began taxi-ing trials at Yate aerodrome, but on the 26th of that month the machine sustained considerable damage when it turned on its side. Repairs were undertaken and, later that year, the autogiro was taken to Andover for flight testing. Unfortunately J9038 crashed on a take-off attempt on 5 November, 1928, and no further flights were attempted.

The engine, undercarriage and rotor support structure of the C.10. (*T I Jackson Ltd*)

Contemporarily in competition with the Parnall C.10 was the Avro-built Cierva C.9 J8931, which was in the hands of the RAE at Farnborough.

The second Parnall-built Cierva Autogiro, the C.11, was of similar layout to the earlier C.10, but was a civil machine with the registration G-EBQG (Parnall c/n P1/5281).

The completed C.10. (*J M Bruce/G S Leslie collection*)

Built in 1927, the C.11, known as the Parnall Gyroplane, incorporated an airframe designed by Harold Bolas, and was powered by a 120 hp ADC Airdisco eight-cylinder air-cooled vee-type engine which, at 2,000 rpm, was capable of a maximum 140 hp. At the normal 1,800 rpm this powerplant was rated at 128 bhp, and it also had a reduction gear ratio of 2:1 which reduced the propeller speed to 900 rpm, thus making possible the

The Parnall-built Cierva C.10 Autogiro J9038 after its accident during tests at Yate in April 1928. (*George Jenks*)

George Parnall (nearest) with the C.10 after its accident. (*Mark Parnall*)

installation of a highly efficient, large diameter four-blade propeller.

Despite the more powerful engine, however, the C.11 Autogiro came to grief at Parnall's when it crashed on Yate aerodrome with Juan de la Cierva himself at the controls. It appears the rotor had not gained

Powered by a 120 hp Airdisco engine, this was the civil C.11 Autogiro built by Parnall at Yate. It has a four-bladed propeller, tandem cockpits and neat engine cowling. Harold Bolas designed the airframe incorporating his rounded style of vertical tail surfaces. (*Royal Aeronautical Society*)

sufficient momentum to provide the required lift when the designer/pilot tried to take off.*

The C.11 was repaired at Yate, while at the same time a simpler design of pylon was fitted and modifications incorporated into the drive shaft so that it spun the four rotor blades before take-off. This worked in conjunction with a new transmission shaft, clutch and gearing, the intention being to implement more effective lift characteristics in the C.11, but no further success was recorded.

This second Parnall-built Cierva Autogiro ended its days at Hamble, where it was used as an instructional airframe by Air Service Training.

Cierva C.10

Single-seat experimental military Autogiro. 70 hp Armstrong Siddeley Genet I seven-cylinder air-cooled radial engine.
Rotor diameter 30 ft; span approx 17 ft; length approx. 22 ft 8 in.
Maximum take-off weight about 1,100 lb.
Rotor speed 135 rpm.

Production

One built under contract No.642578/25. See Appendix A.

Cierva C.11 (Parnall Gyroplane)

Single-seat experimental civil Autogiro. 120 hp ADC Airdisco eight-cylinder vee air-cooled engine, rated at 128 bhp at 1,800 rpm.
Rotor diameter approx 35ft 3¼ in.
No other data recorded.

Production

One built. See Appendix A.

---

*Long after the accident Harold Bolas came to the conclusion that ground resonance was the cause of the accident.

De Havilland D.H.9A Contracts

Throughout aviation history there have been aircraft which could be singled out as outstanding for their time. In the Royal Air Force one such aeroplane, noted for its longevity and reliable service both at home and abroad, was the de Havilland D.H.9A. It was this type that provided Parnall with much needed work in the mid-1920s for, although the company was at that time engaged with several prototype projects, the D.H.9A construction contracts awarded by the Air Ministry produced the means by which Yate works could continue to function on a more secure footing.

Parnall was among firms involved in refurbishing and building new de Havilland D.H.9As for the RAF during the mid-1920s. This example, E9891, was produced by the Vulcan Motor & Engineering Co at Southport. (*K E Wixey collection*)

The D.H.9A was derived from the D.H.9, a First World War two-seat bomber that was a disappointment because of its Siddeley Puma engine. A converted D.H.9 was fitted with a 375 hp Rolls-Royce Eagle VIII, but the eventual standard powerplant installed was the American 400 hp Liberty 12, an engine produced after the United States entered the war.

Over typical hostile terrain in Iraq during the 1920s are three D.H.9As from No. 30 Squadron, J7124, H3633 and H3632. (*MAP*)

A two-seat, twin-bay conventional biplane, the D.H.9A was of mainly wooden construction and fabric-covered. Although based on the D.H.9 design, the D.H.9A possessed wings of greater chord and span, incorporated wire bracing for the fuselage structure instead of plywood bulkheads, and had a frontal radiator. The type lent itself admirably to the aircraft manufacturing techniques of woodworking companies such as George Parnall.

In addition to those D.H.9As kept in store after the war, some new machines were built having had modifications introduced. As a consequence several Air Ministry contracts were issued to various manufacturers including Parnall, whose first order was for a batch of eighteen D.H.9A rebuilds (J8172–J8189).

These aircraft were from a batch of 130 D.H.9As (J8096–J8225) produced after the First World War, the contracts being distributed by the Air Ministry between Westland Aircraft, de Havilland Aircraft, Short Brothers, S.E. Saunders, Blackburn Aircraft and George Parnall.

In January 1927, an order for a further thirty-five D.H.9As was placed by the Air Ministry, one contract for twenty-three machines (J8460–J8482) going to Westland Aircraft Co. Ltd., while the remaining twelve aircraft (J8483–J8494) were contracted to Parnall at Yate, all these machines being the dual-control training version.

Familiarly known as the 'Nine-Ack' ('Ninak' for short), the D.H.9A became one of the most widely used aircraft in RAF service during the 1920s. It operated both as a bomber and general purpose type, and served with at least twelve home-based and nine overseas squadrons, the latter based mostly in the Middle East. The D.H.9A shared with the Bristol F.2B the difficult job of policing Iraq and the North West Frontier of India for a

D.H.9A E8407 as originally produced by the Aircraft Manufacturing Co (Airco). (*Real Photographs*)

This photograph, of poor quality but very rare, shows two Parnall-built D.H.9As at Yate in the mid-1920s. (*K E Wixey collection via F E Draycott*)

number of years. Those 'Ninaks' abroad were fitted with a tropical radiator beneath the nose, and normally carried a spare wheel on the side of the fuselage.

A distinctive D.H.9A built by Parnall was J8177, which was the personal aircraft of the AOC in Iraq around 1929, Sir Robert Brooke-Popham and was finished in an all-over deep red. D.H.9As saw service with the Auxiliary Air Force, and as trainers at RAF Flying Training Schools, the type not being finally withdrawn until 1931.

Some reflections on the test flying of certain D.H.9As from Parnall's second batch (J8483–J8494) can be found in these notes from Frank Courtney's log, when he was contracted as test pilot to the Yate works.

14.3.27	Two flights in D.H.9As which were from batch by George Parnall & Co at Yate. These machines were J8484 (30 minute recondition test flight) and J8483 (40 minute recondition test flights, three in all).
21.3.27	Parnall-built de Havilland 9A J8485. 40 minute production test flight. A second Parnall D.H.9A, J8486, taken on 30 minute production test flight from Yate also on the same day.
29.3.27	Parnall-built D.H.9A, J8487. 10 minute production test flight from Yate.
5.4.27	Parnall-built de Havilland 9A, J8489. 30 minute production test flight from Yate.
30.4.27	Parnall-built de Havilland 9A, J8490. 30 minute production test flight from Yate. Second production test flight followed with D.H.9A, J8491, and a third similar test flight with Parnall-built D.H.9A, J8492, of 30 minutes' duration concluded work at Yate for this particular day.
17.5.27	Parnall-built de Havilland 9A, J8493. 30 minute production test flight from Yate. Second D.H.9A, J8494, taken up later same day on 35 minute production test flight also at Yate.

de Havilland D.H.9A (as built by Parnall)

Two-seat general purpose and training biplane. 400 hp Liberty 12 twelve-cylinder vee water-cooled engine.

Span 45 ft 11½in; length 30 ft 3 in; height 11 ft 4 in; wing area 488 sq ft.

Empty weight 2,695 lb; loaded weight 4,645 lb.

Maximum speed 114 mph at 10,000 ft; climb to 10,000 ft, 15 min 45 sec; service ceiling 16,750 ft; endurance 5¼ hr.

One fixed forward-firing .303-in Vickers machine-gun and one Scarff-mounted .303-in Lewis machine gun. Bomb load 660lb (normally two 230lb or four 112lb bombs).

Production (Parnall only)

First contract 18, second contract 12. See Appendix A.

Parnall Peto being catapulted from HM Submarine M.2. The derrick fitted above the aircraft hangar was for hoisting the Peto aboard after a flight. (*K E Wixey Parnall collection*)

Parnall Peto

The idea of conveying an aeroplane aboard a submarine for use as a spotting aircraft was first conceived in the years preceding the First World War. In conjunction with the British & Colonial Aeroplane Company, a young naval officer, Lieut Charles Dennistoun Burney, designed a hydroplane of which three are known to have been constructed under very tight security. These machines were known as the 'X' type Bristol-Burney Hydroplanes, and were designated the X.1, X.2 and X.3, one machine

The prototype Peto, with Saunders 'Consuta' floats and Bristol Lucifer three-cylinder engine. The photograph was taken at Felixstowe in 1926. (*Imperial War Museum*)

being developed as a collapsible type to facilitate its operation from a submarine.

In 1916 two Sopwith Schneider seaplanes were carried aboard the British submarine E.22 in an experimental capacity, but it was not until the mid-1920s that further types emerged to fulfil the submarine-borne aeroplane concept. Among these was the German Caspar U 1, the United States Navy's Martin MS-1 and Cox-Klemin XS-1 and Italy's Macchi M.53 and Piaggio P.8. Later, during the Second World War, both Germany and Japan built experimental submarine-borne aircraft in the form of the Arado Ar 231 and Aichi Sieran respectively.

Meanwhile probably the most ambitious and successful attempt at operating aircraft from a submarine was the conversion, completed in April 1928, of the British submarine M.2. The vessel's 12-in gun was replaced by a seaplane hangar in which was housed the Peto, a small two-seat biplane produced at Yate by George Parnall.

Harold Bolas designed the Peto in response to Air Ministry Specification 16/24, which called for a two-seat naval reconnaissance seaplane that could be carried and operated from the confined space of a submarine.

Obviously the wing span would be necessarily short, the wings being able to fold, and considerable ingenuity in design would be required if the proposed aircraft was to show a useful air performance as well as prove itself seaworthy.

In the event the Parnall Peto prototype, N181, appeared in 1926 as a compact two-seat biplane with staggered wings of unequal span and pronounced sweepback. The upper centre-section was on a level with the

Seen off Felixstowe on Saunders 'Consuta' floats, is prototype Peto N181 powered by a Bristol Lucifer engine. (*Imperial War Museum*)

eyes of both crew members to give maximum view without altering the Peto's flight path.

Only the upper wing had dihedral. Mainplane construction incorporated spruce spars, ribs and drag struts braced internally with tie-rods, and externally by means of stainless steel streamline struts in the form of a Warren girder. The centre-section was supported and braced to the fuselage by stainless steel struts of tubular section.

The Peto's fuselage comprised spruce longerons braced together with spruce and stainless steel struts. Tie-rod bracing was practically eliminated with the exception of one bay forward of the observer's seat. The top fuselage decking was dome-shaped and joined to the upper centre-section by a faired cabane, while the fuselage was fabric-covered up to the front cockpit. Forward of this, quickly detachable aluminium panels were fitted. A system of levers and cranks situated alongside the cockpits actuated the ailerons, which extended full-span along the upper mainplanes.

The Peto's tail unit was of composite construction, the stainless steel fin and rudder extended well below the fuselage to reduce the height for stowage, while the rear spar carrying the balanced rudder was attached to the upper and lower longerons. The tailplane, located atop the rear fuselage, was a mainly wooden framework and was adjustable in flight. The entire tail unit was fabric-covered.

The seaplane undercarriage consisted of streamlined N-struts, cross-braced with cables in the front and rear panels. Twin duralumin single-step floats were attached and carried cantilever fashion on the front and rear

A three-cylinder Bristol Lucifer radial, very similar to that installed in the Parnall Peto. In this picture the Lucifer is fitted to a Bristol Type 73 Taxiplane. (*Rolls-Royce Bristol*)

booms. These floats were of V-bottom long type, and had water rudders. Alternative twin floats for the Peto were produced by S E Saunders, these being constructed in accordance with the well-known Saunders 'Consuta' system in which mahogany plywood was used sewn together by copper wire. In the early days of its career, the Peto was fitted with a land undercarriage, the oversize wheels being 'borrowed' from the much larger Parnall Pike reconnaissance aircraft.

Some confusion has arisen in the past as to how many Peto seaplanes were actually built. This is understandable because, although only two prototypes were completed as new (N181–N182), the first machine was later rebuilt and allotted the serial N255. To confuse matters further, the two original Petos were, at varying stages of their careers, fitted with no less than six different wing designs. These includes the RAF 15 Section type (unslotted with rounded tips) and a similar slotted type; the RAF 31 Section type (unslotted with blunt tips) and a similar slotted version; and the RAF 31 Section type (unslotted with rounded tips) as well as a similar slotted design. In all cases it was specified that hand-holes should be provided at the wingtips, but these were not always apparent.

The object of these various wing experiments was to determine by trial and error the most satisfactory combination, both in wing design and type of slots, that would result in the most efficient all-round performance.

The ultimate aim was to achieve 110 mph coupled with a low landing speed, factors which the Peto was to prove itself capable of during trials.

Despite its diminutive size, the Peto was reported to be quite manoeuvrable on water, and found to taxi easily across wind and tide. When folded for ground/ship handling and stowage the aircraft was ideally suited for its intended role as a submarine-borne type.

The first prototype Peto was initially powered by a 135 hp Bristol Lucifer IV three-cylinder radial engine, but this was later replaced by a 135 hp Armstrong Siddeley Mongoose. The powerplant was supported by a simple girder-type plate attached to the fuselage by stainless steel tubes, while the engine's cowling was easily and quickly detachable. A 14½ gallon capacity gravity fuel tank was located inside the fuselage beneath the centre-section, and immediately below it was a 1½ gallon capacity oil tank.

The use of stainless steel throughout the Peto's structure was obviously

The first Peto, at Yate, powered by a 135 hp Armstrong Siddeley Mongoose IIIC. Duralumin floats with water rudders have been fitted. (*K E Wixey Parnall collection*)

to combat the effects of corrosion on metal components; the Royal Navy and Royal Air Force were acutely aware of the damaging results that could accrue when metal used in aircraft operating over the sea was exposed to the elements. True, the inclusion of stainless steel in the Peto's airframe made the machine more expensive, but Parnall emphasised the fact that the extra cost would be offset by reduced maintenance charges.

The second Peto prototype was first flown at Felixstowe in the summer of 1926 powered by a Bristol Lucifer engine driving a two-blade wooden propeller. The Lucifer was reported as developing 127.8 hp at 1,700 rpm, and the performance of the Peto was contained in the MAEE Felixstowe report, submitted by Flg Off O E Worsley in July 1926.

The aircraft was recorded as handling well, both in calm water and in the air, although on rough water the machine was difficult to handle, a fault offset by the Peto's good flying qualities and ease of maintenance. The report went on to state that the Peto was of robust construction, easy to trim, and the type of floats employed were quite satisfactory. However, the first prototype was unable to reach the required service ceiling of 11,000 ft called for in the specification, and could only attain a maximum altitude of 9,550 ft.

One unusual feature of the Peto was the method of starting the engine; a hand-turning gear was installed, not in the pilot's cockpit, but in the observer's front position, so that the hapless observer found one of his first tasks was to 'crank' the starting handle until the engine fired.

The first prototype came to grief in the early part of 1930 when, while operating from HM submarine M.2 at Gibraltar, the Peto alighted heavily on the water and was damaged. After being dragged from the waters of

On its dolly at Felixstowe, the second prototype Peto (N182) has earlier type floats without water rudders, and the engine is a three-cylinder Bristol Lucifer radial. (*K E. Wixey Parnall collection*)

HM Submarine M.2 at Gibraltar, with Peto N181 standing at the end of its catapult. (*Eric Harlin*)

Gibraltar Harbour by a dockside crane, N181 was hoisted unceremoniously on to the wharf by its tail to lie dejectedly beside Fairey IIIF seaplane S1334, which had also been 'dumped' after a heavy alighting.

The prototype Peto inside Parnall's Yate works. It is seen at the time when its Saunders 'Consuta' floats had been exchanged for duralumin type floats with water rudders. The engine is a 135 hp Armstrong Siddeley Mongoose. (*K E Wixey Parnall collection*)

The Peto prototype, N181, fitted with duralumin floats, and powered by a 135 hp Armstrong Siddeley Mongoose, circa, late 1920s. (*K E Wixey Parnall collection*)

This was not the end for the first prototype Peto however, for it was later returned to George Parnall's Yate works and rebuilt as N255. The aircraft was modified to have a 135 hp Armstrong Siddeley Mongoose IIIC radial driving a Fairey-Reed duralumin propeller, a combination resulting in a rating of 169.2 hp at 2,035 rpm. Other improvements included the fitting of heavier duralumin floats with steep-fronted bows giving increased

After being rebuilt as N255, the original Peto is seen here being prepared for a catapult launch from its mother ship, the Royal Navy's submarine M.2. (*Fleet Air Arm Museum*)

buoyancy and greatly enhancing the water handling characteristics of the aircraft.

Special gear was installed which connected or disconnected the water rudders and main rudder as required; wings having square tips and equipped with slots were fitted and facilities provided for the Peto to undertake deck catapult launching.

The Admiralty had decided the most obvious choice of Royal Navy submarine for conversion to an 'aircraft carrier' was the large M class. Four of these vessels (M.1, M.2, M.3 and M.4) had been ordered during the First World War, the original intention being to use them for shore bombardment. Each of these submarines was to have a 12-in gun which had been modified to have an electrically-controlled watertight muzzle cap, and a simple sighting device enabling the gun to be fired from the

Following a flight, the Peto was hoisted back on board M.2 by means of the vessel's derrick as shown here. (*Fleet Air Arm Museum*)

control room. There was little traverse, but the gun could be elevated up to 30 deg. One method of attack involved the submarine being taken up to periscope depth, firing a single shell with the muzzle above water, diving, and returning to the surface to repeat the procedure so that the time spent on the surface was less than eighty seconds between firings. This system of bombardment was known as dip-chick, and it proved very effective on exercises.

Submarines M.1 and M.2 were built by Vickers, and M.3 and M.4 by Armstrong, although the M.4 was never completed. M.1 was launched and completed in time to serve in the Mediterranean and the Dardanelles, but was sunk on 12 November, 1925, after a collision off Start Point. M.3 was converted as a very successful minelayer, ending her days in the scrapyard in 1932. The M.4 was launched in July 1919, unfinished and only in order to clear the slipway. She was sold for scrap in 1921.

Thus it befell the M.2 to become partners with the Parnall Peto, and in 1927 this large submarine was commissioned as an 'aircraft carrier'.

The 12-in gun was replaced by an aeroplane hangar which was constructed as a watertight structure to withstand external pressure at the submarine's operating depths. This hangar, which was rounded on the outside with a hemispherical top, was fitted with a door measuring 9 ft 3 in by 8 ft 9 in. Above the hangar was located a derrick for recovery of the Peto, or hoisting out for a take-off if required, although the aircraft was normally launched by means of a short, inclined catapult fitted to the submarine's forward deck casing. This catapult was designed by R Falkland Carey and worked via a system of pulley wheels, wire cables and a ram powered by compressed air, or alternatively, cordite. The catapult was designed to launch an aircraft weighing some 7,000 lb into the air at a speed of 45 mph over a distance of 34 ft, the crew being subjected to a force of some $2\frac{1}{2}$ g. In order that the Peto could be kept operational for a month at sea, fuel tanks were located in the hangar with a capacity of 200 gallons, and there was tankage for twenty gallons of oil.

The M.2 had her conning tower raised to clear the aircraft hangar, and also to afford some protection for the crew while the Peto was being recovered after alighting beside its mother ship. The submarine's 3-in anti-aircraft gun mounted aft was retained.

When stored inside its hangar with wings folded the Peto rested on a trolley which, in turn, stood on a short set of rails. In the event of an aircraft launch the large hangar door was lowered to form a platform over which a further set of rails, connecting the catapult rails with those inside the hangar, were quickly laid. The Peto was then rapidly pushed out on its trolley, locked into position on the rear end of the capatpult, and the wings unfolded and secured in position.

Once the Peto's pilot had his engine running at sufficient speed for take-off he would raise his hand as an indication to the submarine's captain that he in turn could signal to a waiting seaman and stoker that they could release the lever operating the catapult. The Peto then shot forward to become airborne in seconds, much to the discomfort of the two-man crew. The first men to fly the Peto from M.2 were Lieut C W Byas and Lieut C Keighley-Peach, both of whom received double rates of pay; one as naval airmen and the second for being submariners!

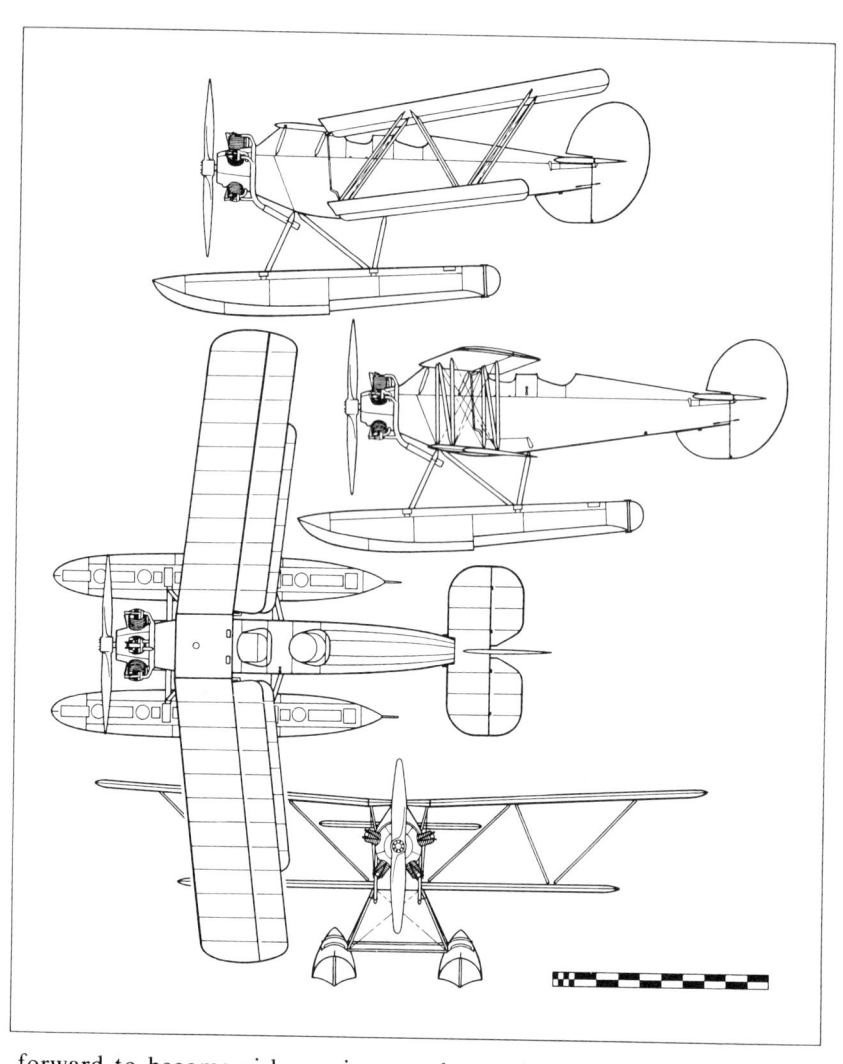

The first Peto prototype had two periods of service aboard M.2, in the first instance as N181 until damaged in the aforementioned Gibraltar mishap, and later as the rebuilt N255, the form in which it became involved in the tragedy that occurred on the morning of 26 January, 1932, when M.2 failed to resurface after making a routine dive off Portland. Later that day an Admiralty announcement stated: 'News has been received this evening that submarine M.2 dived at about 10.30 this morning off

Portland, and since then no further communcation has been received from her. Destroyers and submarines are searching the area in which she was last known to be, and every endeavour is being made to establish communication with her'. In due course a further Admiralty communiqué was issued which said: 'An object, believed to be submarine M.2, has been located three miles west of Portland Bill, in seventeen fathoms on a sandy bottom. Salvage craft and divers have been sent from Portsmouth'.

Confirmation that it was the ill-fated M.2 came on 3 February, when the submarine was discovered at a depth of 108 ft. Sadly seven officers, fifty-one petty officers and ratings, and two RAF leading aircraftsmen perished with her. The Peto was removed from the hangar of the doomed vessel despite strong currents which made it very difficult to disentangle the aircraft from the wreck.

After being transported to Portland Harbour, the Peto was found to be in a very sorry state, with its framework battered and the Fairey-Reed propeller bent out of shape. It was decided that to try to repair the aircraft would be a waste of time and money, and N255 was written off for scrap.

As for the submarine M.2, the Royal Navy tried in vain to resurface the large craft, but on 8 September, 1932, after she had been raised to within eighteen feet of the surface, a strong gale blew up and the M.2 had to be allowed to sink back again. Three months later salvage work on the submarine was abandoned and M.2 rests to this day somewhere off Portland.

At the MAEE, Felixstowe, the second Peto, N182, shows to advantage the Warren girder system of interplane bracing, early style floats and Bristol Lucifer engine. (*Imperial War Museum*)

Why M.2 sank has remained a matter for conjecture over the years, but when the Royal Navy divers originally went down they found the hangar door, the hatch from the pressure hull into the hangar and the conning tower hatch, all open. This discovery led inevitably to a number of theories: the hangar door was accidentally left open; the hangar door was unable to withstand the underwater pressure; an order had been badly misinterpreted; the after ballast tanks had started filling when M.2 surfaced due to the vent valves being inadvertently left open; a hydroplane had failed; or there might have been an engine transmission break-down.

The true cause will probably never be known, but one thing is certain, the Royal Navy, aware of the problems outweighing the advantages in operating spotter aircraft from submarines, stopped any further experiments in that field.

Meanwhile the second prototype Peto had at one time flown from M.2, this aircraft causing something of a sensation on the morning of Sunday 29 June, 1930. It appears N182 had been launched from M.2 off Ryde a little before mid-day, and intended to land at the Naval Co-operation School at Lee-on-Solent.

Unfortunately as the Peto flew over Stokes Bay Beach on its approach to Lee-on-Solent, the aircraft stalled above a row of beach huts. It force-landed, ploughing through half-a-dozen beach huts and ending up on its nose, and although fortunately no one was injured, one hapless occupant of a beach hut was obliged to hurriedly evacuate his hut in the nude! After the Peto had been recovered from this incident, its usefulness as a military type was apparently expended, for it was sold privately to a F C H Allen,

The second Peto has here been modified to have duralumin floats with water rudders, an enlarged fin and rudder and a 135 hp Armstrong Siddeley Mongoose engine. (*Imperial War Museum*)

who later entered the rebuilt Peto on the British civil register as G-ACOJ. The machine was prepared for its C of A at Ford aerodrome in Sussex during 1934 and 1935, but for some unknown reason the work was abandoned and the second Peto went into storage. Its ultimate fate is uncertain, and it can only be assumed that it was finally dismantled. Perhaps one day some old barn somewhere will reveal yet another aviation historical relic, bearing the faded letters G-ACOJ on its fuselage and/or wings!

Once again we find Frank Courtney's flight log providing descriptions of the first Peto's initial flight and early test flying sequence of both Peto prototypes.

4.6.25	Peto N181	10 minute straight hops at Yate, followed by 10 minute first flight proper.
5.6.25	Peto N181	20 minute test flight at Yate. Later same day at Yate, N181 taken up on 35 minute test flight.
6.6.25	Peto N181	20 minute test flight at Yate.
29.6.25	Peto N181	15 minute test flight from Yate for propeller test.
6.8.25	Peto N181	30 minute test flight from Yate aerodrome. Air-intake and propeller tests (three flights in all).
23.8.25	Peto N181	45 minute general water tests at Felixstowe.
24.8.25	Peto N181	10 minute test flight, full load with No.2 propeller at Felixstowe. Aircraft's designer, Harold Bolas on board. Later same day, Parnall Peto N181 on 1 hr 30 min fully-loaded duration test flight at Felixstowe. Mr Healey on board.
13.9.25	Peto N181	30 minutes (two flights) on contractor's trials. Light load test, Felixstowe. Second flight same day; 20 minute test flight on contractor's trials of Peto N181 with full load at Felixstowe. Aircraft's designer Harold Bolas on board.
3.10.25	Peto N181	35 minute test flight from Felixstowe with new propeller and centre-section. Later same day made 1 hr 5 min as finish of contract trials with this aeroplane at Felixstowe. Mr Healey on board.
1.3.26	Peto N182	1 hr 15 min contract test flights from Felixstowe. (Second prototype)
2.3.26	Peto N182	Further test flights from Felixtowe 2 hr 45 min.
27.4.27	Peto N182	30 minute contractor's trials flight at Felixstowe.

Parnall Peto

Two-seat naval reconnaissance seaplane from operation from submarines. 135 hp Bristol Lucifer IV three-cylinder air-cooled radial or 135 hp Armstrong Siddeley Mongoose IIIC five-cylinder air-cooled radial engine.

Span 28 ft 5 in upper, 20 ft 5 in lower; width folded 8 ft; length 22 ft 6¼ in; height 8 ft 11 in; wing area 174 sq ft.
Empty weight 1,300 lb; loaded weight 1,950 lb.
Maximum speed (Mongoose) 113 mph at sea level, 107 mph at 5,000 ft/min; rate of climb 600 ft/min; climb to 5,000 ft, 11 min; service ceiling (Lucifer) 9,550 ft; endurance 2 hr.

Production

Two prototypes only. See Appendix A.

The one-off Parnall Pike, N202, at Yate in 1927, with Napier Lion V. The hooks fitted to the axle were intended to connect with the contemporary longitudinal wires employed on British aircraft carriers. (*Parnall & Sons*)

Parnall Pike

In response to Air Ministry Specification 1/24, which called for a dual role naval reconnaissance aeroplane, Harold Bolas designed the Parnall Pike, a two- or three-seat biplane convertible as either a landplane or seaplane.

Making its first flight from Yate in March 1927, the Pike was powered by a 450 hp Napier Lion V water-cooled engine driving a two-blade Fairey-Reed metal propeller.

The aircraft was of mixed construction with wooden wings and a fuselage framework of steel tubing and fabric covering. The wings were of equal span, slightly backward staggered and without taper, the tips being blunt-ended. The interplane struts were based on the Warren girder principle resulting in the elimination of flying and landing wires. The mainplanes folded back along the fuselage sides for ease of stowage, while a quite noticeable feature of the Pike was the broader chord of the upper wings in comparison to the lower ones.

The aircraft's empennage comprised a large rounded fin and horn-balanced rudder, wire-braced tailplane and broad-chord divided horn-

Pike N202 at Felixstowe during its official trials as a seaplane. (*Imperial War Museum*)

balanced elevators with rounded tips.

As a landplane the Pike was fitted with a conventional V-type undercarriage with oleo front legs and cross-axle. A tailskid was fitted beneath the rear fuselage.

In its seaplane form the Pike had twin all-metal floats, which were nearly 34 ft in length. These were carried by six struts of which the forward two extended from beneath the engine cowling to join the front two oleo legs as used on the landplane version.

Two additional struts were positioned at the bottom of the fuselage and inclined aft to connect with the floats just behind their centre point.

Armament consisted of a fixed forward-firing .303-in Vickers machine-gun for the pilot, which was mounted in the port side of the cockpit so that the barrel projected into a short channel incorporated above and to the rear of the port bank of cylinders. An Aldis gun-sight was fitted in front of the pilot's windscreen. Rear protection was afforded by a .303-in Lewis machine-gun mounted on a Scarff gun-ring in the rear cockpit. This gunner's position was rather odd, for as the Pike's upper mainplanes were fitted directly on to the top of the fuselage, the rear cockpit was located well inside the trailing-edge of the upper wings. The Pike was equipped with underwing bomb-racks on which a maximum of four 112-lb bombs could be carried.

When fitted with a landplane undercarriage for use on board an aircraft carrier, the Pike had deck landing wire arrester hooks fitted to the cross-axle, these working in conjunction with the longitudinal arrester wires then in use.

For its intended role the Pike appeared at first to offer good potential, but when the prototype, N202, was sent to the MAEE at Felixstowe for service trials in its seaplane configuration, the test pilots who flew it gave

The Pike at Yate before a test flight. (*T I Jackson Ltd*)

unfavourable reports on both the Pike and its only rival, the Short Sturgeon N199.

Parnall's Pike was stated to be cold and draughty, the cockpit being a source of considerable discomfort to the pilot. The forward view was reported to be good, but otherwise the pilot's vision was very restricted both to the rear and downwards. Complaints were also received regarding the unusually long distance separating the pilot from the observer-gunner. The pilot's cockpit was immediately under the leading-edge of the wing which had a V-shaped cut-out.

Criticism was also made of the Napier Lion engine, which it was said created maintenance problems through its awkward installation. The Pike's flying qualities did not receive very favourable comment either, the controls being reported as sluggish.

On one particular occasion, Frank Courtney recalled how the Pike was fitted with a Curtiss-Reed aluminium-alloy propeller before going on a test flight. The problem was the aircraft would require rebalancing and a major

With Frank Courtney at the controls, Pike N202 about to fly from Yate aerodrome in 1927. (*T I Jackson Ltd*)

modification seemed inevitable until one of the technicians decided that by re-rigging the tailplane to a more negative angle, the pending test flight would not be delayed for so long. This 'modification' having been made Courtney took off and found the machine climbed quite well. The level and cruising flight also proved satisfactory, but when attempting to land (the Pike was in its landplane configuration) Courtney could just not raise the nose of the aircraft high enough to make a normal landing approach. He decided to try a fast landing by holding back the stick and trying to level off by opening the throttle, but although this resulted in a good touchdown, alas, with the tail still high on half throttle and the aerodrome boundary approaching too fast for comfort, the throttle had to be closed. Immediately the big Pike nosed over and the Napier Lion engine was pushed back, trapping Courtney by his legs. Mechanics had to jack up the engine in order to free him, but fortunately he was not seriously injured. In Courtney's own words: 'I suffered my regular damage – a couple of skinned shins'.

It is to Frank Courtney's flight log that we turn to gain some knowledge of the early trials and tribulations involving the Pike.

3.3.27	Five minute straight hops at Yate aerodrome.
4.3.27	Five minute straight hops at Yate aerodrome.
14.3.27	Five minute circuit flight of Yate aerodrome. Tail flutter occurred.
29.3.27	Taken on five minute test flight.
30.6.27	10 minute test flight from Yate aerodrome. Tail wobble occurred. Later same day Pike N202 again taken up with aircraft's designer, Harold Bolas, on board. After five minutes aloft machine crashed ending up on its nose.

Only one Pike was built, and although the serial number N201 was allocated for a second example it was cancelled when the Air Ministry rejected both the Pike and Short Sturgeon, neither aircraft meeting the full requirements of Specification 1/24.

Parnall Pike

Two/three seat naval reconnaissance landplane or seaplane. 450 hp Napier Lion V twelve-cylinder broad-arrow water-cooled engine.

Span 46 ft; length 35 ft 9 in*; height 15 ft 8 in*; wing area 663 sq ft.

Empty weight 4,183 lb; loaded weight 6,350 lb.

Maximum speed 126.5 mph at sea level.

One fixed forward-firing .303-in Vickers machine-gun and one .303-in Mk. III Lewis gun Scarff mounting. Four 112 lb bombs on underwing racks.

Production

One prototype completed, N202. See Appendix A.

*Seaplane version.

This view of the 80 hp Armstrong Siddeley Genet II powered Parnall Imp shows to advantage its unorthodox layout. (*Parnall & Sons*)

Parnall Imp

During 1927 Harold Bolas designed a biplane which was George Parnall's second venture into the civil aircraft market. Named the Imp, this machine was a two-seat sporting biplane intended by Bolas to cater for the competition pilot wanting to participate in speed events.

A cantilever type biplane of unusual style, the Imp's lower one-piece wing was perfectly straight in planform and had no dihedral. In direct contrast the upper mainplane had prominent sweepback, interplane bracing being accomplished on each side by a single wide-chord outward slanting strut. There were no bracing wires, and the only other interplane support consisted of a centre-section cabane situated between the apex of the swept-back upper wing and top fuselage decking forward of the cockpits. The Imp's wing surfaces comprised spruce sheeting overlaid by a protective covering of doped-on Egyptian cotton fabric. The lower wing incorporated full-span trailing-edge ailerons.

The fuselage was of ply-covered stressed-skin construction, and the empennage comprised a small triangular fin, well-rounded rudder, strut-braced tailplane, and squared-off wide-chord elevators. The undercarriage was of the cross-axle type, the rear legs having oleo shock absorbers, while the front bracing struts were quite lengthy and joined the fuselage well forward under the Imp's nose.

The Imp was initially powered by an 80 hp Armstrong Siddeley Genet II air-cooled radial engine.

Registered G-EBTE the Imp prototype made its first flight in 1927, and the following year was entered for the annual King's Cup Air Race, having received a C of A on 4 May, 1928. It was piloted in the race by Flt Lieut D V Bonham Carter, and took eighth place at a speed of 109.93 mph.

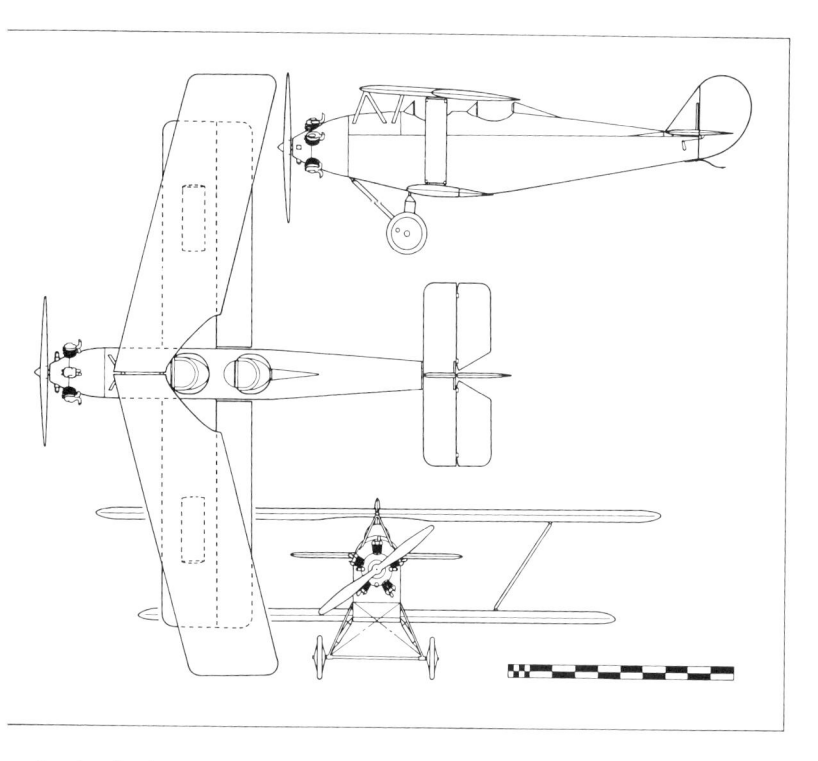

Meanwhile D R Pobjoy of Minster-on-Sea, Sheppey, in Kent, had evolved a new radial engine which he designated the Pobjoy P type. This

The Imp at Yate in 1927. (*T I Jackson Ltd*)

powerplant was intended for the civil light aeroplane market and had seven cylinders. It had ratings of 60 bhp at 3,000 rpm (normal) and 67.5 bhp at 3,300 rpm (maximum).

Parnall was convinced at the time that it would be responsible for producing and marketing the new Pobjoy engine, a fact borne out by the inclusion in Parnall's 1929 brochure of diagrams and details of the Pobjoy radial. Also when a flying test-bed was required for the new Pobjoy powerplant, the choice fell upon the Parnall Imp.

Despite its robust construction the Pobjoy P radial was quite small and had a good power to weight ratio. The cylinder heads and valves ran very coolly thus rendering it possible to practically encase the entire power unit in a cowling, this in turn reducing drag to a minimum.

Modifications were consequently made to the Imp, the original Genet motor being exchanged for the new Pobjoy P, which had not yet flown. The Imp took on a new front profile which was much more refined, streamlined front section being added that terminated in the propeller pointed spinner. A later improvement was the fitting of a raised headrest behind the rear cockpit.

The first flight of the Pobjoy-powered Imp was undertaken by Harold Bolas himself soon after he had learned to fly, which shows how much faith the designer had in the Pobjoy engine, for although this was not the aircraft's first flight, its front section had been considerably modified to accommodate the new engine.

Unfortunately for Parnall, once the Pobjoy P engine had successfully passed its trials in the Imp, Pobjoy, aware that his new powerplant would be a commercial success, decided to start his own business as Pobjoy Airmotors at Hooton in 1930. This move thwarted any plans Parnall had envisaged for the manufacturer of Pobjoy aero-engines at Yate.

The Imp with Pobjoy P engine, streamlined nose and headrest fairing. (*Eric Harlin*

The sole example of the Imp was eventually sold to Flg Off A T Orchard at Worthy Down in August 1933, but in December of that year was scrapped.

Parnall Imp

Two-seat sports biplane. 80 hp Armstrong-Siddeley Genet II five-cylinder or 65 hp Pobjoy P seven-cylinder air-cooled radial engines.
Span 25 ft 6 in; length 21 ft 2 in; height 7 ft 8 in; wing area 176 sq ft.
Empty weight 850 lb, loaded weight 1,320 lb.
Maximum speed (Genet) 102 mph; landing speed 40 mph.

Production

One prototype only. See Appendix A.

Parnall's response to Specification 21/26 was the Pipit with a 495 hp liquid-cooled Rolls-Royce F.XI. The clean lines of the prototype (N232) are apparent as it stands in the sun at Yate, circa, 1928. (*Parnall & Co/T I Jackson Ltd*)

Parnall Pipit

In response to Air Ministry Specification 21/26 calling for a single-seat shipboard fighter, both Hawker and Parnall produced their respective interpretations of the requirements. Hawker submitted the Hoopoe, N237, which could be fitted alternatively with a wheel or float undercarriage, and

The Pipit prototype (N232) under construction at Parnall's Yate works 1927–28. (*T I Jackson Ltd*)

which flew with several different engine installations including the Bristol Mercury and Armstrong Siddeley Jaguar and Panther, all air-cooled radials.

Parnall offered the Pipit, a clean looking machine with a neat streamlined cowling within which was housed a 495 hp Rolls-Royce F.XI twelve-cylinder vee engine.

The Pipit was a single-bay biplane with staggered wings of equal span incorporating dihedral on the upper mainplanes only. Ailerons were fitted on the lower wings only, and the four mainplanes were detachable in two boxed units, jury struts being fitted which obviated slackening the flying wires. Duralumin-formed wing spars comprised three drawn sections riveted together which carried pressed duralumin ribs. The N interplane struts were of stainless steel, and the top centre-section, which contained an auxiliary skin-type radiator, was attached to the fuselage by four steel struts and bracing wires.

The Pipit's fuselage was a rectangular-section structure of square duralumin struts and stainless steel tubes faired to an oval section, the shapely engine cowling being formed from aluminium.

The engine had gravity feed from the two main fuel tanks located in the upper wings. These tanks contained 68 Imp gal, and were supplemented by auxiliary tanks holding a further 18 gal. The engine was fitted onto a riveted stainless steel mounting. An underslung retractable radiator mounted on an adjustable column in the forward part of the cockpit was operated by means of a hand wheel. As the Pipit's cockpit was reputed to be particularly free from draughts at all speeds, this retractable radiator was claimed to obviate the need for electrically heated clothing at altitudes of up to 20,000 ft under winter conditions! In hot weather the cockpit temperature could be regulated by a controllable vent. No pilot's comments have, as far as is known, been recorded on this aspect of flying the Pipit.

Other cockpit equipment included a short-wave radio set attached to a sliding tray and working on a fixed aerial, oxygen apparatus, a Very pistol, a hand wheel for operating the variable gearing on the ailerons and elevators, as well as conveniently disposed service equipment. The pilot was provided with an adjustable seat which, together with good wing disposition and forward fuselage shape, afforded excellent vision for both combat and carrier deck landings.

Design of the Pipit allowed for the type to be operated either as a seaplane or landplane for shipboard or shore-based service. In its seaplane form the Pipit was equipped with lengthy twin floats having single steps and water rudders. The whole seaplane undercarriage was, like the landplane counterpart, built as a self-contained unit, and the two could be interchanged quickly being attached to the fuselage at common fixing points.

The landplane undercarriage was of the cross-axle type with V supports, the front legs incorporating double-acting oleo shock absorbers.

Parnall pinned its hopes on a production order for the Pipit naval fighter, the prototype of which (N232) is seen here nearing completion outside the Yate works. (*T I Jackson Ltd*)

The Pipit had dihedral in the upper mainplanes only. (*Parnall & Sons*)

The wheels were fitted with Palmer type brakes which were servo-acted from the rudder bar. The seaplane floats for the Pipit were of duralumin and specially designed for the aircraft, although the Pipit was rarely seen in its floatplane configuration.

The tail unit was composed of a stainless steel tube framework, fabric-covered, the conventional type fin and rudder being mounted on top of the rear fuselage. The adjustable tailplane was located below it in a mid-rear fuselage position.

Armament for the Pipit comprised two synchronised Vickers machine-guns mounted one each side of the fuselage level with the pilot's seat, the muzzles protruding from troughs in the fuselage sides. Provision was made to carry bombs beneath the lower wings.

The Pipit seemed ideally suited to Air Ministry and Fleet Air Arm requirements, and Parnall was relying heavily on the new fighter to pass its tests and service trials. Success, the company knew, could mean the follow on of a substantial production order. But alas it was not to be.

The Pipit was designed as a high-speed aeroplane employing the latest contemporary constructional methods, and this resulted in the new fighter becoming a victim of flutter, a phenomenon that had plagued aviation from its early days.

As aircraft design had progressed, machines became more complex, more sophisticated, and with all-metal airframes and higher speeds there was a corresponding increase in the violence of vibrations occurring in aircraft wing and tail units. So severe was this oscillation on some aeroplanes, structural disintegration followed resulting in the complete loss of an aircraft. In some cases there was tragic loss of life, not only among test pilots, but civil and Service pilots also.

The reason for this was because the flutter problem did not always adhere to prototype aeroplanes only; an outstanding example of a Service

Much blame for Pipit accidents was attributed to the tail-light bracket, just visible here, fitted to the rudder's trailing edge just aft of the serial. (*Parnall & Sons*)

type which encountered flutter troubles was the Gloster Gamecock fighter. A number of RAF pilots lost their lives in Gamecocks due to wing flutter, a malady that had manifested itself in the earlier Gloster Grebe fighter. In the Gamecock the problem was virtually solved after Gloster's designer, Henry Folland, introduced V-type interplane struts on the outer wing panels, although even then certain manoeuvres were severely restricted in RAF Gamecocks.

Meanwhile the first prototype Pipit, N232, flew to the A & AEE at Martlesham Heath for its official trials in October 1928. During one test flight the Pipit was put into a terminal velocity dive and serious tail flutter developed. The pilot was Flt Lieut J 'Oojie' Noakes, an experienced test pilot at Martlesham, which was then the RAF's main experimental station. So severe did the flutter become it caused the tailplane spar to fracture, and the Pipit went out of control. In an effort to try to get the aeroplane down in one piece, Noakes stayed with the machine, but to no avail. The Pipit crashed and was a complete write off. Miraculously Noakes, who had often been referred to as the 'crazy flier' because of his daring antics as a pilot, was rescued from the wreckage alive, but with a broken neck! Later, however, he flew again and, by 1930, had risen to the rank of Squadron Leader.

Meanwhile, at Yate a second Pipit was under construction and Harold Bolas was involved with a mathematical analysis of the flutter problem. At the time Hubert Broad, the distinguished airman and test pilot, was on hand to help the Parnall team with his experience and advice on the flutter problem.

The second Pipit, although allotted the serial number N233, became something of an anomaly in that it emerged from the Yate works as N232 bearing the same number as the first ill-fated Pipit. The obscurity of N233 puzzled many air historians for years, but the mystery was unravelled in

This view of the Pipit shows the ailerons on the lower wing, gun trough in the fuselage side, the exhaust stubs for the Rolls-Royce F.XI, and the cumbersome tailskid. (*T I Jackson Ltd*)

comparatively recent times by Norman Hall-Warren, who was at one time on George Parnall's design team with Harold Bolas.

The second Pipit was somewhat modified in relation to the first prototype, the fin and rudder shape having been altered to include a large horn-balance. The tailplane was this time strut-braced to the fuselage, while ailerons, operated by push-rod connections, were now incorporated

The Pipit at Yate in 1928. (*T I Jackson Ltd*)

into all four mainplanes. These improvements instilled new hope and faith in the Pipit by Parnall's employees, and the modified aircraft began its flight tests early in 1929. All went well until the morning of Sunday 17 February. That morning test pilot Flt Lieut H N 'Poppy' Pope had the Pipit up on a routine test flight when suddenly violent tail flutter set in and the second Pipit went out of control.

It appeared that, despite the modifications, the aircraft's sternpost snapped resulting in the fin and rudder breaking away. Pope was forced to abandon the Pipit and parachute to safety. The aeroplane ended up as a pile of wreckage on the railway embankment at Westerleigh near Yate.

The scattered pieces of wreckage that had been the second Pipit symbolised the equally shattered hopes that Parnall had in its new naval fighter. If the Pipit's tests had been successful, it appears more than likely the type would have provided Parnall with a lucrative production run. This in turn might well have resulted in further Air Ministry contracts for any new design of future Parnall aeroplanes, and could have established the Yate company as a producer of military aircraft for the RAF, RN and possibly export. Such was the importance placed on the Pipit by the company.

One thing is certain, the two Pipit crashes brought the problem of wing and tail flutter to a head. The milder form of flutter experienced with earlier aeroplanes had now developed into a vicious and highly potential killer, a fact attributed to the contemporary metal airframes which,

The first Pipit built (both had serial N232) standing on Yate aerodrome in 1927. Despite its clean lines, this aeroplane was plagued by flutter problems. (*MoD*)

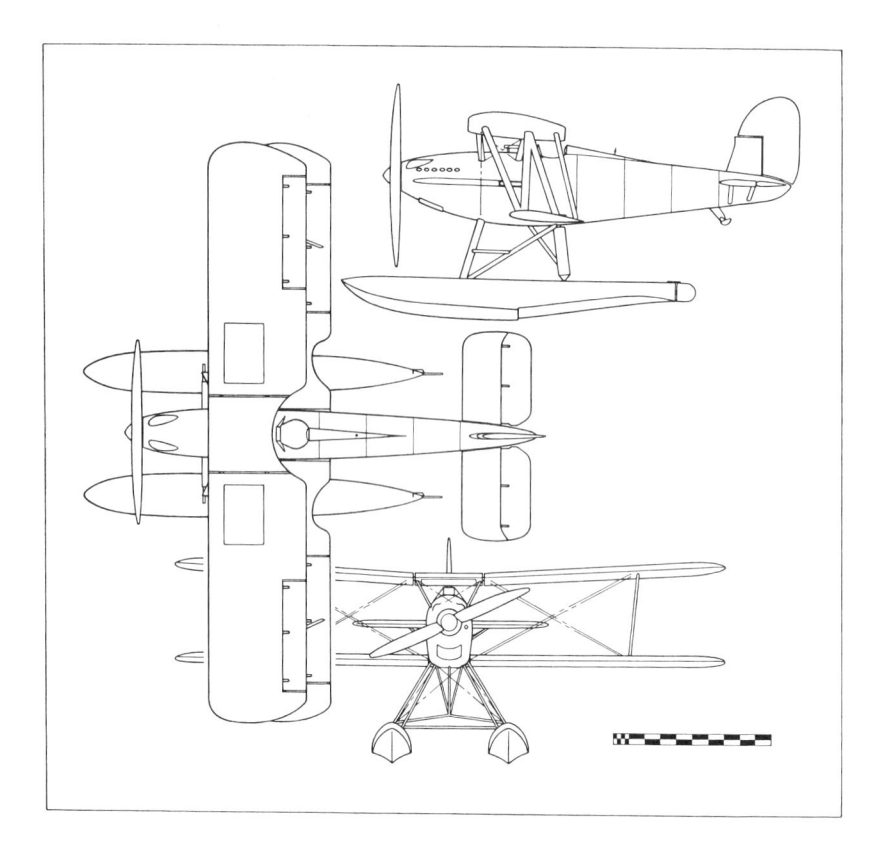

together with more powerful engines and consequent higher speeds, revealed an acute susceptibility to oscillation.

The Pipit accidents were the subject of an investigation by the Flutter Sub-Committee. Tests were also conducted with a one-eighth scale model of the Pipit in a wind tunnel. The first Pipit crash was caused by failure of the tailplane spar, and the committee came to the conclusion that the second Pipit was destroyed through tail flutter of the rudder-fuselage type and fin failure. The findings written in the report went on to comment that flutter would not have occurred if the rudder had been dynamically balanced, and could even have been avoided if a rather 'heavy' tail light bracket had not been fitted to the trailing-edge of the rudder.

A description of the Pipit investigations was contained in Aeronautical Research Committee Reports and Memoranda R & M No 1247 issued in May 1930, and titled *Tail Flutter of a Particular Aeroplane* by W J Duncan and A R Collar.

The result was an intensive research programme under R A Frazer and W J Duncan, which eventually produced a formula of preventive design rules. These were published in Aeronautical Research Committee Reports and Memoranda R & M No 1225 issued in 1931 entitled *The Flutter of Monoplanes, Biplanes and Tail Units*. The main recommendations of the report stated: 'Tail of the fuselage must be very stiff in flexure and torsion. Tailplane, elevators, fin and rudder must be very stiff. The elevators should be rigidly connected together to make it impossible for one to move without the other. The elevators and rudder should be well underbalanced aero-dynamically, and most importantly, the elevators and rudder should be mass balanced to bring the centres of gravity of the surface up to the hinge-lines'.

These brief quotations from the relative reports and findings emphasise the importance attached to the invaluable knowledge gained from the Pipit accidents, knowledge that went a long way in helping to solve one of the most difficult problems encountered in the evolution of high-speed metal aeroplanes. This of course was little consolation to Parnall at the time, for the Pipit, which had shown such promise as a fine naval fighter with production potential, was sacrificed, albeit not in vain, in the process of analysis.

The demise of the two Pipits appeared to seal the fate of Parnall at Yate as far as large-scale aircraft production was concerned. It was true that other designs would follow, and small contracts be awarded, but no large Government sponsored orders were placed with the firm for any of its subsequent military aircraft designs.

Parnall Pipit

Single-seat shipboard fighter landplane or seaplane. 495 hp Rolls-Royce F.XI twelve-cylinder vee liquid cooled engine.

Span 35 ft; length 26 ft; height 10ft $5\frac{1}{2}$ ins; wing area 361 sq ft.

Empty weight 3,050 lb; loaded weight 3,980 lb.

Maximum speed 138 mph at sea level, 173 mph at 3,000 ft, 168 mph at 10,000 ft; climb to 7,000 ft 1 min, to 10,000 ft $7\frac{1}{2}$ min; landing speed 55 mph.

Two fixed forward-firing .303-in Vickers machine-guns. Provision for four 20 lb Cooper bombs on underwing racks.

Production

Two prototypes only, both with serial N232. See Appendix A.

Parnall Parasol

During the 1920s the United States National Advisory Committee for Aeronautics (NACA) made a number of experiments in which large aircraft models were towed in an inverted position well beneath an aeroplane. The purpose was to study, under actual flight conditions, the behaviour of aircraft wings in relation to the stall, tendency to spin and

K1228, the first of the two Parnall Parasol monoplanes. (*Parnall & Sons*)

other phenomena associated with aerofoil surfaces. Apparently this system was not a great success as it never came into general use despite reports of some fairly good results. The chief aid to aerodynamic research still remained the wind tunnel, but even the large high-density wind tunnels, capable of producing full-scale test effects, could not compensate for the type of investigation that could be made in full-scale flight with an aeroplane.

In Great Britain the Air Ministry, while appreciating the value of wind tunnels and their use with model aircraft, was of the opinion that it would be advantageous to employ a full-size aeroplane designed and built to perform as a pure research type in which wing testing could be undertaken during flight. As a consequence Parnall was awarded a contract to produce two prototype research aircraft.

Harold Bolas designed a parasol monoplane in which the wing was so attached to the fuselage that it was free to make restricted movements in

Parasol K1228 with blunt-tipped parallel-chord fully-slotted wing of RAF 28 section. A recorder can be seen below the port wing. (*Parnall & Sons*)

relation to the fuselage. A dynamometer was incorporated into the wing supporting system in order that forces acting on the wing at various angles of incidence could be accurately measured.

Known simply as the Parnall Parasol, the two 'flying laboratories' emerged from Yate late in 1929 bearing the military serials K1228 and K1229. The fuselage was of composite steel-tube and spruce construction with removable forward side fairings providing access for the inspection, adjustment and lubrication of the wing support mechanism. These detachable fairings were so designed that they ensured the streamlining of the fuselage as well as maintaining the Parasol's aerodynamic cleanness, which was an asset in an experimental type where the interference of the free flow over the wing should be kept to a minimum.

The Parasol was a two-seater in which both cockpits were very roomy and gave a wide field of vision to both the pilot and observer. The seats were arranged to take the standard Irvin parachute, and provision was made for the stowage of special experimental equipment likely to be required aboard a research aircraft of that type. Certain instruments, the air log for example, could be lowered and suspended in flight. The pilot occupied the rear seat and was provided with an adjustable rudder-bar to suit various leg lengths. A lever operated by the pilot actuated a hydraulic brake on the propellers; this device stopped the engine to allow dynamometer readings to be taken in gliding flight without interference from the slipstream. Once the readings and glide were completed the engine was restarted by an RAE Mk II. gas starter.

Control of the dynamometer gear was the responsibility of the observer whose front cockpit contained the dynamometer control wheel, as well as a special observer's instrument panel. The reading obtained from a particular wing setting gave the extent of air forces acting on the wing, but to ascertain the direction of those forces together with the drag and lift coefficient required a second reading.

This was obtained by altering the attachment points of the wing bracing struts on the fuselage by means of a swinging frame that could provide up to three different incidence positions. High-tensile steel tubing was employed in the construction of this swinging cradle on which the wing was supported, and was also the material used for the wing bracing struts. These struts featured adjustable plywood fairings allowing for the alignment required for a particular strut position in use at a given time.

The parasol wing itself was supported by two inverted-V steel tubes attached to the upper fuselage longerons by hinges. These tubes were located at the wing's centre-line, while outboard parallel struts were pivot-jointed to the fuselage lower longerons by adjustable members, movement of the parallelograms being limited by a member fixed to the dynamometer. This member sloped down to a forward crank beneath the fuselage, the crank being connected to the dynamometer by a horizontal tube. It was this link between the crank and dynamometer that allowed the permissive 'play' of the wing under test.

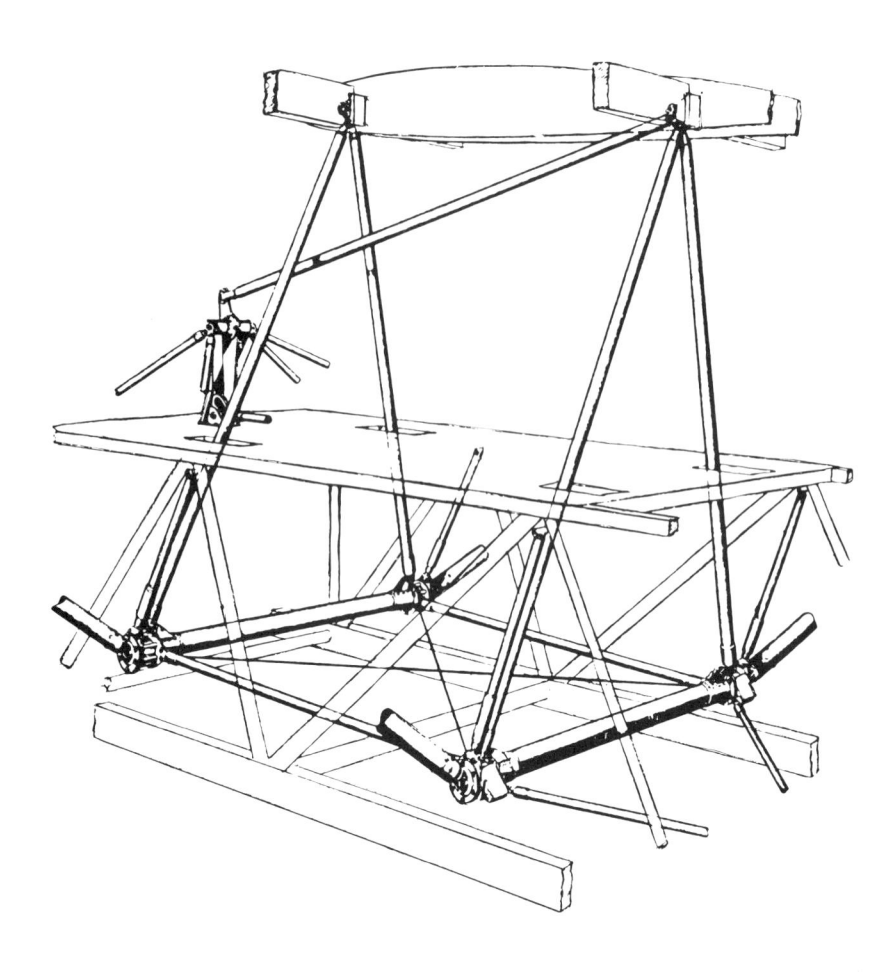

Up to three wing incidence positions could be obtained through use of this specially constructed swinging frame, which was installed in Parnall's experimental Parasol monoplane as shown in this 1926 sketch. (*K E Wixey Parnall collection*)

For wings fitted with slots or other high-lift aids requiring the measuring of forces acting upon them up to high angles of incidence, the Parasol was fitted with alternative wing attachment points. It was a feature of the type of structure used in the Parasol that changes in bracing strut attachment positions could be made with comparative ease and rapidity.

In side elevation all the struts on the Parasol were parallel, and together with wing members at the upper ends and fore-and-aft members at the lower ends, resulted in variable parallelograms. To limit the wing movements the dynamometer was provided with twin rollers, one each side, which were restricted by cams.

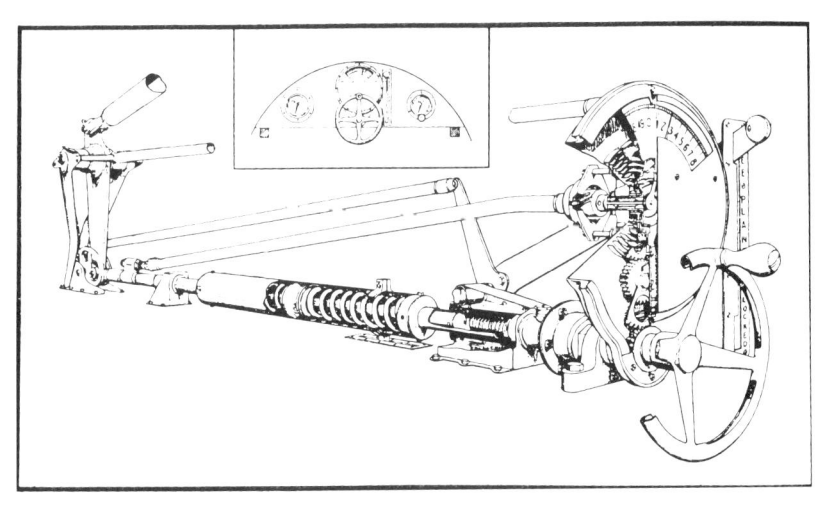

A 1926 diagram showing the dynamometer gear system, mechanism and observer's control wheel as fitted to the Parasol monoplane. Inset is the observer's instrument panel. (*K E Wixey Parnall collection*)

These cams rotated through 90 deg by means of a lever in the pilot's cockpit. They varied in width along the dynamometer's length, one end fitting the roller, while the opposite end had a clearance of 6 mm. This represented the wing movement and was sufficient to obtain a reading. The equipment was so designed that, in the event of a failure of the dynamometer gear, the safety of the aeroplane would not be in jeopardy.

The Parasol's strut-braced tailplane was located atop the rear fuselage foward of the rudder, which was of the rounded comma-type. Ample elevator surfaces and an adjustable tailplane allowed for control and stability in flight according to the wing incidence angle under test, the incidence adjusting gear being operated by a wheel in the pilot's cockpit.

The sturdy divided-type undercarriage incorporated Parnall's patented combined oleo and rubber compression shock absorbers; a conventional style tailskid was fitted beneath the rear fuselage.

An unusual feature of the Parasol's test programme was the fitting of a tripod-mounted camera well above the rear fuselage to allow the behaviour of wool tufts, stretched in rows from tip to tip of the mainplanes, to be recorded on film.

In order to minimise the time taken to reach the required operational altitude, both Parasols were powered by a supercharged 226 hp Armstrong Siddeley Lynx seven-cylinder radial engine, which gave a faster rate of climb than the standard model. However, although this super-charger worked up to a height of 14,500 ft, the normal altitude for dynamometer tests was only 7,875 ft.

Initially the first Parasol (K1228) was fitted with a fully-slotted, square-tipped parallel-chord wing of RAF 28 Section.

Clearly seen in this picture of the first Parasol (K1228), is the tripod-mounted camera on the rear fuselage, and the wool tufts attached to the upper surfaces of the experimental wing. (*MAP*)

The second machine (K1229) was tested with wings having a full-span split trailing-edge, and the ailerons were outrigged so that a narrow gap separated them from the upper wing surfaces.

In the role for which it was designed the Parasol performed well, and was found capable of testing various types of wing design. Its usefulness was determined by the number of aerofoils that could be employed in wing designs, and the aircraft's main restriction was due only to stability and strength limitations.

The first machine went to the RAE at Farnborough, where it was taken on charge on 3 September 1930, the second Parasol following on 9 October. Both aircraft were employed at the RAE in trials involving wing control surfaces and lift devices. The second Parasol was eventually struck off charge in August 1936, but the first machine continued flying until the following January when it too was finally withdrawn from service.

Performance figures obviously varied for the Parasol as different wing forms were tested, and the following data refer to a machine fitted with the RAF 28 Section wing.

Parnall Parasol

Two-seat experimental and research aircraft. 226 hp Armstrong Siddeley Lynx IV seven-cylinder supercharged air-cooled radial engine.

Span 42 ft; chord 7 ft; length 30 ft 4 ins; height 9 ft 6 in; wing area 294 sq ft.

Empty weight 2,222 lb; loaded weight 2,869 lb.

Maximum speed 110 mph at sea level, 118 mph at 8,000 ft; climb to 575 ft at sea level 1 min, to 8,000 ft, 12.4 min; stalling speed 50 mph at sea level, 56 mph at 8,000 ft; absolute ceiling 29,200 ft; recommended operational height for wing testing 8,000 ft.

Production

Two prototypes built to Air Ministry contract. See Appendix A.

Flying low across Yate airfield in 1929 is the first Parnall Elf sporting biplane, powered by a 105 hp ADC Cirrus Hermes I engine. The aircraft had yet to receive its registration, G-AAFH. (*Parnall archives*)

Parnall Elf

Having ventured into the civil light aeroplane market with its earlier Pixie and Imp sporting machines, Parnall was represented at London's Olympia in the 1929 International Aero Exhibition by a new two-seat private and sporting biplane named the Elf. Appearing on Stand 92 of the exhibition, Parnall's new aeroplane was powered by a 105 hp Cirrus Hermes I four-cylinder inline engine, and carried no markings, although it was later registered G-AAFH, receiving a C of A on 25 June, 1930.

The Elf was readily convertible from a landplane to seaplane configuration, its main improvements over previous Parnall civil types including a better view for both pilot and passenger, easier maintenance, improved performance and the advantage of folding wings which reduced the aircraft's size considerably to facilitate ground transport. In many contemporary light biplanes the pilot, and often the passenger, were seated beneath the upper wings, thus greatly restricting both forward and upward vision. In the Elf, however, with its staggered wings and centre-section on a level with the eyes of the occupants, a much improved field of view was afforded. This factor was further enhanced by having the main fuel tank installed in the Elf's fuselage, which allowed a thinner centre-section to be used.

In order to reduce maintenance to a minimum on the Elf, the usual wing bracing wires were eliminated by the use of Warren girder-type interplane struts, an arrangement resulting in greater rigidity, an asset for aerobatic

The prototype Elf. (*Parnall & Sons*)

manoeuvres. It also obviated the trueing-up process necessary on wire-braced biplanes.

The Elf was designed by Harold Bolas to meet the growing demand at the time for a cruising speed of 100 mph, yet without impairing the aircraft's landing speed. With a normal certificate of airworthiness the Elf could also carry sufficient fuel for a long-distance flight up to a total gross weight of 1,900 lbs.

An excellent feature of the Elf was its extremely narrow width of 7ft 1in with wings folded. This was approximately 1ft 6in less than contemporary similar types of light aeroplanes, and was intended to facilitate ground handling of the aircraft 'through gateways' in the event of a forced landing.

This view of the prototype Elf shows the unusual wing bracing for a light aeroplane (*Parnall & Sons*)

The Elf's fuselage was of the three-ply box-type reinforced with spruce members, the pilot and passenger cockpits being in tandem and fitted with seats capable of accommodating either a parachute or seat cushion! The pilot was provided with a standard Smiths instrument panel, while the controls were constructed in one unit and secured to the fuselage bottom as a complete section. An exceptionally large luggage compartment was provided immediately behind the pilot, an auxiliary locker being incorporated forward of the passenger's seat. This locker contained a tool kit and a spare can of petrol for emergency use!

The wings were of wooden construction braced internally with tie-rods and externally with streamline-section steel tubes. The upper mainplanes incorporated full-span ailerons, the span being greater than that of the lower mainplanes. The aileron controls consisted of external steel tubing and no cables or tie-rods were used in their construction. Also, because of the excellent rigidity of the Warren girder bracing, no jury strut was required to support the front spar for folding.

The upper wing centre-section was of composite construction with wire-braced steel spars of tubular section. The ribs were purposely reduced in depth to extend the field of view for both pilot and passenger. The whole upper centre-section was supported on the fuselage by four streamline steel tubes braced by diagonal struts in side elevation, and streamline wires transversely. The entire mainplane surfaces were fabric-covered.

The tail unit, which was also of composite construction and fabric-covered, was attached to the top of the rear fuselage as a complete unit. It was braced with steel struts and provision was made for the adjustment of the tailplane incidence on the ground. All the controls were carried within the fuselage.

With wings folded the width of the Elf was 7 ft 1 in. (*T I Jackson Ltd*)

This view shows the trailing edge of the lower wing folded forward when the Elf's wings were folded. (*Parnall & Sons*)

The Elf's undercarriage was of the divided V-type and this normally had a compression rubber shock absorbing strut, but a double-acting oleo gear could be fitted as an extra. The tailskid was of the laminated spring type clamped to the underside of the rear fuselage, and it was fitted with an easily replaceable cast-iron shoe. The wheels were interchangeable with a seaplane chassis which consisted of long single-step floats equipped with

The then unregistered prototype Elf over Yate. (*Parnall & Sons*)

Another revealing shot of the prototype Elf as it stands in front of the Yate hangars. (*the late A J Jackson*)

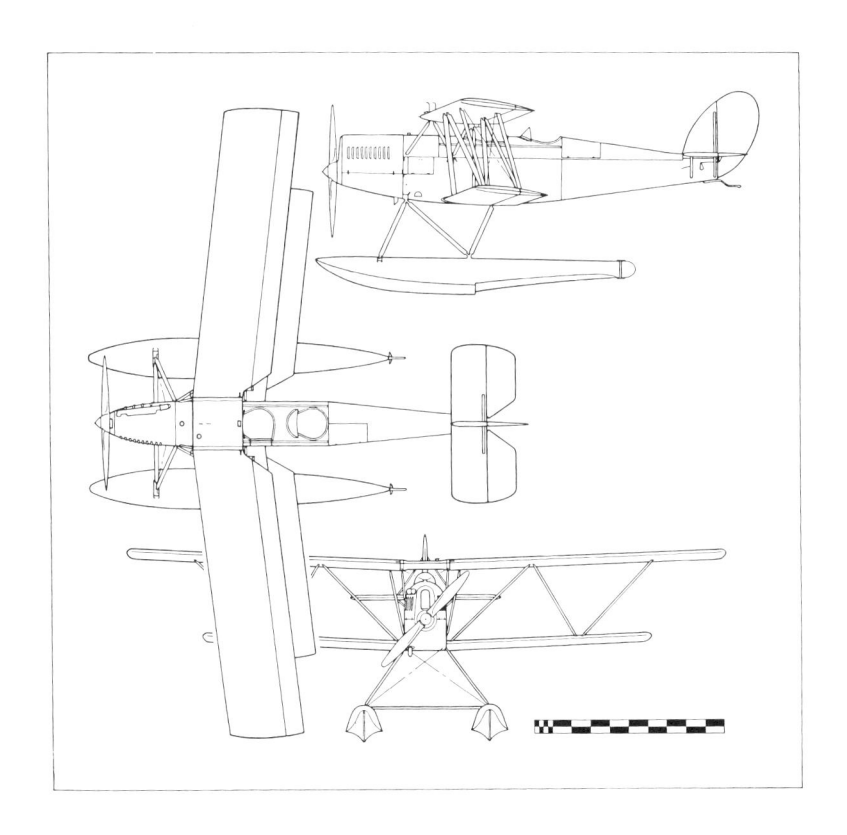

water rudders. These floats were attached to the Elf by means of braced and angled N struts.

The engine mounting was a self-contained unit constructed of welded steel tubes attached to the fuselage bulkhead by four bolts. The fuselage-mounted petrol tank held 18 Imp gal, and a pump mechanically fed a small 3 gal gravity tank located in the centre-section from which the petrol flowed to the engine.

The four-cylinder air-cooled upright inline Cirrus Hermes power unit installed in the first Elf developed 105 hp at the normal 1,900 rpm, and 115 hp at the engine's maximum of 2,200 rpm. With a dry weight of 318 lb, this engine, with its weight to power ratio of 2.9 lb/hp, gave the Elf a very good performance. So much so that when it flew in the 1930 annual King's Cup Air Race, it finished fifth out of a field of eighty-eight aircraft.

An aesthetically pleasing aeroplane for a biplane, the Elf also possessed a very businesslike look and, in many respects, resembled a military type rather than a light civil machine. It became renowned for its excellence as an aerobatic mount and was flown with great zeal by those pilots who were acutely aware of the Elf's reputation as a thoroughly robust and reliable aeroplane with few vices.

The controls were reported as well balanced and functioned efficiently and positively at all speeds down to the stall, which was said to give the machine a safe and docile feeling when manoeuvering. The cockpit layout was considered excellent for its comparatively unrestricted view and comfort, while the deep fuselage and ample wind screening was reported as precluding any draughts. The seats were deep and extremely well cushioned, the controls in exactly the right position, and there was no noticeable vibration from the Hermes engine. The Elf's undercarriage was recorded as functioning well when landing or taxi-ing, and the machine was reported as being easy to steer on the ground.

The first two Elf biplanes, G-AAFH and G-AAIO, at an aviation meeting in the early 1930s. (*the late A J Jackson*)

Seen at a prewar flying meeting is the second Elf built (G-AAIN), powered by an uprated 120 hp ADC Cirrus Hermes II, and with horn-balanced rudder. The unusual paint scheme on the rudder gives the appearance that it is shorter than designed. The colours were silver and red. (*Parnall archives*)

The first prototype Elf with its 105 hp Cirrus Hermes engine was known as the Mk. I, and was sold to Lord Apsley of Badminton in December 1932.

At one time this aeroplane flew with the Cornwall Aviation Company of St Austell, which was in fact a 'flying circus' run by a Capt Philips. With two Avro 504s and apparently the first Elf, this company gave joy-rides to the public as well as exciting exhibitions of crazy flying as it 'barnstormed' around the west country.

It was further east, however, that the first Elf, G-AAFH, was lost. On 20 March, 1934, while flying near Rickmansworth in Hertfordshire, the aircraft suffered a fuel pump failure and had to make a forced landing at Herongate. In the ensuing crash it was damaged beyond repair.

A second Elf, designated the Mk. II, appeared in September 1931, this being an improved version with an uprated 120 hp Cirrus Hermes II engine. This aircraft also featured half-span ailerons, an inflight incidence adjustment for the tailplane and a horn-balanced rudder in place of the original type. This second Elf, G-AA10, received a C of A on 2 September, 1931, and was later sold to R Hall of the Cotswold Aero Club in November 1933. This aircraft crashed at Sapperton, Gloucestershire, on 13 January, 1934, and was burned out. Tragically the Elf's owner and his son were killed in the crash. Again this accident was attributed to a faulty fuel pump.

The third and final Elf, G-AAIN, emerged from Parnall's Yate works in June 1932, and like the original was sold to Lord Apsley of Badminton.

The second Elf built, G-AAIN, emerged in 1932, and was sold to Lord Apsley. This aeroplane is seen here at a prewar flying meeting. (*Parnall & Sons*)

During the Second World War this aeroplane was stored, and after the war went to a W J Nobbs, who undertook some restoration work on it. Eventually, however, the last of the Elf trio was cancelled as 'withdrawn from service' on 12 May, 1950.

Fortunately this was not to be the last of the old biplane, for in July 1951, it was purchased by the Shuttleworth Trust, and moved to Old Warden aerodrome, where it was to be fully restored to flying condition. In 1972, G-AAIN was loaned to the Southend Historic Aircraft Museum, but later returned to Old Warden

After the Shuttleworth Trust had patiently restored the surviving Parnall Elf to airworthy condition, this grand old biplane flew again on 25 June, 1980, when it made its first flight for over forty years. George Parnall and Harold Bolas would have been proud of her.

There is little doubt that the Elf, notwithstanding the fuel pump failures with the first two machines, did live up to the expectations of its designer, for in planning it Harold Bolas had envisaged an aeroplane that would not require a complicated upkeep. After a thorough study of the best methods of aircraft manufacture, combined with the most economical processes, Bolas produced the Elf in accordance with those ideas, and made provision for a production order of some magnitude. Dies and jigs for all metal detail fittings were manufactured together with well designed assembly jigs for each component. Interchangeability was guaranteed and George Parnall's company prepared itself for a substantial production run with the Elf. They realised that with its robustness and an estimated top speed of 110 mph, this aeroplane had great potential, not only as a sporting machine, but as an asset to private owners, flying clubs, and, perhaps, the military flying schools.

The only surviving Parnall aeroplane, Elf G-AAIN at Old Warden in June 1981 after restoration by the Shuttleworth Trust. (*John A Long LRPS*)

Alas for Parnall it was not to be. Following the trio of Elves, no further orders were forthcoming.

It has always been the contention that one of the main contributory factors to this lack of interest in what was undoubtedly a fine aircraft, was the overwhelming success of the de Havilland D.H.60 Moth series, a type which had been proving increasingly popular with the light aircraft fraternity since 1925. Had the Elf appeared on the market sooner it would, in all probability, have proved a winner for, in 1930, the price of a complete Elf varied between £875 and £890.

Parnall Elf

Two-seat private-owners and sports biplane. 105 hp Cirrus Hermes (Mk.I) 120 hp Cirrus Hermes II (Mk.II) four-cylinder air-cooled inline engine.

Span 31 ft 3½ in upper, 26 ft 9 in lower; length 22 ft 10½ in; height 8 ft 6 in; wing area 195 sq ft; wheel track 5 ft 6 in.

Mk. II empty weight 900 lb; loaded weight 1,700 lb; loaded weight (aerobatic C of A), 1,500 lb.

Mk. II maximum speed 116 mph at sea level, 112 mph at 5,000 ft; cruising speed 103 mph; stalling speed 40 mph; climb to 800 ft, 1 min, to 10,000 ft, 21 min; ceiling 16,000 ft; range 400 miles.

Production

Three built. See Appendix A.

Parnall Prawn

Another one-off venture was launched by George Parnall & Co during 1930 in the form of a diminutive single-seat flying-boat named the Prawn. This machine was built as an experimental type for the Air Ministry, and its chief purpose was to determine the effects which would result from installing a powerplant in the prow of a flying-boat!

The use of stainless steel was much in evidence in the Prawn's construction, and J E Draycott, Parnall's ground engineer and works inspector at the time, recalls inspecting stainless steel components for the aircraft. However, according to Mr Draycott, the S.60 type of steel employed in the Prawn's structure did not come up to the required standards. Nevertheless the dainty little Prawn emerged from the Yate works in 1930, and was prepared for its trials, which were to take place at the Marine Aircraft Experimental Establishment at Felixstowe.

The Prawn was powered by a 65 hp Ricardo-Burt liquid-cooled engine, similar to the type envisaged as being suitable for use as an auxiliary power unit in the R101 airship. This engine was mounted well above the Prawn's bow, the main problem being how to obtain clearance for the propeller from the spray thrown up as the flying-boat accelerated through the water. This hazard was overcome by fitting a special pivoting device at the rear end of the engine, this enabling the angle of thrust to be altered by raising the complete power unit, if necessary, to a maximum elevation of twenty-two degrees. To further reduce the effects of spray a four-bladed propeller of the smallest practical diameter was fitted. In the lowered position the airscrew spinner formed the actual prow of this unique flying-boat.

In its elevated position the engine, together with the radiator, situated as

The Parnall Prawn had straight leading edges to its wings, but there was a pronounced taper to the trailing edges. The engine is in the raised position. (*Parnall & Sons*)

The Prawn with its 65 hp Ricardo Burt engine in raised and normal thrust positions. (*Parnall & Sons and MoD*)

it was centrally on top of the cowling, must have severely restricted the pilot's view when taking off.

The Prawn had an all-metal single-step hull into which was incorporated the open cockpit. The pilot was provided with a headrest which was faired into the rear fuselage, and a windscreen was fitted for his protection.

The Prawn had a parasol monoplane wing, fabric-covered and with a fairly wide and deep trailing-edge cut-out above the cockpit. Wing leading-edges were straight, but the trailing edges had a pronounced taper, the outer wing panels incorporating broad-chord ailerons. A gravity feed fuel tank was located above the centre-section and supported on the top decking by an inverted V-type cabane constructed of steel tubing. Four main bracing struts, two each side, ran parallel from the hull's lower sides and sloped upward and outward to the wing undersurfaces.

Two stabilising floats were fitted outboard supported by normal N-struts, while a pair of diagonal struts was located between each float and the undersurface of the wing.

The Prawn at Felixstowe in about 1930. The very small diameter airscrew is obvious when it is realised that the wing span was about 28 ft. (*Imperial War Museum*)

The Prawn experimental flying-boat was on trials at the MAEE, Felixstowe, when this photograph was taken. (*Imperial War Museum*)

The Prawn's empennage comprised ample fin and rudder surfaces, while the tailplane, rectangular in planform, and the fairly large elevators, were situated slightly above the top decking of the hull and attached to the fin. The tailplane was strut-braced to the hull below and wire-braced to the fin above.

Completed in an all-over silver metal finish, with the exception of the main supporting struts, which were black, the Prawn carried the standard British red, white and blue roundels on the fuselage and upper and lower wing surfaces, while the contemporary national rudder stripes covered the entire rudder surface.

Superimposed across the vertical red, white and blue rudder stripes, in the style then customary on British military types, was the Prawn's military serial number S1576.

In photographs of the Prawn, the Parnall part numbers P1/6213 and

Taken at Felixstowe this photograph shows most of the features of the Prawn. (*Imperial War Museum*)

P1/6214 can clearly be discerned on the starboard side of the rudder and fin respectively. On the starboard stabilising float can be seen the letters and numerals SB4289, indicating that the stabilising floats were probably supplied by Short Brothers. The oil drainage point is clearly indicated on the forward starboard side of the hull in black lettering.

When ashore the Prawn was transported for beaching and maintenance purposes on a small two-wheel dolly.

After undergoing its trials at Felixstowe the Prawn was used at the MAEE for experimental purposes, but for how long has never, as far as is known, been established. The ultimate fate of this remarkable little flying-boat remains uncertain.

Parnall Prawn

Single-seat experimental flying-boat. 65 hp Ricardo-Burt water-cooled inline engine.
Span 28 ft*; Length 18 ft*; height on dolly 7 ft.
Maximum speed approximately 100 mph.

Production

One built in 1930. See Appendix A.

*Approximate

Parnall G.4/31

In the immediate aftermath of the First World War, the newly fledged Royal Air Force suffered a drastic retrenchment programme and, due to political expediency, was reduced from the world's most powerful air arm to one possessing only a handful of squadrons. The cutbacks and

The Parnall G.4/31 making a low, fast run across the aerodrome at Yate, with Howard Saint at the controls. (*Rolls-Royce*)

curtailments of new programmes would persist for a number of years, allowing only a few new aircraft types (mostly fighters) to be produced. As a result the North West Frontier of India and Iraq were still being patrolled by ageing D.H.9As and Bristol F.2Bs of the First World War vintage up until the late 1920s. By the early 1930s the Westland Wapiti and Fairey Gordon biplanes were in service, but although they gave yeoman service, these types were not so much of an advance in concept over their predecessors.

It came as no surprise therefore when, in July 1931, the Air Ministry issued Specification G.4/31 which called for a new aeroplane in the general purpose category. The requirements of the specification demanded an aircraft of exceptional versatility as it was to be capable of day and night bombing, dive-bombing, overland reconnaissance, army co-operation, aerial photography, and in an amendment of October 1931, to be able to undertake the role of a torpedo-bomber and coastal reconnaissance aircraft.

The inclusion of dive-bombing was unusual as a requirement in a British specification for, although it was becoming recognised as a precision form of attack in other countries (especially the United States and Japan), the British apparently frowned on the dive-bomber concept.

The dive-bombing stipulation was in fact later dropped from the specification, but not before those aircraft entered for the competition had been designed to include dive-bombing as one of their functions.

This extremely rare picture shows the Parnall G.4/31 general purpose biplane before its metal structure was covered by fabric. Note, the unusual profile of the fin and rudder. (*T I Jackson Ltd*)

Response to Specification G.4/31 was quite promising and resulted in the emergence of several interesting prototypes from British manufacturers. These included the Armstrong Whitworth A.W.19, Blackburn B.7, Bristol Type 120, Fairey G.4/31 Mks.I and II, Hawker PV4, Handley Page H.P.47, Vickers Type 253, Westland PV7 and Parnall G.4/31.

Harold Bolas's place as chief designer at Parnall had been taken by H V Clarke, and it was he who was responsible for Parnall's G.4/31 design. The aeroplane was a large two-bay biplane of fabric-covered metal construction and incorporated wings of unequal span. These were braced in a rather unorthodox manner by N-interplane struts having attachments from opposite corners to those normally associated with biplanes. The upper mainplanes had a span of 57 ft, the roots having a sharp dihedral angle which resulted in a noticeable gull-wing effect. Ailerons were fitted to all four wing surfaces. Complementing the normal interplane struts were

The Parnall G.4/31 at Martlesham in about 1935. (*Imperial War Museum*)

195

two sturdy N struts. Located each side of the fuselage these sloped upwards and inwards from the inboard interplane struts at an angle to a point just below the top fuselage decking beneath the upper centre-section.

The tail unit comprised an exceptionally large fin which, together with the horn-balanced rudder, gave the vertical tail surfaces an unusual appearance. The strut-braced tail plane was situated on top of the rear fuselage section.

The well proportioned elevators incorporated full-length broad-chord trim-tabs, and there was a fairing between the bottom of the rudder post and a point beneath the fuselage aft of the tailwheel.

A divided-type undercarriage was fitted with the wheels enclosed in streamlined spats, each unit being supported by a tripod-type set of undercarriage legs.

Parnall's G.4/31 was powered by a 690 hp Bristol Pegasus IM3 nine-cylinder air-cooled radial engine driving a two-blade wooden propeller. The Pegasus was enclosed by a short-chord Townend ring cowling which incorporated shallow cylinder-head fairings or helmets. Fuel was supplied from two main tanks located in the upper mainplanes, one each side, and situated in the dihedral sections of the wing roots.

A crew of two was carried, the pilot being housed in an enclosed cockpit well above the nose of the aircraft and level with leading-edge of the upper wings. The observer/gunner sat in an open cockpit aft, which was equipped with a gun ring on which was mounted a .303-in Lewis machine-

The upper gull wing of the Parnall G.4/31 is well shown in this view, while the sun angle helps to show the interplane strut layout. (*Parnall & Sons*)

gun. Forward armament consisted of a fixed .303-in Vickers machine-gun mounted in the port side of the fuselage and synchronised to fire through the propeller arc. Offensive armament could comprise either an aerial torpedo slung between the undercarriage legs, or alternatively a load of bombs carried on underwing racks beneath the lower wings.

A sizeable unglazed cabin was incorporated between the mainplanes filling the whole gap, this enabling passengers or stretcher cases to be carried. For use in an emergency over the sea, an inflatable rubber dinghy was provided and carried in the upper port mainplane.

Parnall's prototype was the largest of the entries in the G.4/31 competition, and also the last of the contenders to be completed.

Despite its development to a 1931 specification, the machine did not make its first flight until 1935, when it flew from Yate piloted by Capt Howard Saint. It carried the serial number K2772.

Subsequent test flights showed Parnall's big biplane possessed excellent potential in the performance and duty requirements of the G.4/31 specification.

However, despite the various aircraft manufacturers' ready response, and the excellent prototypes resulting, the Air Ministry, wishing to obtain aircraft capable of more sophisticated roles, shelved the general purpose concept. The only contender seriously considered was the Vickers Type 253, but although a contract was actually drawn up, this machine was cancelled in favour of the more advanced Vickers Wellesley monoplane.

Parnall G.4/31

Two-seat general purpose biplane. 690 hp Bristol Pegasus IM3 nine-cylinder air-cooled radial engine.

Span 57 ft; length 35 ft 9 in; height 15 ft; wing area 687 sq ft.

Loaded weight 6,800 lb.

Maximum speed approximately 165 mph at 5,000 ft.

One fixed forward firing .303-in Vickers machine-gun and one wing-mounted .303-in Lewis machine-gun. Provision for torpedo or underwing bombs.

Production

One prototype only. See Appendix A.

Hendy 302/302A

Although Parnall had suffered a severe setback with the unfortunate fate of the Pipit fighter prototypes, and had been unsuccessful in securing production orders for military aircraft since the small run of Plovers in the early 1920s, the firm did nevertheless continue with other aircraft construction work. In addition to its own prototypes, this included several

The Hendy 302, G-AAVT, in its original form as built by George Parnall & Co at Yate, powered by a 105 hp Cirrus Hermes I engine. (*via Parnall archives*)

civil contracts among which was one to build the Hendy 302 for the Hendy Aircraft Company.

The 302 was designed by Basil B Henderson, known familiarly as 'Hendy' Henderson, and was of advanced concept for its time. Produced at a time when biplanes were mainly in vogue, the Hendy 302 was an aesthetically pleasing long-wing cantilever monoplane incorporating a tandem two-seat enclosed cockpit. The fuselage was a rectangular structure with a domed top and was constructed of spruce with a plywood covering.

The mainplanes were of fabric-covered wooden construction and comprised two I-section spars built up with a plywood web. Rectangular-section spruce strips formed flanges on each side, and the spars were interconnected by a lattice arrangement of spruce strips. The spar joints and intersection points consisted of plywood gusset plates, while the ribs were of three-ply capped with spruce strips.

The Hendy 302's empennage was the conventional monoplane style of unbraced tailplane with divided elevators, curved fin and horn-balanced rudder.

The non-retractable undercarriage was of the divided-type comprising vertical compression legs each side which incorporated oleo and coil-spring shock absorbers.

The top ends of these legs were attached to the front wing spar, the

After changing hands in 1933, when its new owner was C S Napier, the Hendy 302 was updated to have a more powerful 130 hp Cirrus Hermes IV engine, a redesigned fully-glazed cockpit canopy and streamlined wheel spats. It also acquired a new paint scheme as well as being redesignated the Hendy 302A. (*The Riding Photograph Collection*)

bottom ends being hinged on the centre line of the fuselage underside by a steel tube V.

As originally built by Parnall in 1929, the Hendy 302 was powered by a 105 hp Cirrus Hermes I engine very neatly enclosed within a faired metal cowling. Fuel was contained in a main 16 Imp gal wing tank, while a 9 gal gravity-feed tank was housed in the fuselage. An optional 16 gal tank could be additionally installed if required.

The cockpits were enclosed by a coupe top, which was hinged on the port side to allow access to the two seats.

Registered G-AAVT (c/n 1) the Hendy 302 obtained a C of A on 27 June, 1930, the aircraft's first owner being Capt E W Percival. Entered in the 1930 King's Cup Air Race, the Hendy 302, flown by Percival, achieved an average speed of 121.51 mph, and a year later, when competing in the 1931 Heston to Newcastle race, again with Percival at the controls, the Hendy 302 covered the course at an average speed of 145 mph.

In July 1931, the Hendy 302 was sold to Cirrus Hermes Engineering Co Ltd, the aero-engine manufacturers, who used it as a flying test-bed. Later, in 1933, the machine changed hands again, the new owner being Carill S Napier, who had the Hendy 302 rebuilt at Croydon.

The Cirrus Hermes I was replaced by a 130 hp Cirrus Hermes IV, while structural modifications undertaken included a fully glazed cockpit canopy and the introduction of streamlined wheel spats. The aircraft was redesignated the Hendy 302A, and flew in the 1934 King's Cup Race in which it averaged 133.5 mph.

The Hendy 302A also participated in a number of other sporting events including the 1935 Wakefield Cup Race. In 1936 the aircraft had its inverted Hermes IV engine replaced by a 150 hp Cirrus Hermes Major II, for which it served as a flying test-bed. The Hendy 302A survived until 1938, when it was finally withdrawn from use at Gravesend.

Hendy 302

Two-seat private-owners' and sports monoplane. 105 hp Cirrus Hermes I four-cylinder inverted inline air-cooled engine.

Span 35 ft; length 22 ft 10 in; height 7 ft 3 in; wing area 178 sq ft.

Empty weight 1,045 lb; loaded weight 1,900 lb.

Maximum speed 132 mph; cruising speed 112 mph; stalling speed 37 mph; climb to 850 ft, 1 min, to 5,000 ft, 7.1 min; ceiling 16,000 ft.

Hendy 302A

130 hp Cirrus Hermes IV.

Dimensions as Hendy 302.

Empty weight 1,050 lb; loaded weight, 1,900 lb.

Maximum speed 135 mph; cruising speed 117 mph; stalling speed 37 mph; climb to 900 ft, 1 min, to 5,000 ft, 6½ min; ceiling 17,000 ft.

Production

One only, modified to 302A. See Appendix A.

F G Miles running up the 75 hp Pobjoy R in the Parnall-built Miles Satyr. (*the late A J Jackson*)

Miles M.1 Satyr

During 1931 Frederick George Miles approached Parnall to make arrangements for the Yate works to construct a small sporting biplane, to be named the Satyr. F G Miles and his wife, Blossom, collaborated in the design of the Satyr* and, together they supervised the construction of the little biplane.

Intended as a purely aerobatic and exhibition aeroplane for the personal use of Miles, the Satyr was, at that time, the smallest aircraft in Great Britain, and had the appearance of a half-size contemporary RAF fighter.

Of fabric-covered wooden construction, the Satyr had a conventional box-section fuselage with the top decking faired to an oval shape. The single open cockpit was fitted with a small windscreen and the pilot's headrest was faired into the top of the fuselage.

The wings were of unequal span, well staggered and of parallel chord. A distinctive feature of the Satyr was the incorporation of single I interplane struts, which were of quite broad chord, streamlined and widely faired into the upper and lower mainplanes. These single struts were complemented by bracing wires and small N centre-section struts. Ailerons were fitted to the upper mainplanes only, while all four wings had blunt tips.

The Satyr had a conventional style tail unit consisting of well proportioned fin and rudder, and a broad-chord tailplane, which was unbraced and located between the top of the rear fuselage and the fin.

The undercarriage was of the cross-axle V-type, cross-braced with wires, and fitted with quite large diameter wheels for the size of the aeroplane. A tailskid was fixed at the extreme rear of the fuselage beneath the stern-post.

Power was provided by a 75 hp Pobjoy R seven-cylinder air-cooled radial engine, and fuel was supplied from the main tank, which was situated in the upper centre-section.

The Parnall-built Miles Satyr made its first flight from Parnall's aerodrome during August 1932. It was painted in an overall silver finish and carried its civil registration, G-ABVG, in red lettering above and below the wings and on the fuselage sides.

Test flying of the Satyr, c/n 1 (later J.7), was undertaken by F G Miles, who flew the machine from Yate with much zeal. He found the aircraft extremely manoeuvrable and possessing a very fast rate of climb. On concluding the test flight programme, Miles flew the Satyr from Yate to Shoreham, a flight that was inadvertently to have some significance in British aviation history. This came about when Miles, on his way across country, decided to land for lunch at the Reading Aero Club's aerodrome at Woodley in Berkshire. Arrival of the Satyr and its pilot created quite a stir, and the Aero Club's chief flying instructor took the diminutive biplane up to perform a series of aerobatics. He landed full of praise for the aeroplane, his enthusiasm arousing the interest of Charles Powis of Philips & Powis who was also at the club.

Over lunch Powis and Miles discussed a light, low-wing monoplane design which Miles was contemplating, and as a result an immediate

*At some stage the Satyr was given the Miles designation M.1.

A rain-soaked aerodrome provides the backdrop for the Miles Satyr, built at Yate by Parnall for the personal use of F G Miles. (*MAP*)

agreement was signed between the two men, whereby Miles Aircraft Ltd and Philips Powis Ltd would build and sell aeroplanes from premises envisaged at Woodley. From this lunchtime meeting was to evolve development of the Miles Aircraft company, a concern which was to produce numerous types of private and sporting aeroplanes for the civil market as well as a number of well-known training aircraft for the Royal Air Force.

After receiving a C of A on 1 February, 1933, the Satyr was sold the following May to the Hon Mrs Victor Bruce, who owned a firm known as Luxury Air Tours. Mrs Bruce was also involved with Hospital Air Pageants, a touring air show, and the Satyr often took part in their air displays piloted by John B Pugh. It was in a finish then of red and white chequers, and continued flying until September 1936, when this delightful little biplane was written off after flying into telephone wires.

Miles M.1 Satyr

Single-seat aerobatic biplane. 75 hp Pobjoy R seven-cylinder air-cooled radial engine.
Span 21 ft; length 17 ft 8 in; height 5 ft 9 in; wing area 117 sq ft.
Empty weight 594 lb; loaded weight 900 lb.
Maximum speed 125 mph; landing speed 40 mph; climb to 1,400 ft, 1 min.

Production

One built. See Appendix A.

The Percival Gull prototype as designed and constructed at Maidstone, by Capt Edgar Percival and his team. (*the late A J Jackson*)

Percival Gull Four

The most significant of the civil contracts undertaken by Parnall was that awarded the company in the early 1930s for the construction of the first production batch of Percival Gull Four three-seat cabin monoplanes.

The prototype Gull Four was designed by Edgar Percival, who also supervised construction of the aircraft. This took place in a small workshop at Maidstone, Kent, premises that had first been used by C H Lowe-Wylde for the building of gliders.

When the prototype Gull Four was completed Percival undertook the test flight programme. Later, on 8–9 July, 1932, Percival flew the new monoplane, G-ABUR, in the round-Britain King's Cup Air Race and, although not gaining a winning place, managed to cover the course at an average speed of 142.73 mph, a performance that revealed the benefits of the new type's advanced design and aerodynamic efficiency. The Gull Four was the first low-wing cantilever monoplane to go into production in the Commonwealth, and it was reputed to possess greater all-round efficiency than that of the earlier Schneider Trophy racing aircraft according to the Everling formula.

During 1933, G-ABUR was powered for a time by a 160 hp Napier Javelin III engine, and its top speed was better than that of many contemporary military fighters. When powered by a de Havilland Gipsy Major engine, the prototype Gull Four became a familiar sight around much of Europe, but unfortunately the aircraft was written off in Northern Rhodesia during the Cape record attempt in 1935 by Man Mohan Singh.

Before 1945, the prefix type number given to Percival aeroplanes was widely published as P. This was in fact a letter used wrongly by some as a means of convenient publicity. The proper designation of the original Gull

The prototype Gull, G-ABUR, after modifications to the cockpit canopy roof, a new paint scheme and racing number on its fin and rudder. (*the late A J Jackson*)

Four powered by a Cirrus Hermes engine was in fact the Percival Type D.1, with subsequent versions having this correct 'D' type number prefix.

The Gull Four was of wooden construction with a fuselage of box-section, the top decking being formed to an oval. The material used in the aircraft's structure consisted mainly of plywood with plywood skinning. Entrance to the enclosed cabin by the pilot and two passengers was on the port side, access being gained by raising the cabin roof and lowering the port side window sections.

This Parnall-built Gull Four, G-ABUV, was powered by a 130 hp Cirrus Hermes IV engine. Initially sold to C S Napier in March 1933, it crashed at Nice in November 1936 while under the ownership of M Maxwell. (*K E Wixey collection via P Mills*)

The wings were of spruce and plywood construction, fabric-covered, and of low-wing cantilever monoplane layout. For ease of stowage and ground transport the wings could be folded backwards to lie parallel to the fuselage.

The empennage was of conventional wooden construction, the vertical and horizontal surfaces being fabric-covered.

The main undercarriage wheels were enclosed by streamlined spats, the top sections of which partly encased the undercarriage legs and bracing struts. A tailskid was fixed to the stern-post at the extreme end of the fuselage.

Power was provided by a 130 hp Cirrus Hermes IV four-cylinder inverted air-cooled engine driving a two-blade wooden propeller.

Following the success of the prototype Gull Four the Percival Aircraft Company was formed by Edgar Percival and Lieut-Cdr E W B Leake, and it was decided to entrust the first production batch of Percival D.1 and D.2 Gull Fours to Parnall's factory at Yate.

Being of all-wooden construction the Gull Four was ideally suited to the manufacturing techniques of Parnall with its proven expertise in wooden airframe production. The contract came also at a very opportune time for Parnall, for just then the company's order books were very bleak indeed.

The production Gull Fours were powered by the Cirrus Hermes IV engine normally, but alternatively a 130 hp de Havilland Gipsy Major, or 160 hp Napier Javelin III could be installed, the two variants being designated the D.1 and D.2 respectively.

Among those Gull Fours built at Yate was G-ABUV, which went originally to C S Napier in March 1933. It then passed to Surrey Flying

Production Gull Four (G-ACPA) built at Yate in 1933 by Parnall it was powered by a 160 hp Napier Javelin engine. It was converted to Gull Six standard by Percival Aircraft. (*MAP*)

Direct descendant of the Gull Four via the Gull Six and Vega Gull was the Percival Proctor. This Mk.3 Proctor (G-AOGE) is seen on 22 April, 1979, at a flying meeting at Henstridge. (*Roger P Wasley*)

Services with which it flew as a charter and photographic aeroplane until October 1935, when it was sold to M Maxwell. It was still in his ownership when, on 2 November, 1936, it crashed at Nice and was written off.

Other Parnall-built Gull Fours included G-ACFY used by A V Roe and its communications aircraft based at Woodford; G-ACIS which went to Air Service Training before being sold to Indian National Airways in 1935; and G-ACHM acquired by the British Air Navigation Company in 1933, this aircraft being employed on fast newspaper duties.

Among privately-owned Parnall-built Gull Fours were G-ACGR owned by Sir Philip Sassoon who, at his own request, had the machine fitted with a Napier Javelin III engine; G-ACLG which belonged to the Hon Loel Guinness, this aircraft also being sold in 1935 to Indian National Airways; and G-ACAL, named *Leicestershire Fox*, owned by W Lindsay Everard MP. This Gull Four was eventually acquired by the British Air Navigation Company of Heston and, like the firm's other Gull Four, G-ACHM, was used on express newspaper assignments. Unfortunately G-ACAL was wrecked when it crashed during a bad storm while on a return flight from the Continent. The pilot, A J Styran, and the company's manager, I C MacGilchrist, both lost their lives in the crash.

One Parnall-built Gull Four, G-ACJV, became famous when it was used by Sir Charles Kingsford Smith on his record England to Australia flight in October 1933. Kingsford Smith had travelled by sea to the United Kingdom during September to find the Gull Four waiting for him at Heston. He promptly named the monoplane *Miss Southern Cross* and, on 4 October, Kingsford Smith took off in G-ACJV from Lympne. On 11 October, 7 days 4 hr 33 min later, he touched down at Wyndham. Kingsford Smith received a congratulatory telegram from HM King George V, and the Australian Government presented him with a tax-free grant of £3,000. The Gull Four used by Kingsford Smith remained in Australia and was registered there as VH-CKS.

The Percival Gull Four as a type found its way to a number of countries, where overseas buyers acquired them second-hand in places as far apart as Australia, Brazil, France, India and the Netherlands. One Gull Four, VH-UTP, was still known to be flying in Australia as late as the mid-1950s.

Edgar Percival having established his own aircraft manufacturing company meant that no further contracts were issued to Parnall for the construction of Percival aeroplanes.

Of the twenty-three production Gull Fours built by Parnall during 1933-34, one machine, G-ACHA, was modified by Percival to have a de Havilland Gipsy Six engine installed before being sold to an Australian buyer. In addition it is believed, according to available records, that Percival modified three other Parnall-built Gull Fours to Gull Six standard with Gipsy Six engines. These were G-ACUL (sold to a New Zealand customer as ZK-AES), G-ACPA and G-ACXY, the last being sold to a French buyer as F-AOXY.

These aircraft were representative of a revised version of the Gull Four, designated the D.3 and known as the Gull Six, in which the 200 hp de Havilland Gipsy Six engine was installed. More than twenty Gull Sixes were produced at Gravesend by Percival before the company's move to Luton.

Percival Gull Four D.1/D.2

Three-seat cabin monoplane. 130 hp Cirrus Hermes IV four-cylinder inverted inline air-cooled engine (D.1), 130 hp de Havilland Gipsy Major or 160 hp Napier Javelin III four-cylinder inverted inline air-cooled engine (D.2).

Span 36 ft 2 in; width folded 13 ft 2 in; length 24 ft 9 in; height 7 ft 4½ in; wing area 169 sq ft.

D.1/D.2 with Javelin. Empty weight 1,170 lb; D.2 with Gipsy Major 1,290 lb.

Loaded weights 2,050 lb D.1, 2,250 lb D.2 with Javelin, 2,300 lb D.2 with Gipsy Major.

Maximum speed 145 mph (Hermes IV), 155 mph (Gipsy Major), 160 mph (Javelin); cruising speed 125 mph (D.1), 133 mph (D.2 Gipsy Major), 140 mph (D.2 Javelin); climb to 850 ft, 1 min (D.1); ceiling 16,000 ft (D.1), 18,000 ft (D.2 Gipsy Major); range 700 miles (D.1), 745 miles (D.2 Gipsy Major), 700 miles (D.2 Javelin).

Production

First 23 production aircraft built at Yate. See Appendix A.

Parnall F.5/33 Project

During 1934 Parnall undertook the design of a new two-seat fighter to Air Ministry Specification F.5/33 in which it was stipulated that a front gun station should be included.

Unfortunately no drawings or sketches of this interesting project have survived, but a copy of details relating to the aeroplane, issued by Parnall, has recently been found. Dated May 1934 it contains the following information:

Note:
Owing to pressure of work in the design staff, it has been impossible to present this design in as complete a manner as has been our custom. Equipment and services which are of stereotyped design have, therefore, been briefly dealt with in the description, and in certain cases have been omitted from drawings.

Careful and studied attention has, however, been devoted to the design, but only items of importance and interest have been dealt with in detail.

General Design:
The layout here submitted is that which incorporates a forward gun turret rotatable about a vertical axis fixed in the aircraft, and a horizontal axis, square with the gunner, fixed in the turret. This differs from the turret shown in Design No. 2 of the Specification in so far as in that case the horizontal axis was fixed to the machine; the vertical one moving with the turret.

With this arrangement it is impossible to depress or elevate the gun when the turret is yawed through 90°, while at smaller angles movement about the horizontal axis will be completed with a 'rolling' rotation of the turret.

These disadvantages do not occur with the design submitted.

The question of balancing the aircraft leads to the pusher type in order to get the engines aft of the c/g. Were it not for this fact, there is little to recommend the pusher, and it will be safe to assume that no-one would select this type of machine if a tractor were available. A rough comparison shows that for equal wing loadings the tractor is superior in the following cases:-

(a) Run to take-off; (b) Climb; (c) Ceiling; (d) Parachute exit for pilot. With this in view the necessary weight distribution has been coupled with the tractor's advantages.

Gun Turret:
This unit is a spherical sheet metal shell built on formers. The main loads are taken on a pair of circular girders which act also as the elevation tracks. These tracks are mounted on rollers attached to a ring at the bottom of the turret. Centrally disposed between these elevation tracks is a rack driven by an electric motor, through an irreversible worm drive, both of which are mounted on the base ring (referred to on the drawing as the inner ring).

This inner ring is carried on an outer ring, and under normal motor operation both are keyed together.

The outer ring carries a series of rollers which are housed in a fixed channel-shaped ring thus allowing relative rotational movement, similar to a Scarff ring. This fixed ring forms part of the main fuselage structure being supported on its lateral diameter by two pylons.

Moments about the attachment points are taken on a pair of built-up girders on the under surface.

The traverse motion is derived from another motor secured to the main structure through a worm drive.

The hand operating mechanisms have taken the form of handles on the two sides of the turret. Elevation is by means of a direct sun and planet gear driven on to a torque arm growing from the inner ring. The traverse drive is obtained by the handle shaft passing through the hinge point to a bevel gear, and thence by a pair of universal coupled rods to a pinion fixed to the inner ring and geared to the outer ring.

Under motor-driven conditions this pinion acts as a key, causing the two rings to move simultaneously as described above. To operate the hand-driven elevation gear, the elevation rack is disengaged by a sideways movement.

Both motors are actuated from rheostats by movements of the guns. The guns are linked together, a small amount of free angular play being provided both horizontally and vertically. The levers attached to the rheostats are spring-loaded. The greater the load applied to the gun handle the bigger the rheostat displacement, with resultant higher motor speed.

Owing to the difficulty of taking rigid pipes from the outside to inside the turret it has been thought advisable to equip the gunner with his own independent oxygen supply/gear. The upper forward quadrant is capable of rearward rotation and when opened, forms the doorway. The remainder of the equipment is of the usual form and needs no special description.

Pilot's Cockpit:
The equipment here also follows stereotyped lines (as can be seen from the drawings).

Two Lewis guns are mounted in the wings clear of the airscrew, the cocking handles being operated via cables and levers situated on the sides of the seat.

The guns are fired from the standard ring-type control column handle, as described in the following section. It will be noticed (on reference to the No. 2 drawing) that as an alternative to the Lewis guns in the wings, two Vickers guns can be mounted/housed in the cockpit. The fuselage is very wide by virtue of the front turret and it was thought, that although the specification calls for wing guns, this installation might be worth considering on account of the ability to clear jams.

Armament:
The types of gun have been mentioned above. The two Lewis guns are housed within the leading-edge of the wing on each side of the fuselage, and clear the airscrew disc.

A rapidly removable cover is provided on the upper surface for access to the gun and drums for removal. The main supports are attached by a braced structure to the wing-spar and are taken on the gun lugs in such a way as to provide at these points universal joints. Screws are provided here for adjusting the setting of the guns in the vertical plane.

The rear ends of the guns are held by means of horizontal guides embracing the upper parts of the handles. These take vertical loads. Lateral loads are taken, and adjustment supplied, by two screwed clamps bearing on each side of the handles.

Removal of the guns can be carried out very quickly, without dismantling any part of the mountings. In the case of the Lewis gun installation a standard three lever ring type control column handle is employed; one of the levers operating the camera gun.

In order to minimise the effort required for firing and to secure simultaneous action of the two guns, a hydraulic servo system is employed for the Lewis guns.

This can most conveniently be carried out by taking a branch pipe from the C.C. secondary pipe near the C.C. reservoir. This pipe then proceeds to the Lewis guns' trigger motor.

The light series bomb carried is conveyed under the fuselage in a trough, so that only half the diameter of the bombs protrudes into the wind stream. The forward clearance is 80°. The controls will be mounted on the starboard side of the pilot's cockpit.

R/T:
This unit is housed in a compartment behind the pilot's head, and is mounted on a removable tray carried on four spring boxes. The whole unit can be withdrawn through a door. Remote controls are provided on the top starboard longeron.

Power Unit:
The engines chosen are Bristol Aquilas. The mountings take the form of two fore and aft braced members secured to the wing-spar by removable pins affording cantilever support for the engine. These members span the Townend ring and at their rear ends are connected by traverse members which pick up the engine mounting bolts. At these points the local loads are taken up and into a pylon structure. The normal airscrew hub is replaced by a special splined disc. The airscrew is driven through an extension shaft. The coupling is broken by removing the retaining cap which is in principle a union nut of large diameter. The forward end of the shaft is carried in a housing containing radial and thrust ball bearings.

To dismantle the engine, the pins mentioned above are removed and the coupling broken, thus affording detachment of the complete engine unit. Access to the rear of the engine is obtained by removing the tail fairing. Forward of the spar are the gravity-feed tanks, both fuel and oil, the tank having the oil cooler incorporated into its upper surface.

It will be noticed that the tractor airscrew arrangement allows the engine to be within easy reach of the ground, thus obviating the use of trestles for ground maintenance work.

Fuel System:
The main tank is in the fuselage, from which the fuel is pumped to the gravity tanks in the engine nacelles. The system has no special features needing detailed descriptions.

Flying Controls:
The control column is of the standard ring type, supported in a self-aligning bearing, housed in a bracket built on the seat pan. The lower end is attached to a tube. This tube acts as a torque tube for the ailerons and as a connecting rod for the elevator motion.

Pilot's Seat:
The seat is adjustable over a total range of 4 inches. Raising the seat in no way affects the positions of either elevator or the ailerons. The torque tube is attached at the rear end to a bell crank lever on the front countershaft, which extends from the middle to the port side of the fuselage.

Elevator Control:
Fore and aft movements of the torque tube rotate this countershaft, transmitting motion to the elevator push rods via a lever.

Aileron Control
Lateral movement of the control column rotates the torque tube, thus producing angular displacement of the bell crank lever. The motion then proceeds via levers and push rods to the aileron lever. The push rods are established by idler levers at frequent intervals.

Tail Adjusting Gear:
The tail adjusting gear is operated from a handwheel on the left side of the cockpit. The wheel does not rise with the seat but is, nevertheless, accessible over the normal range of adjustment. The drive is by chain and cable to a worm box in the rear of the fuselage.

The tailpiece is hinged to the longerons at the front spar while the rear spar is adjusted by struts connected to levers on the worm box, the gear ratio being so chosen that the system is irreversible. The chief advantage of the worm box over the screw is the ease of lubrication and high-speed replacement.

Rudder Control:
The rudder pedals are adjustable fore and aft over a range of 4 inches which is achieved by the rotation of a foot-operated starwheel placed centrally between the pedals. The pedals are of the parallel motion type, being square to the foot in all positions.

The auxiliary rudder bar carries a central operating lever, which projects forwards. The lateral motion of this lever is communicated to a transverse rod, and thence to the cable lever via a bell crank and another rod.

The rudder is trimmed by a servo flap which also serves to assist the normal horn balance, the gearing being so chosen as to produce a rudder hinge movement linear with angular displacement.

Alighting Gear:
The main undercarriage is of the usual split type with the addition of a retracting gear, operated by means of a screw and gear train from a handwheel placed on the starboard side of the pilot's seat. In all positions of the undercarriage chassis other than when fully extended, a red indication light will show on the instrument panel.

The tail wheel can rotate through a complete revolution but is restrained normally to 90° each side of the central position. The stop can be removed by turning a handle near the wheel.

Brakes:
Wheel brakes of the hydraulic type will be fitted. To reduce the landing run an airbrake of approximately 6 square feet area is mounted over the fuselage.

Fuselage:
This is a tubular steel structure. The joints are of a tubular riveted fish plate construction, the tube ends being squared and non-abutting for ease of manufacture and repair. Wire bracing will be avoided.

The portion forward of the pilot will be of monocoque construction with removable panels for access to the electrical apparatus, oxygen bottles and compressed air cylinders.

The remainder will be fabric-covered, doors being provided at the rear end for inspecting controls. Along the port side the controls run in a duct, having sectional hinged covers to assist inspection and maintenance.

Wing Structure:
This unit has all-steel primary structure; light alloy only being used for fairings and the like. Frise ailerons are used, the operating levers being totally enclosed within the wing.

A single spar system is employed. The spar will be built up of segments; each segment will have corrugations and the edges will be turned outwards. These flanges can then be riveted together. By this means the gauge around the perimeter and along the length can be economically graded.

A word may be said here with reference to the torsion produced by the engine. The spar is approximately 20 inches diameter.

Although ordinary engineer's theory does not hold for such structures, and estimates of the strength can be made on these assumptions, estimates of wing weight show that the allowable weight per foot of centre-section spar is 15 lb. This gives a mean thickness of .07 inches. the extra shear stress due to the engine will only be 2½ tons per square inch.

From the point of view of wing flutter, the torsional stiffness can be adjudged by calculating the angular displacement of the wing tip. This can be calculated for CPF factor and is ½°.

Tail Unit:
This is all-steel, but the spars will be of normal dumb-bell section in the case of the tailplane, and round tubes for the other components.

General Particulars (Parnall Design to A.M. Spec. F.5/33)
All up weight, 6,350 lb.
Gross wing area (including body), 355 sq ft.
Nett wing area, 321 sq ft.
Gross wing loading, 17.9 lb/sq ft.
Nett wing loading, 19.8 lb/sq ft.
Aileron area, 44.6 sq ft.
Tailplane and elevator area, 50 sq ft.
Fin and rudder area, 25 sq ft.
Maximum speed at 1,500 ft, 225 mph.
Rate of climb at ground level, 1,450 ft/min at rated boost;
  1,770 ft/min at maximum boost.
Service ceiling, 30,000 ft.
Landing speed, 70 mph.
Total weight of power unit, 1,962 lb (30.9% of a/c weight).
Total fuselage weight, 665 lb (10.5% of a/c weight).
Total wing weight, 1,036 lb (16.3% of a/c weight).
Total u/c weight, 288 lb (4.5 of a/c weight).
Total tail structure weight, 107 lb (1.7% of a/c weight).
Total tankage (fuel & oil), 1,537 lb (24.2% of a/c weight).
Total contract load, 775 lb (11.9% of a/c weight).
Total weight of aircraft, 6,350 lb.

This ends the report submitted by Parnall giving brief details of the proposed new two-seat turret fighter. The company was obviously quite involved with this project, and although the aircraft was never built, it does nevertheless help to show the technical ability of the company in dealing such an advanced military aeroplane for its time.

The prototype Hendy Heck (G-ACTC) built by Westland Aircraft. Designed by Basil Henderson, this aircraft was powered by a 200 hp de Havilland Gipsy Six, and had a retractable undercarriage. (*Westland Helicopters*)

Parnall Aircraft Limited 1935–1939

Parnall Heck

On selling his aircraft business and retiring in 1935, George Parnall left behind him a legacy of fine achievement in aviation design and technology. The family name of Parnall was retained in the trading name of his successors, Parnall Aircraft Ltd, a company formed jointly by the Hendy Aircraft Company and Nash & Thompson Ltd, a concern which became famous for its Frazer-Nash range of aircraft gun turrets.

When Parnall Aircraft took over at Yate, the only Parnall-built aeroplane still on the premises was the G.4/31 general purpose biplane. The new company's priority was in the conversion of sixty-two Hawker Demon two-seat fighters to what became known as the 'Turret Demon' in which Frazer-Nash specially designed 'lobster-back' turrets were installed. Plans were also afoot at Yate for the future production of hydraulically-operated gun turrets for British monoplane bombers, but in the meantime during 1935–36, the company undertook a small amount of work involving Hendy Heck monoplanes.

The Heck was a small low-wing, two-seat cabin monoplane with a retractable undercarriage, and was designed as a sporting machine with a high cruising speed.

The prototype, G-ACTC, was built in 1934 by Westland Aircraft at Yeovil. It was produced for Whitney Straight to the design of Basil Henderson, and, initially designated Hendy 3308, it became known as the Hendy Heck.

The Heck's fuselage was built of spruce members forming an oval section, the whole being ply-covered. The pilot and passenger sat in tandem beneath a well glazed, hinged canopy which afforded a good all-round view.

The wings had spruce and plywood spars and ribs, the surfaces being ply-skinned. An unusual feature for this type of aircraft was the incorporation of camber-changing flaps and leading-edge Handley Page slots. These were fitted to comply with the requirements of Whitney Straight, who had specified an aeroplane with a fast cruising speed, but which must have the ability to take off and land in a small space. The wing leading- and trailing-edges were tapered to semi-oval tips, and large root fairings were fitted.

The empennage was of conventional layout with the tailplane and elevators having straight leading and trailing edges and rounded tips. The vertical tail surfaces comprised a well proportioned triangular fin and horn-balanced rudder.

Power was provided by a 200 hp de Havilland Gipsy Six six-cylinder inline inverted air-cooled engine. This was enclosed in a neat streamlined cowling and drove a two-blade de Havilland metal propeller fitted with a pointed spinner.

To ensure the maximum effect of the Heck's aerodynamically clean

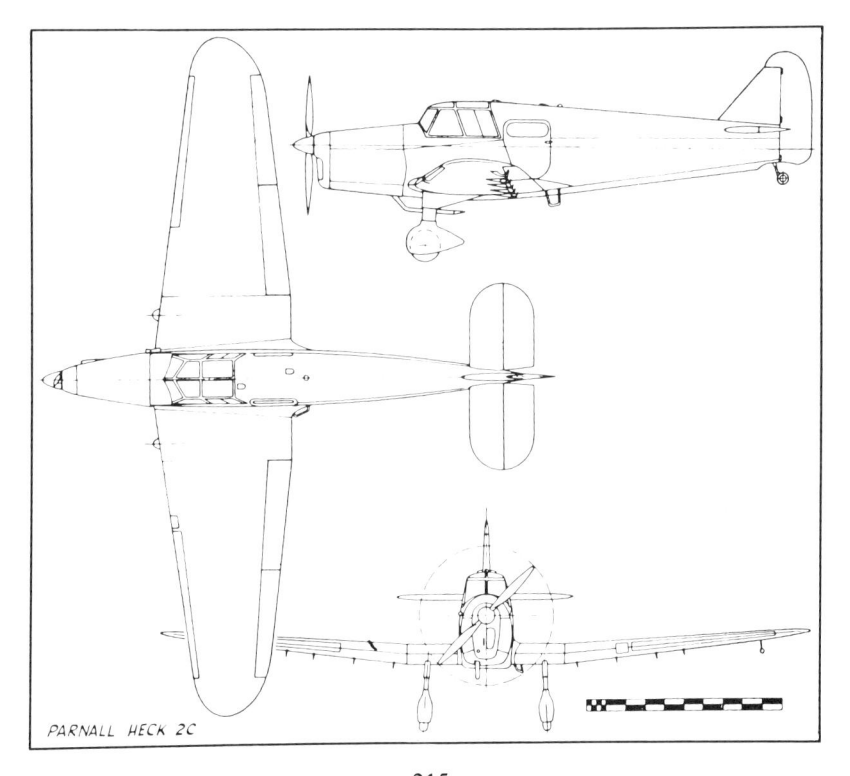

PARNALL HECK 2C

Parnall Heck 2C K8853 modified to have .303-in Browning machine-guns installed in conjunction with contemporary gun-sight trials. (*Parnall & Sons*)

outline in attaining a fast cruising speed, the prototype was installed with a manually-operated retractable undercarriage that retracted outwards into wheel wells in the underside of the wings. A non-retractable tailwheel was fitted at the extreme rear of the fuselage beneath the stern-post.

The prototype Heck made its initial flight in July 1934, in an overall red undercoat finish, and it was intended that the machine would be entered in the 1934 King's Cup Race.

However, while the aircraft was en route for the A & AEE at Martlesham Heath to undergo its airworthiness trials, it was obliged to make a forced landing in a field and sustained damage when colliding with a cow! As a result the Heck was unable to compete in the race, but its performance did create a stir when it achieved a maximum speed of 170 mph and a landing speed of only 44.8 mph.

On the formation of Parnall Aircraft, the Heck became the Parnall Heck, and was publicly demonstrated at Hanworth and the SBAC Show at Hendon in July 1935. The pilot was Flt Lieut R Duncason of Aircraft Exchange & Mart, a company prepared to handle sales of the Heck if Parnall put it into production. The Heck was entered for the 1935 King's Cup Race, but was again prevented from participating because of a wheels-up landing at Hanworth.

The machine was then prepared at Yate for an attempt on the United Kingdom–Cape Town record. The crew was Capt David Llewellyn and Mrs Jill Wyndham, and Parnall's ex-employee Margaret Fry can recall the pair staying at the Railway Hotel at Yate as they waited for their Heck monoplane to be overhauled. For days they sat around in the flight shed waiting for the aircraft's finishing touches to be applied. This included the doping on of Japanese silk over the Heck's plywood skinning.

Eventually, on 8 October, 1935, the Heck took off from Hanworth on its record attempt, but forced landings en route meant the machine did not arrive in Cape Town until 29 October, rendering the outward journey

Seen here at Yate is the first Parnall Heck 2C with its civil registration, G-AEGH. During the Second World War this machine was impressed as NF749, and flew as a communications aircraft with No. 17 Group. It was scrapped at Kemble in May 1944.
(*MAP*)

unsuccessful. On the return flight, however, the Heck beat the previous best time and landed at Lympne 6 days 8 hr 27 min after leaving Cape Town.

It was decided to enter the Heck prototype in the 1936 King's Cup Race, for the third year running, but yet again the pilot's efforts, in this case J D Kirwan, were thwarted when the port undercarriage collapsed as the Heck was taxi-ing at Whitchurch on 10 July.

During the same year it was decided to put the Heck into production at Parnall's Yate factory, and the first of six Heck 2C production machines appeared in the autumn of 1936. This first machine went to Hanworth in September for demonstration purposes carrying the registration G-AEGH, and was in the light and dark blue colour scheme of Aircraft Exchange & Mart.

The Heck 2C differed from the prototype in having three seats, a cabin entrance door replacing the hinged canopy, and small elongated oval-ended side windows instead of the extensive cockpit glazing of the prototype. Also, after the undercarriage problems with the prototype, the wheels on production Heck 2Cs were locked down permanently, the undercarriage legs being encased in trousered fairings. These were later replaced by fixed single-leg undercarriage units enclosed with streamlined spats and fairings.

The prototype Heck was eventually sold to Mrs L Elmhurst of Yeovil, but by December 1935 had passed to Aircraft Exchange & Mart. After its C of A had expired in April 1937, the aircraft was scrapped.

The first three production Heck 2Cs from Parnall (G-AEGH, G-AEGI, G-AEGJ) were all chosen as communications aircraft in accordance with the requirements of the RAF expansion scheme, and each machine was given a coat of all-over dark grey paint. They served as liaison types

The non-retractable undercarriage with streamlined spats, camber-changing flaps and underslung pipe identify this as a Parnall Heck 2C communications monoplane as operated during the war. (*Real Photographs via MAP*)

operating between Parnall at Yate and RAF units.

By that time the Yate works had become increasingly involved with armament programmes in connection with RAF bombers including the Whitley and Wellington, and the Heck 2Cs often flew daily trips of around 1,000 miles as they conveyed staff between Yate and RAF squadrons in the field, or other manufacturers' sites.

Heck G-AEGH was later impressed by the RAF and allotted the serial NF749. Based at Tolworth initially, it was later transferred to RAF Turnhouse, where it operated with the Communications Flight of No. 17 Group. On 21 January, 1944, this aircraft was flown to 5 MU, Kemble, where it remained until 27 May the same year, when it was struck off charge. This particular Heck did, however, have a brief respite from its military duties when, during 1938, together with Heck 2C G-AEGI, it was released to take part in the King's Cup Race with Hubert Broad as pilot. The other machine was in the hands of J A C Warren, and both Heck 2Cs had a lap average of 159 mph, G-AEGH being placed 14th and G-AEGI 10th.

In September 1944, G-AEGI was sent to the British Parachute Co at Cardiff, where it served for the remainder of the war. During 1946, this aircraft returned to Hanworth, where it was renovated and fitted with a 200 hp de Havilland Gipsy Queen 3 engine. The aircraft was then sold to Lieut-Cdr J G Crammond and based at Rochester.

On 29 July, 1949, G-AEGI flew in the King's Cup Race at Elmdon airport, finishing 13th at an average speed of 145.5 mph. The following

Last of six production Heck 2Cs, this machine (K8853) was built to Air Ministry contract and used for experimental purposes. It was delivered to the A & AEE, Martlesham, on 1 April, 1937. (*MAP*)

year it flew into 7th place in the same event, held at Wolverhampton, and actually averaged 159 mph as it had done in 1938. Unfortunately this Heck 2C was severely damaged after the race when Spitfire G-AISU collided with it during the Spitfire's landing run.

The Heck's rear end was smashed, and it was put into a hangar at Wolverhampton, where it languished for some time. It was at one stage offered for sale at £50.00, this being less than the Gipsy engine was worth, but no-one seemed interested. The machine was still at Wolverhampton in May 1953, but late that summer its Gipsy engine was removed from the airframe, and G-AEGI was burnt.

Heck 2C G-AEGJ had a short career, its C of A, which expired on 5 September, 1939, not being renewed. This aircraft was in fact cannibalised to provide spare parts for the other Heck 2Cs.

A clerical error resulted in the registration G-AEMR being applied to the fourth Heck 2C instead of G-AEGK. This aircraft went to the British Parachute Co in September 1944, and remained with it until 1948 at Cardiff, where it was reduced to scrap the same year.

The fifth Heck 2C, G-AEGL, was employed as a test-bed for the 225 hp Wolseley Aries air-cooled radial engine, and was used for a time at the RAE on experimental duties.

The sixth and last production Parnall Heck 2C was supplied under contract 486334/36 to the Air Ministry, and was allotted the military serial K8853. This aircraft was taken on charge by the A & AEE at Martlesham Heath on 1 April, 1937. Just over two years later, on 26 April, 1939, it was transferred to the RAE at Farnborough, where it was used as a test-bed for trial installations of Browning machine-guns. These guns were mounted outboard of the undercarriage, two each side with the barrels protruding from the wing leading-edges, and underwing fairings were introduced in connection with the guns.

Other trials were conducted on this Heck 2C with reflector gun-sight installations for use on Hawker Hurricane and Supermarine Spitfire fighters. This aircraft was also employed on a number of aerodynamic flight tests.

While serving at the two experimental establishments, K8853 was fitted with a modified cabin layout, powered by a Gipsy Six Series II engine, and fitted with a variable-pitch propeller. Initially this Heck 2C was in an all-over silver/metal finish and had standard RAF roundels, but later, as with the other Hecks employed on flying duties, this aircraft received the standard contemporary camouflage finish then used for RAF training and communications aeroplanes.

Later transferred to the RAF, K8853 served as a communications machine at Andover and Heston, eventually going to RAF Hucknall, where it became the personal aircraft of Air Marshal Smart. After being struck off charge this Heck 2C was relegated to a ground instructional airframe bearing the number 3125M.

Parnall Heck 2C

Three-seat cabin monoplane. 200 hp de Havilland Gipsy Six six-cylinder inverted inline air-cooled engine.

Span 31 ft 6 in; length 26 ft 1½ in; height 8 ft 6 in; wing area 105.2 sq ft.

Empty weight 1,750 lb; loaded weight 2,700 lb.

Maximum speed 185 mph; cruising speed 160 mph; climb to 1,000 ft, 1 min; ceiling 16,700 ft; range 605 miles.

Production

Six built. See Appendix A.

Parnall Type 382 (Heck Mk.III)

During 1938, the last aeroplane to bear the name of Parnall rolled out of the Yate works. It was a two-seat ab initio trainer built to Air Ministry Specification T.1/37. This machine was designed by Basil Henderson, and was based on the earlier Heck 2C cabin monoplane. Indeed it became officially known as the Parnall Heck Mk.III.

Specification T.1/37, issued during 1937, called for an elementary two-seat training monoplane larger and heavier than the Miles Magister and Hawk trainers then in service. It was stipulated that the resulting design should ideally be powered by the 200 hp de Havilland Gipsy Six.

Parnall's offering was the Type 382, which incorporated identical outer wing panels and a similar tail unit and undercarriage to the Heck 2C, while

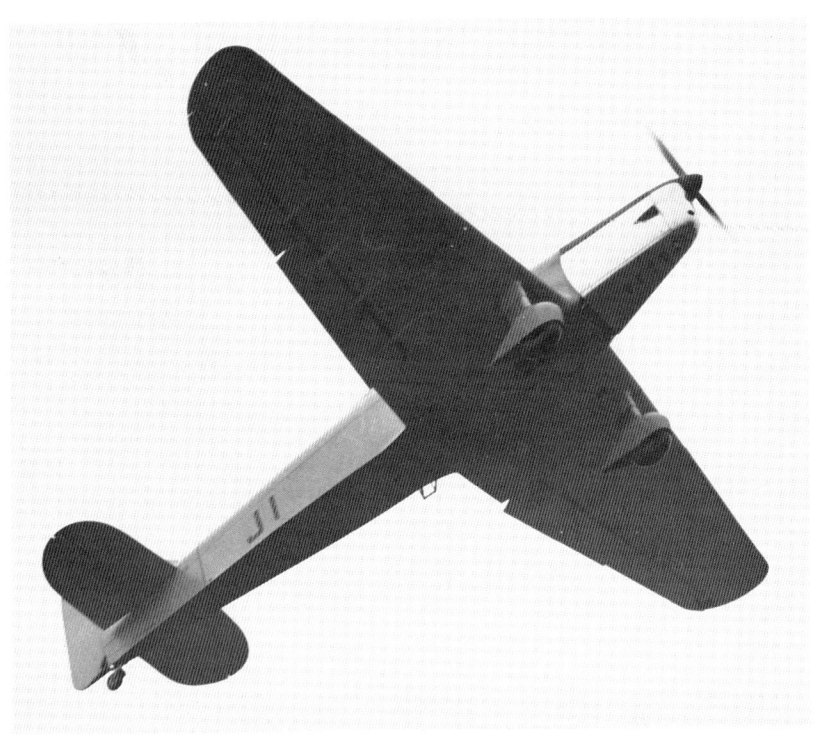

The Parnall Type 382 class B marking J1. (*Parnall archives*)

The Parnall Type 382 with flaps and rear cockpit door lowered. (*MAP*)

The Type 382 with camber-changing flaps lowered. (*Parnall archives*)

the same type of 200 hp Gipsy Six was employed. The pupil and instructor sat in tandem open cockpits, which were embodied into a fuselage constructed mainly of spruce and plywood. The sides were assembled as whole units, and the complete fuselage was constructed in two halves, which were joined aft of the cockpit.

The cockpits were almost identical in layout, the pupil's front position containing all starting controls and the necessary electrical equipment. Although the undercarriage was not retractable, an undercarriage retraction control facsimile was included, and a folding blind-flying hood could be raised to fit inside the windscreen when required. Both seats were vertically and horizontally adjustable and designed to accept a parachute pack.

Particularly neat Perspex windscreens were fitted to both cockpits, evidence of Nash & Thompson's expertise in the moulding of Perspex, which was of course used in their bomber gun turrets. The Parnall 382 was later equipped with a coupé cockpit enclosure for the instructor's cockpit. This canopy was of the sliding type and could be pushed back on runners situated each side of a fairing, the front of which included a headrest for the instructor.

The engine mounting was of welded construction and attached to the front of the fuselage by four bolts, and rapid changing of the Gipsy Six was facilitated by the incorporation of quick-release couplings in each pipe line.

The cantilever wing tapered in both planform and thickness and was constructed in three sections, the outer section leading-edges carrying Handley Page automatic slots, while flaps were fitted to eighty per cent of the trailing edges. The inner sections of these flaps could be lowered to a 45 deg angle while the outer sections, which also acted as ailerons, could be lowered 15 deg, and still function normally as ailerons when depressed to the full extent. The flaps were manually-operated by means of a screw jack

In this view the Parnall 382 is not unlike the Miles Magister. (*Parnall archives*)

device with Teleflex controls, the flap operating wheel being on the same shaft as the tab control.

Four turns of the flap-operating wheel lowered the flaps completely, while various other settings were indicated on the control panel. The elevator trim tabs also operated through Teleflex controls and were actuated via a torque shaft in the tailplane.

The flap and aileron hinges were located on outriggers beneath the wings, but the Handley Page slots ran on three tracks borne on roller bearings and were independent of the flap gear. The slots had light springs fitted to hold them in the closed position, and a locking device was installed in the instructor's cockpit.

The wing structure comprised two main I-section spars of spruce and plywood, the entire wing surfaces being ply-covered.

The tail unit was of wooden construction, the tailplane being fixed to the fuselage top longerons by steel-plate fittings. Horizontal trim was adjusted by the elevator tabs. The elevator hinges were fitted in such a manner that very little gap was discernible at the junction with the tailplane, while the fin was built as a unit and fixed to the rear of the fuselage in such a way that side loads were transferred to the fuselage at the fin post, and at a point two bays further forward. The rudder, which was hinged to the fin post in a similar manner to that used on the tailplane and elevators, was of fabric-covered wooden construction, differing only slightly from that used on the Heck 2C in having no horn balance. Instead mass balance weights were carried on streamlined tubes attached to the top of the rudder spar. The tailplane and fin were ply-covered, but the elevators, like the rudder, were fabric-covered.

In a head-on view the Heck 2C's outward sloping undercarriage was quite noticeable, but the Type 382 possessed a straight landing gear in which each wheel was supported on Lockheed legs and Parnall forks. The undercarriage unit was attached to the front wing spar by means of built-

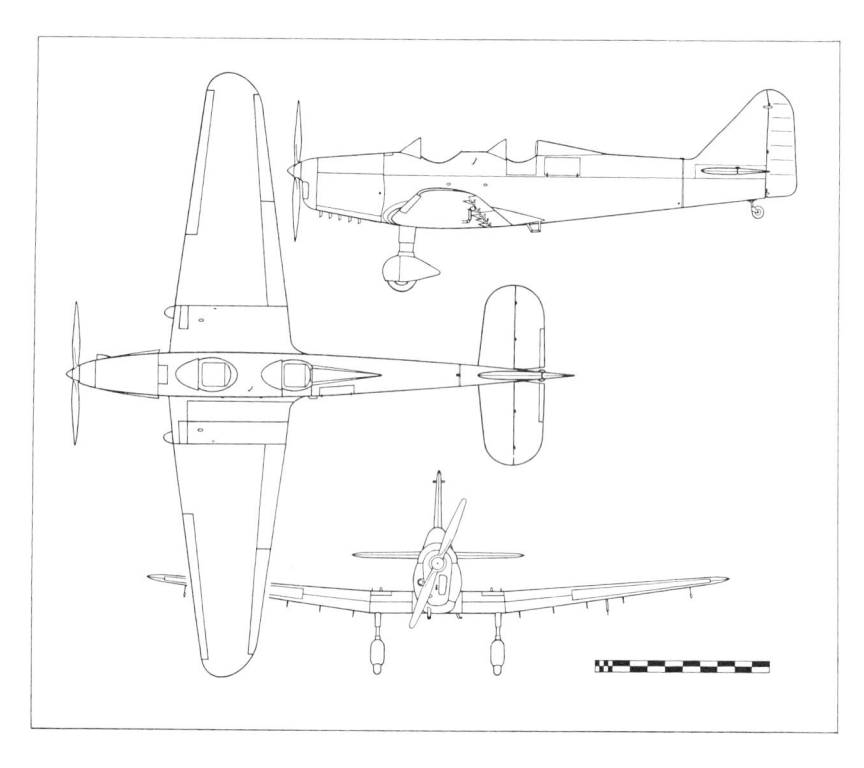

The first primary trainer to be so fitted, Parnall's Type 382 had interconnected slots and flaps. (*Parnall & Sons*)

up duralumin fittings bolted to the spar at the wing joint assembly. The undercarriage leg fairings were designed to give added stiffening against brake loads, while the wheels, fitted with Dunlop hydraulic brakes operated by a lever in the pilot's cockpit, were enclosed by streamlined spats divided transversely.

Fuel was supplied from two wing tanks containing 36 Imp gal, sufficient for a three hour cruising flight.

Inspection doors were located at various points in the Type 382's fuselage and on the wing surfaces.

With the use of slots and flaps the new Parnall trainer could be flown at 43 mph with the engine on, and the stall was not reached until the angle of incidence was over thirty degrees, a factor that eliminated the possibility of accidentally stalling in a glide.

Test flying at Yate of the Type 382 was undertaken by Parnall's test pilot at the time, J A C Warren, who dived the aircraft at a speed of 265 mph.

Report M/734, issued by the A & AEE in 1939, noted that the Parnall T.1/37 could be flown solo from either cockpit without the necessity of changing ballast, and that the machine could be started electrically in conjunction with a ground battery. There were some reservations about the lack of an engine starting battery, insufficient fuel capacity to fulfil the requirements of the specified endurance, and the absence of night flying equipment.

Generally the Parnall 382 was stated to be comfortable with good views from both cockpits when taxi-ing or taking off, except when waiting for the tail to rise during actual take-off, the view directly over the aircraft's nose then being poor. The machine was reported as having satisfactory systems, which included flaps and locking devices, and a rudder bar lock. However, the brake system came in for criticism and it was recommended the Parnall T.1/37 should be fitted with a standard brake control system as used on such types as the Gloster Gauntlet, Hawker Hurricane, Supermarine Spitfire and others.

Take-off and initial rate of climb were reported as acceptable, although a modification to the fin was found necessary.

Controls, elevators, ailerons and vertical tail surfaces responded pleasantly and harmoniously enough, while lateral, longitudinal and directional stability received favourable comments.

When testing for stalling characteristics it was found the slots opened at around 75 mph ASI, and the stalling speed with flaps up was about 50 mph. With flaps down and slots free a straight stall occurred at 40 mph with a slight wing drop being easily remedied by use of the ailerons. The stalling speed with flaps up and slots locked out was 58 mph, but with flaps down and slots locked shut the stalling speed was reduced to 42 mph.

The Type 382 received an excellent aerobatic report, and the type's gliding ability and landing characteristics also received praise.

In spinning and diving tests it was found the Type 382 could be spun easily with flaps up, but with flaps down the machine did not spin so readily. Spin recovery was reported as easy and rapid with flaps up or down and slots locked or free. During dive tests the trainer was considered quite satisfactory, the aircraft remaining steady during dives and enabling the pilot to keep the nose of the aeroplane easily on target. When increasing the diving speed controls became heavier, but once the maximum dive speed was attained, the aircraft's controls behaved well and were moderately light and effective.

The conclusions of the report were that, with certain reservations and a small number of minor points needing rectification, the Parnall T.1/37 was an aeroplane easy and pleasant to fly and, in view of its characteristics near the stall, was considered a type which would make a good ab initio trainer.

Despite favourable comments and findings on the aeroplane, the Type 382 did not go into production, and neither did its rival in the competition, the Miles M.15, which was of similar form, but with elliptical outer wing panels.

The sole Type 382/Heck Mk.III flew initially with the class B marking J 1, but this was later replaced by the civil registration G-AFKF. After the start of the war, the Type 382 was, like many of its contemporaries in the lightplane class, impressed into service with the RAF, where it was allotted the serial R9138. The machine was eventually delivered to No.24 Squadron on 16 June, 1941, but on 16 August was involved in a minor accident and returned to Parnall's Yate works for repairs. On 30 April, 1942, R9138 flew to 5 MU, Kemble, from where it was released to No. 637 Air Training Corps Squadron at Pontypool on 19 February, 1943. The aircraft then became ground instructional airframe No. 3600M, and was housed at Abersychan Secondary School, West Monmouth (No. 3 Welsh Wing). The Parnall Heck Mk.III/Type 382, or T.1/37, call it what you will, was unceremoniously scrapped before the end of the war.

Parnall Type 382 (Heck Mk.III)

Two-seat elementary trainer. 200 hp de Havilland Gipsy Six six-cylinder inverted inline air-cooled engine.

Span 33 ft 6 in; length 28 ft 8 in; height 7 ft 9 in; wing area 155 sq ft.

Empty weight 1,655 lb; loaded weight 2,450 lb.

Maximum speed 155 mph at sea level, 139 mph at 3,000 ft; cruising speed 135 mph; climb to 780 ft, 1 min; service ceiling 17,000 ft; range approximately 620 miles; endurance 3 hr at cruising speed.

Production

One prototype. See Appendix A.

APPENDIX A
Individual Aircraft Notes

Unfortunately much information, works drawings and other relevant details of Parnall-built aircraft, perished in the German air attacks on the Yate works in 1941. However, some records have survived and the author, with the kind assistance of individual air historians, especially Bruce Robertson, Eric Harlin, G Stuart Leslie and the late A J Jackson, has compiled the following available details regarding individual aeroplanes produced by the respective Parnall factories between 1916 and 1935.

Sub-Contracts (Parnall and Sons Ltd)

Avro 504B (1916), Contract No. CP111730/16. Military serials 9861-9890 (c/ns believed P31-P60): 504B 9890 armed with forward-firing .303-in Vickers machine-gun; Nos. 9862, 9863, 9864, 9870, 9875 to RNAS Cranwell; Nos. 9865, 9866, 9867 to RNAS Redcar; No. 9880 to RNAS War School, Manston.

Avro 504B (1916), Contract No. CP139233/16. Military serials N6010-N6029 (c/ns P62-P81): Machines N6015-N6029 transferred to RFC. Known transfers, N6018-N6021 became B382-B385; N6022-N6025 became B389-B392; N6026-N6027 became B395-B396; N6028-N6929 becaṃe B1390-B1391.

Avro 504, Contract No. not available. RNAS serials and c/ns unknown, but three transferred to RFC as A9975, A9976 and A9977.

Avro 504B Armament Trainers (1917), Contract No. CP103733/17. Military serials N6650-N6679 (c/ns P82-P111): N6650-N6656 transferred to RFC.

Avro 504A/J/K (1917/18), Contract No. AS20353 (believed associated with RFC transfers). Military serials B8581-B8780 (c/ns P1/1671-P1/1870). B8758 and B8774 later became G-EABH and G-EAEB respectively.

Avro 504K (1917/18), Contract No. AS41535 (believed associated with RFC transfers). Military serials D9281-D9380 (c/ns not available). D9303, D9329 and D9341 later became G-EAIB, G-EADU and G-EACS respectively.

Avro 504K (1918), Contract No. 35/A228/C.1038. Military serials E3254-E3403 (c/ns P1/8000-P1/8149). Machines E3390-E3397 were fitted with 100 hp Gnome Monosoupape engines and served with the Grand Fleet. The following machines were later sold to civil operators and

227

entered on the civil register: E3292 (G-EADI); E3293 (G-EADW); E3358 (G-EANT); E3363 (G-EAFP); E3364 (G-EAHW); E3399 (G-EAMI); E3387 (G-EBPO).

Avro 504K (1918), Contract No. not available. Military serials F8696-F8863; F8883-F8945 (no confirmation how many from these were built by Parnall). Machines F8812 and F8834 converted to 504Ns.

Short 827 (1915/16), Contract No. CP48104/15. Military serials 8218-8229 (c/ns P1-P12). 8219 to No.8 Naval Squadron (East Africa), later transferred to Belgian forces. 8226, 8227, 8228 and 8229 fitted with dual controls; 8226 served at RNAS Killingholme, 8222 Great Yarmouth, 8228 and 8229 at Calshot.

Short 827 (1915/16), Contract No. CP48104/15 (extended order). Military serials 8250-8257 (c/ns P13-P20).

Short Bomber (1916), Contract No. CP105536/16. Military serials 9771-9780 (c/ns P23-P30). 9777-9780 (c/ns P27-P30) later cancelled. 9776 with No. 5 Wing, RNAS, Coudekerque; 9772 transferred to RFC from No. 3 Wing, RNAS, Luxeuil.

Hamble Baby Seaplane (1916/17), Contract No. AS7718. Military serials N1190-N1219 (c/ns P112-P141). Fitted with 110 hp Clerget.

Hamble Baby Seaplane (1916/17), Contract No. AS10058. Military serials N1960-N1985 (c/ns P142-P167). Fitted with 130 hp Clerget.

Hamble Baby Convert landplane (1916/17), Contract No. AS10058 (part of above seaplane contract, but for 74 as landplanes). Military serials N1986-N2059 (c/ns P1/1 to P1/74). Fitted with 130 hp Clerget. Machine N2002 (Parnall No. P1/17 below serial) was 193rd aircraft produced by Parnall & Sons, and 17th Hamble Baby built by the company.

Parnall Scout/Zepp-Chaser (1916), Contract No. CP124455/16/24486. Military serials N505-N506 (c/n P61) as only one (N505) built.

Parnall Panther N.2A (1917/20), first prototype, Contract No. not available. Military serial N91. Arrived Martlesham Heath (A & AEE) 23.4.18 for type testing. At Parnall 17.10.18 and 31.12.18 for repairs/modifications.

Parnall Panther second prototype. Military serial N92. To Turnhouse for Fleet trials 22.6.18.

Parnall Panther third prototype. Military serial N93. Completed July 1918. To Isle of Grain for flotation tests 18.8.18. At Parnall, Bristol, 17.10.18, but not on 31.12.18.

Parnall Panther fourth prototype. Military serial N94. To Royal Aircraft Factory, Farnborough, 22.5.18 for loading trials. Still at RAF on 17.10.18.

Parnall Panther fifth prototype. Military serial N95. To Turnhouse for tests with Grain flotation gear. Later allocated to ACA.

Parnall Panther sixth prototype. Military serial N96. Brought up to production standard.

Parnall Panther production (1919/20), Contract No. AS26370. Military serials N7400-N7406 (c/ns P871-P877). Built by Parnall.

Parnall Panther production (1919/20), Contract No. AS26370 (as above). Military serials N7407-N7426 (c/ns P878-P879); believed Parnall built up to N7426.

Production Panther (1919/20), Contract No. 38/988/C.1035. Military serials N7400-N7549 (c/ns as above for Parnall-built machines). Contract replaced earlier AS26370 (above) when taken over by British & Colonial Aeroplane Co, but N7400-N7426 believed built, or partly built, by Parnall at request of British & Colonial, which completed N7427-N7549. Panther N7530 was completed at Filton by Bristol Aeroplane Co. on 23.6.20. It was converted to the civil-registered G-EBCM, and flew in the Royal Aero Club race at Croydon on 17.4.22.

Production Panther (1920), Contract No. not available; two built for US Navy with USN serials A5751 and A5752 (Bristol c/ns 5889 and 5890 respectively). Shipped to United States 1920.

Production Panther (1920/21), Contract No. not available; 12 built for Imperial Japanese Navy. Military serials not known (Bristol c/ns 6128-6139). Shipped to Japan 1921.

Second contract for 162 production Panthers, allotted military serials N7680-N7841, cancelled.

George Parnall and Company

Parnall Puffin (1920/21), built to Air Ministry Specification Type 21. Military serials N136-N138.

Parnall Plover (1922), first prototype built as landplane with Bristol Jupiter. Military serial N160.

Parnall Plover (1923), second prototype built as amphibian with Bristol Jupiter IV. Military serial N161.

Parnall Plover (1923), third prototype built as landplane with Armstrong Siddeley Jaguar. Military serial N162.

Parnall Plover (1923), first production batch of three (N9608-N9610), of which first two were landplanes and third an amphibian. All powered by Jupiter IV.

Parnall Plover (1923), second production batch of seven (N9702-N9708), all landplanes powered by the Jupiter IV. N9705 became G-EBON (C of A 7.7.26), entered in King's Cup Air Race of 1926. Crashed January 1929.

Parnall Possum (1923), two built as postal aircraft with triplane configuration. Used experimentally; powered by one 450 hp Napier Lion driving two propellers via extension shafts. Military serials J6862 and J6863.

Parnall Pixie Mk.I (1923), civil single-seat monoplane with 29 ft wing span and 500 cc Douglas engine. No c/ns issued for Pixies, and this aircraft not registered initially, but flew as No.9 in 1923 Lympne Light Aeroplane Trials.

Parnall Pixie Mk.II (1923), was Mk.I Pixie with 18 ft wing span and 736 cc Douglas engine. Not registered when it flew as No.24 in 1923

Lympne Light Aeroplane Trials. Was afterwards converted to Pixie Mk.III for 1924 Lympne trials.

Parnall Pixie Mk.II (military training version); two ordered by Air Ministry as single-seat trainers. Military serials J7323 and J7324, of which J7324 later became G-EBKM.

Parnall Pixie Mk.III (1924), two-seat monoplane with detachable upper wings and powered by Bristol Cherub. Registered as G-EBJG, and flew in 1924 Lympne Light Aeroplane Trials as No.18.

Parnall Pixie Mk.III (1924), two-seat monoplane with detachable upper wing and powered by Blackburne Thrush. As Mk.IIIA flew in 1924 Lympne Light Aeroplane Trials in biplane form, being allotted the competition number 19.

Parnall Perch (1926), experimental two-seat side-by-side naval training biplane powered by 220 hp Rolls-Royce Falcon III. Alternative land or seaplane undercarriage. only one built, with military serial N217.

Parnall (Cierva) C.10 Autogiro (1926), built by Parnall at Yate. Military serial J9038.

Parnall (Cierva) C.11 Autogiro/Parnall Gyroplane (1926), built by Parnall at Yate. Civil registration G-EBQG.

Parnall-built de Havilland D.H.9A (1926/27), thirty machines built and/or rebuilt at Yate as part of Air Ministry contract to various manufacturers for 165 refurbished and new D.H.9As. Military serials of Parnall-built machines were J8172-J8189 and J8483-J8494. Those aircraft of the second batch (J8483-J8494), together with 23 from Westland Aircraft (J8460-J8494), completed as dual-control trainers.

Parnall Peto (1926), two built as submarine-borne reconnaissance aircraft. First prototype serialled N181 later rebuilt as N255, in which condition it was lost (scrapped after recovery of aircraft only) aboard HM submarine M.2, which sank in 1932. Second Peto serialled N182 was later registered G-ACOJ.

Parnall Pike (1927), only one of two ordered built, powered by Napier Lion. Military serial N202; second prototype to have been serialled N201, but this order cancelled.

Parnall Imp (1927), sporting biplane. Only one built and registered G-EBTE. Scrapped 1933.

Parnall Pipit (1928/29), single-seat naval fighter. First prototype, serial number N232, crashed October 1928. Second prototype built, allotted serial N233, but flew with same serial as first prototype (N232). Crashed 14.2.29.

Parnall Elf Mk.I (c/n 1), two-seat private-owner/sporting biplane/flying club type. Built 1929 and powered by 105 hp Cirrus Hermes. Crashed 20.3.34.

Parnall Elf Mk.II (c/ns 2 and 3). Civil registrations G-AAIN and G-AAIO (later had c/ns J6 and J5 respectively). Both fitted with uprated 120 hp Cirrus Hermes II. G-AAIO crashed 13.1.34. G-AAIN restored and now owned by Shuttleworth Trust.

Parnall Prawn (1930), built as experimental single-seat flying-boat (c/n P1). Military serial S1576.

Parnall Parasol (1931), two built as experimental monoplanes to test wing loadings and performance in flight. Both powered by 226 hp Armstrong Siddeley Lynx IV supercharged radial. Military serials K1228 and K1229.

Parnall-built Hendy 302 (c/n 1). Civil registration G-AAVT; two-seat cabin monoplane designed by Basil Henderson. Powered by 105 hp Cirrus Hermes I. Rebuilt 1933 by C S Napier to become Hendy 302A with 130 hp Cirrus Hermes IV. The aeroplane was wfu at Gravesend in 1938.

Parnall-built Miles Satyr (1932), built to design of Mr and Mrs F G Miles as single-seat sporting and aerobatic biplane (c/n 1 later became J7). Powered by 75 hp Pobjoy 'R' radial. Civil registration G-ABVG. Crashed and w/o September 1936.

Parnall-built Percival Gull Fours (1933), first prototype of which designed and built by Edgar Percival. First production batch of this three-seat cabin monoplane built by Parnall. Various powerplants installed: Gull Four D1, Cirrus Hermes IV; Gull Four D2, D.H. Gipsy Major or Napier Javelin III. Those Gull Fours built by Parnall were registered (as far as can be gathered) as follows:
G-ACAL (D.21) Napier Javelin III; G-ABUV (D.22) Cirrus Hermes IV; G-ACFJ (D.23) Gipsy Major; G-ACAT (D.24) Hermes IV. Later with Gipsy Major; G-ACGC (D.25) Gipsy Major; G-ACFY (D.26) Hermes IV. This was Avro's communications aircraft; G-ACLG (D.27) Javelin III. Later Gipsy Major, and sold to Indian National Airways in 1935; G-ACGP (D.28) Javelin III; G-ACGR (D.29) Javelin III; G-ACHA (D.30) Javelin III. Later Gipsy Six and sold to an Australian buyer; G-ACHM (D.31) Gipsy Major. Used by British Air Navigation Co Ltd; G-ACHT (D.32) Gipsy Major; G-ACIP (D.33) Javelin III; G-ACIR (D.34) Javelin III; G-ACIS (D.35) Gipsy Major. Used by Air Service Training. Later sold to Indian National Airways; G-ACJP (D.36) Gipsy Major; G-ACJR (D.37) Gipsy Major; G-ACJW (D.38) Gipsy Major; G-ACJV (D.39) Gipsy Major. Made record flight to Australia in December 1933 piloted by Sir Charles Kingsford Smith. Later registered VH-CKS; G-ACLJ (D.40) Javelin III; G-ACXY (D.42) Gipsy Major. Later believed to have been modified to Gull Six standard by Percival Aircraft and sold to French buyer as F-AOXY; G-ACPA (D.44) Javelin III. Later believed to have been modified to Gull Six standard by Percival Aircraft; G-ACUL (D.45) Gipsy Major. Later modified to Gull Six standard by Percival Aircraft, and sold to New Zealand buyer as ZK-AES.

Parnall Aircraft Ltd

Parnall Hendy Heck (prototype Westland-built), two-seat cabin monoplane designed by Basil Henderson. Later transferred to Parnall at Yate. Renamed Parnall Heck. Initially 'P' under class B registration, became

G-ACTC. Scrapped 1937.

Parnall Heck 2C first production (1935), three-seat development of original Hendy Heck by Parnall. Powered by 200 hp D.H. Gipsy Six engine. Civil registration G-AEGH (c/n J10); transferred to RAF as NF749. Struck off charge at 5 MU, Kemble, 27.5.44.

Second production Parnall Heck 2C (1935). Civil registration G-AEGI (c/n J11). To British Parachute Co, Cardiff, during Second World War. Flew after war until 1953, when subsequent to a ground collision with civil-registered Spitfire G-AISU, it was scrapped.

Third production Parnall Heck 2C (1935). Civil registration G-AEGJ (c/n J12). Cannibalised in September 1939, after expiry of C and A.

Fourth production Parnall Heck 2C (1935). Civil registration G-AEMR (c/n J13), allotted through clerical error; should have been G-AEGK. This machine to British Parachute Co 1944. Scrapped in 1948.

Fifth production Parnall Heck 2C (1935). Civil registration G-AEGL (c/n J14). Used as test-bed for 225 hp Wolseley Aries. Transferred to RAE as experimental type.

Sixth production Parnall Heck 2C (1935/36). Ordered under Air Ministry Contract No. 486334/36. Military serial K8853 (c/n J15). Used to test Browning machine-gun wing installations and as a test-bed for Hurricane and Spitfire reflector gun-sights. Eventually became ground instructional airframe No. 3125M.

Parnall G.4/31 (1931/35), general purpose biplane built to Air Ministry Specification G.4/31. Military serial K2772. Only one built powered by 630 hp Bristol Pegasus IM3.

Parnall Type 382 (T.1/37) Heck Mk.III. Initially this two-seat monoplane trainer carried J 1 on fuselage under class B conditions. Later registered as G-AFKF. Impressed into RAF service, allotted military serial R9138. Served for time in 1941 with No.24 Squadron. Eventually became ground instructional airframe No. 3600M. This aircraft, powered by a 200 hp Gipsy Six, was scrapped at the end of the Second World War.

APPENDIX B
Dispositions of Certain Parnall-Built Aircraft on Naval Duty 1918

Hamble Baby Seaplane N1201. At Talikna (Mediterranean District No. 15 Group, Mudros), June 1918.

Hamble Baby Seaplane N1209. Recorded for deletion (probably damaged beyond repair (dbr) from No. 64 Wing, Alexandria, 27 September 1918.

Hamble Baby Seaplane N1219. Dundee (North Western Area, No. 22 Group, East Fortune), 17 October and 31 December, 1918.

Hamble Baby Seaplane N1962. Westgate (South Eastern Area, No. 4 Group, Felixstowe), 17 October, 1918.

Hamble Baby Seaplane N1981. Otranto (No. 6 Group, Taranto) 1 October, 1918.

Hamble Baby Seaplane N1982. Aboard HMS *Riviera*. Recorded for deletion (probably dbr). With No. 6 Group, Taranto, 1 October, 1918.

Hamble Baby Seaplane N1983. Aboard HMS *Riviera*. Recorded for deletion (probably dbr). With No. 6 Group, Taranto, 1 October, 1918.

Hamble Baby Seaplane N1984. At Talikna (Mediterranean District No. 15 Group, Mudros), during June 1918.

Hamble Baby Seaplane N1985. Aboard HMS *Ark Royal* (Mediterranean District No. 15 Group, Mudros), 1 October, 1918.

Hamble Baby Convert Landplane N1989. Taranto (No. 6 Group, Taranto), 1 October, 1918).

Hamble Baby Convert Landplane N1990. Taranto (No. 6 Group, Taranto), 1 October, 1918.

Avro 504Ks E3390-E3397 (100 hp Gnome Monosoupape). In transit to Turnhouse on 17 October, 1918. At Turnhouse 31 December, 1918.

Parnall N.2A Panther first prototype N91. Arrived Martlesham Heath for type testing 23 April, 1918. Recorded at Parnall, Bristol, for repairs 17 October, and 31 December, 1918.

Parnall N.2A Panther third prototype N93. Arrived Isle of Grain 18 August, 1918, floating trials. Recorded at Parnall, Bristol, 17 October, 1918.

Parnall N.2A Panther fourth prototype N94. Arrived RAF, Farnborough, 22 May, 1918, loading trials. Still recorded at Farnborough, 17 October, 1918.

Parnall N.2A Panther fifth prototype N95. Ready for delivery 17 October, 1918. Still waiting delivery 31 December, 1918, after being allocated to Turnhouse. Later to ACA.

Bibliography

Aeromodeller. October 1980; January 1981.
Aeronautics. July 1941.
Aeroplane, The. 24.6.36; 6.11.42; 8.1.43; 26.3.43; 15.10.43.
Aeroplane Monthly. May 1973.
Aerospace. January, March 1970: February 1971.
Air-Britain Digest. May 1960.
Air Clues. October 1959; July 1960.
Air Pictorial. May 1958.
Aircraft Engines and Airmen. Scarecrow Press Ltd 1972.
Aircraft Illustrated Annual 1981. Martin Horseman (editor). Ian Allan Ltd 1980.
Aircraft of the 1914–1918 War. O G Thetford and E J Riding, Harleyford Publications (Harborough Publishing Co Ltd) 1954.
Aircraft of the Fighting Powers Volumes I, II, III, IV, VII, Harborough Publishing Co Ltd.
Aircraft of the Royal Air Force Since 1918. Owen Thetford, Putnam & Co Ltd (1957/1968 editions).
Aircraft, of the World, The. William Green and Gerald Pollinger. Macdonald & Co (Publishers) Ltd 1955.
Aircraft of World War I. Kenneth Munson. Ian Allan Ltd 1977.
A Picture History of Flight. John W R Taylor. Hulton Press 1955.
Bombers 1939–45. Kenneth Munson. Blandford Press Ltd 1972 (reprint).
Bristol Aircraft, The Book of. D A Russell. Harborough Publishing Co Ltd 1945.
Bristol Aircraft since 1910. C H Barnes. Putnam & Co Ltd 1964.
Bristol: an Aircraft Album. J D Oughton. Ian Allan Ltd 1973.
Bristol Cornish Association. Booklet.
British Aeroplanes 1914–18. J M Bruce. Putnam & Co Ltd 1957.
British Civil Aircraft since 1919. Volume III. A J Jackson. Putnam & Co Ltd 1974 (2nd edition).
British Military Aircraft Serials 1911–1971. Bruce Robertson. Ian Allan Ltd 1971 (4th revised edition).
British Naval Aircraft since 1912. Owen Thetford. Putnam & Co Ltd 1958 edition.
Combat Aircraft of the World. John W R Taylor. Ebury Press & Michael Joseph 1969.
Control Column. August 1972.
Cross & Crockade Journal. Volume 9 No. 2.

Encyclopaedia of Aviation. Sqn Ldr C G Burge. New Era Publishing Co Ltd 1937.
Encyclopaedia of World Aircraft. John W R Taylor. Odhams Books Ltd 1966
Famous Bombers of the Second World War. William Green. Macdonald & Co (Publishers) Ltd 1959 (1st edition).
Famous Bombers of the Second World War. William Green. Macdonald & Co (Publishers) Ltd. 2nd impression of second series 1962.
Flight. 13.10.27; 11.7.29; 17.4.31; 25.9.34; 25.6.36; 23.3.39; 22.11.57; 29.11.57; 6.4.61.
Flight Path. Capt F T Courtney. William Kimber 1972.
Gloster Aircraft Since 1917. Derek N James. Putnam & Co Ltd 1971.
Gloster Meteor, The. Edward Shacklady. Macdonald & Co (Publishers) Ltd 1962.
Janes All the World's Aircraft 1938. C G Grey and L Bridgman. Sampson Low Marston 1938 (David & Charles 1972 reprint).
Jet Aircraft of the World, The. William Green and Roy Cross. Macdonald & Co (Publishers) Ltd 1955.
Miles Aircraft, The Book of. A H Lukins and D A Russell. Harborough Publishing Co Ltd 1944.
Military Aircraft Serial Markings. Peter R March. Ian Allan Ltd 1981 edition.
Pictorial History of Air Warfare, The. Christopher Chant. Octopus Books Ltd 1979.
Pictorial History of the RAF. Volume I (1918–1939). John W R Taylor and Chaz Bowyer. Ian Allan Ltd 1980 edition.
Pilot. November 1973.
Shell Aviation News. No. 367, 1969.
Shuttleworth Collection, The. Wg Cdr T E Guttery. Shuttleworth Collection Publication, 2nd edition, 1st impression, June 1969.
Speed Seekers, The. Thomas G Foxworth. Macdonald & Janes 1975.
Weapons and Warfare. Nos. 99 and 102. Phoebus Publishing Co Ltd.
Westland Aircraft, The Book of. A H Lukins and D A Russell. Harborough Publishing Co Ltd 1944.
Who's Who in Aviation. 1928 edition.
World Aircraft 1. (Origins–World War I). E Angelucci and P Matricardi. Sampson Low 1977.
World Aircraft 3. (World War II, part 1). E Angelucci and P Matricardi. Sampson Low 1978.
World Aircraft 5. (World Commercial Aircraft 1935–1960). E Angelucci and P Matricardi. Sampson Low 1978.
World Encyclopedia of Military Aircraft. E Angelucci. Janes Publishing Co Ltd 1981.
World War I Aeroplanes. C G Davies. Ward Lock Ltd 1974.

General Index

A&AEE (Martlesham), 92, 116, 117, 127, 133, 135, 137, 171, 195, 216, 219, 225, 228, 233
Admiralty, 9, 16, 19, 28, 36, 69, 72, 85, 88, 89, 154
Admiralty Air Department, 18
Aeronautical Research Committee, 174, 175
Aircraft carriers, 88, 89, 96–98, 105, 160, 161
Aircraft Disposal Co, 98
Aircraft Manufacturing Co, 8, 144
Air Ministry, 9, 19, 21, 30, 31, 34, 38, 49, 50, 52, 55, 56, 97, 101, 103, 105, 107, 112, 115, 124, 127, 133, 142, 144, 147, 160, 163, 167, 170, 176, 194, 197, 207, 220, 219, 229, 230, 232
Aircraft Exchange & Mart, 216, 217
Aircraft Repair Depot No 3 (Western), 39, 59
Air Service Training, 142, 206, 231
Aldis gun sight, 161
Amey, Reg (AID), 50
Apsley of Badminton, Lord, 47, 48, 187, 188
Armistice 1918, 8, 18, 30, 95, 105, 112
Army Aircraft Factory *see* Farnborough
Army Airships *see* Farnborough
Asquith, Herbert (Prime Minister), 7
Auxiliary Air Force, 145
Avery Group, 9, 10, 15, 16, 19–21, 25, 36, 95
Avro, 8, 9, 69, 137, 206

Bath Electric Tramways, 26
Battle, H F U, 127
Bedford Flying Club, 129
Birmingham Aero Services, 48
Blackburn Aircraft Co, 80, 83, 133, 144
Bolas, Harold, 17–19, 37, 38, 44–46, 89, 100, 104, 106, 112, 114, 115, 118, 121, 124, 133, 137, 140–142, 160, 163, 164, 166, 171, 172, 176, 182, 188, 195
Bonham-Carter, Flt Lieut D W, 165
Boulton Paul Aircraft Co, 55
Brazil, Joseph Peter, 25, 27, 30, 31
Brazil Straker Co, 27, 28, 29
Brecknell Munro & Rogers, 31
Brighton, Hove & Preston United Omnibus Co, 27
Bristol Aeroplane Co, 8, 32, 37, 95, 229
Bristol, and Clifton Chess Club, 52
    Cornish Association, 15
    Flying School, 128
    to Gloucester Railway, 42, 57
    Literary and University Club, 52
    and Wessex Aero Club, 128
    Berkeley Square, 38
    Barton Hill, 67
    Brislington, 16–19, 100
    Eastville, 16
    Feeder Road, 37
    Fishponds, 9, 20, 21, 25–35
    Henleaze Lake, 104
    Kingswood, 119
    Narrow Wine Street, 15, 16, 20
    Mivart Street, 16, 18, 37
    Park Row, 9, 10, 16, 21, 36, 42, 95, 97, 100, 116
    Quakers Friars, 16, 18, 37
    St Philips Marsh, 25
British Air Navigation Co, 206, 231
British & Colonial Aeroplane Co, 8, 9. 97, 146, 229
British Parachute Co, 218, 219, 232
Broad, Hubert, 171, 218
Brooke-Popham, Maj, 7
Brooke-Popham, Sir Robert, 145
Browning machine-gun, 56, 216, 219, 232
Bruce, Hon Mrs Victor, 202
Burney, Lieut Charles Denniston, 146
Bussing motor-bus engine, 25
Bussing Patients, 26
Byas, Lieut C W, 156

Camden-Pratt, Adolf, 86, 87
Camm Memorial Hall, 128
Churchill, Winston, 7, 8
Cierva Autogiro Co, 137
Cierva, Juan de la, 141
Cirrus Hermes Engineering Co, 199
Clarke, H V, 195
Coliseum Works *see* Bristol, Park Row
Collar, A R, 174
Cornish Aviation Co, 45, 187
Cosmos Engineering, 20, 29–32
Cotswold Aero Club, 187
Courtney, Capt Frank T, 10, 110, 117, 124, 127–130, 132, 135, 145, 159, 162, 163
Crammond, Lieut-Cdr J G, 218
Cricklewood, 8
Crosby-Warren, J, 54
Curtiss-Reed propeller, 162

D Napier & Sons, 114
Davies, Keith, 86
de Havilland Aircraft Co, 8, 18, 124, 144
Dive-bombing, 94
Douglas, Sqn Ldr W Sholto, 126
Draycott, J E, 47–49, 190
Duncan, W J, 174
Duncanson, Flt Lieut R, 216
Dunlop hydraulic brakes, 225
Dursely, Glos, 64, 66

Elmhurst, Mrs L, 217
England – Cape Town Record, 216
England, Sqn Ldr T H, 117, 127
Esnault-Pelterie, Robert, 28
Everard, W Lindsay (MP), 206

Fairey Aviation Co, 9, 80, 83, 101, 103, 105, 106, 117
Fairey Patent Camber Gear, 81, 82, 84, 107
Fairey-Reed propeller, 153, 157, 160
Farnborough, 8, 18, 49, 87, 95, 110, 116, 139, 180, 219, 228, 232, 233
Fedden, Roy, 27–32, 34, 112

236

Ferdinand, Archduke Franz, 8
Filton, 31, 32, 37, 41, 97, 98, 110, 112, 115, 122, 130, 229
Fishponds Works, 10, 22–25, 27–32, 35
Fleet Air Arm, 97, 98, 110
Flutter, 170, 171, 173
Flutter Sub-Committee, 174
Folland, H P, 9, 171
Frazer-Nash, A G 53
Frazer-Nash turrets, 53, 54, 57, 214
Frazer, R A 174
Frederick Sage & Co, 72, 74
Fry, Mrs Margaret, 46, 47, 55, 62, 63, 216

GEC, 9
German air attacks, 10, 58–63, 66, 67
Gloster Aircraft Co, 8, 9, 97
Gloucester Wagon Co, 25
Grain Flotation Gear, 88, 93–95, 98, 228
Gratton-Thompson, Capt E, 53
Green, F M, 18
Grosvenor Cup Race, 126, 130, 131
Guiness, Hon Loel, 206

Haga-Haig, Flt Lieut R A de, 126
Hall-Warren, Norman, 172
Hawker, Harry, 31
Henderson, Basil B, 198, 214, 231
Hendon, 69
Hendy Aircraft Co, 198, 214
Heston-Newcastle Race, 199
H H Martyn & Co, 8
Hiscocks, S W, 8
Hope, Lieut Linton, 18
Hospital Air Pageants Ltd, 202

Imperial Airways, 32, 34
Imperial Chemical Industries, 53
Imperial Defence Committee, 7
Imperial Japanese Navy, 98, 99, 229
Independent Air Force, 79
Indian National Airways, 206, 231
International Aero Exhibition, 36, 181
International Handicap Race, 130, 131
Ivelaw-Chapman, R, 116, 127
Isle of Grain, 93, 103, 228, 233

Joubert de la Ferte, Capt Philip, 7

Keighley-Peach, Lieut C, 156
Kemble 5 MU, 217, 218, 226, 232
Kent, HRH The Duke of, 66
King's Cup Air Race, 111, 112, 164, 186, 199, 203, 216–218, 229
Kingsford-Smith, Sir Charles, 50, 206, 231
Kirwan, J D, 217

Leake, Lieut Cdr, 205
Le Prieur rockets, 84
Leuchars, 110
Lewis machine-gun, 54, 70, 76, 77, 79, 84, 87, 88, 91, 92, 99, 105, 117, 146, 161, 163, 196, 197, 209, 210
Limerick, Earl of, 50

Llewellyn, Capt David, 216
Lodge Causeway Works *see* Fishponds
London, Bush Lane, 25
  Evelyn House, Oxford St, 38, 41
  Neasden Works, 67
  Nelson St, Blackfriars, 25
London Road Car Company, 26
London General Omnibus Co, 26
London & District Motor Bus Co, 26
London Motor Omnibus Co, 27
Long's Mining Co, 39
Lowe-Wylde, C H, 203
Luxury Air Tours Ltd, 202
Lympne Light Aeroplane Trials, 46, 47, 118, 123–132, 230

Macmillan, Capt Norman, 97, 104, 107, 115, 117, 122, 123
MAEE, Felixstowe, 108, 134–137, 147, 148, 151, 157, 159, 161, 190–193
Mann Egerton Co, 78
May, Miss M *see* Mrs Margaret Fry
Midland Aircraft Preservation Society, 129
Miles Aircraft Ltd, 202
Miles, F G, 200, 201
Miles, Mrs B, 201
Ministry of Aircraft Production, 64, 67
Mitchell, Reginald J, 19
Moore, Maj W G, 95
Muir, A F, 98

NACA experiments, 175
Napier, Carril S, 199, 204, 205
Nash & Thompson Ltd, 52, 53, 55, 56, 192, 222
Newmann's & Co, 50, 57
Noakes, Flt Lieut J, 171

Ogilvie, C P B, 129
Orchard, Flg Off A T, 167
Ortona of Cambridge, 27
Owen, Brazil & Holborow, 25

Parnall Aircraft Ltd, 9, 52, 53–68, 214, 216, 232
Parnall, Alan, 13, 47
Parnall, Basil, 13
Parnall, Dennis, 13, 47
Parnall, George, 9, 10, 13, 15, 16, 18–21, 36–38, 41, 46, 47, 49, 50, 51, 52, 100, 127, 141, 188, 214
Parnall, John, 15
Parnall, William, 15
Parnall and Company, George, 9, 15, 20, 36–52, 55, 100, 103, 106, 108, 113, 116, 122, 125, 129, 135, 137, 142, 144, 145, 147, 151, 153, 164, 166, 170, 173, 175, 176, 187, 188–190, 195, 197, 199, 200, 202, 203, 205, 207, 213, 229
Parnall and Sons Ltd, 9, 14, 15–24, 25, 36, 37, 69–99, 228, 233
Pembereton Billing Ltd, 18
Percival Aircraft Co, 205, 207, 231
Percival, Capt Edgar, 50, 199, 203, 207
Philips & Powis Ltd, 201, 202
Phoenix Dynamo Co, 78
Pierson, Rex, 29
Pobjoy Airmotors Ltd, 166

Pobjoy, D R, 165
Pope, Flt Lieut H N, 173
Powis, Charles, 201
Pugh, John B, 202

Quintin Brand, Sqn Ldr Sir C J, 111, 112

Ranken darts, 84
RAE Mk II Gas Starter, 177
Reading Aero Club, 201
Royal Air Force, 18, 21, 38, 41, 51, 54, 55, 57, 68, 69, 72, 73, 105, 117, 142, 144, 145, 151, 171, 173, 193, 201, 202, 217, 218, 220, 226, 232
Royal Aircraft Factory *see* Farnborough
Royal Aircraft Establishment *see* Farnborough
RAF Hendon Air Pageant, 114, 116, 117, 127, 129
RAF Hendon Museum, 128
Royal Aero Club, 98, 118, 229
Royal Flying Corps, 7, 18, 39, 41, 69, 72, 79, 86
Royal Navy, 19, 151, 158, 173
Royal Naval Air Service, 8, 18, 19, 27, 28, 69, 70–72, 75, 76, 79, 82, 84, 85, 92, 227, 228

Saint, Capt Howard, 194, 197
Samson, Cdr Charles Rumney, 7
Sassoon, Sir Philip, 50, 206
Scarff gun mounting, 70, 115, 161, 163, 209
Schneider Trophy, 19, 31, 203
S E Saunders Ltd, 144, 149
Sempill, Col The Master of, 99
Short Brothers, 8, 9, 78, 144, 193
Shuttleworth Trust, 188, 189, 230
Siddelely Motors Co, 30
Sidney Straker & Squire, 25
Singh, Man Mohan, 203
Smart, Air Marshal, 220
Society of British Aircraft Constructors, 50
Sopwith Aviation Co, 8, 9, 16, 81, 82, 83
Specification A.D./N.2A, 88
  A.M. 9/20, 115
  A.M. 6/22, 105
  A.M. 44/23, 127
  A.M. 1/24, 160, 163
  A.M. 5/24, 133, 134
  A.M. 16/24, 147
  A.M. 21/26, 167
  A.M. G.4/31, 194, 195, 232
  A.M. F.5/33, 207–213
  A.M. T.1/37, 220
Specification RAF Type 21, 101
Squadrons (RNAS/RFC/RAF), 70, 76, 78

St Gennys, Cornwall, 13, 52
Straight, Mr Whitney, 214, 215
Straker, Sidney, 25, 27
Straker Steam Vehicle Co, 25
Straker Omnibuses, 25–27
Straker-Squire Cars, 27, 30
Submarine, HM E.22, 147
  H.M. M.2, 147, 151–158
Sueter, Capt Murray, 7, 79
Sunbeam Motor Car Co, 75, 76, 78
Sutherland, The Duke of, 118

T I Jackson Ltd, 64
Tinson, Clifford, 18
Trenchard, Capt Hugh, 7
Turnhouse (RNAS/RAF), 93, 95, 218, 228, 233

US Navy, 98, 229
US Naval Flying Corps, 98
Uwins, C F, 29

Vane Oil Motors, 53, 68
Vaughn, Lieut-General Sir Ridley, 53
Vickers Aviation Ltd, 8, 86
Vickers machine-gun, 20, 56, 70, 71, 91, 92, 99, 105, 112, 146, 161, 163, 170, 175, 197, 209, 227
Voevodskii, M, 44, 45, 112
Vulcan Iron Works, 25, 27
Vulcan Motor & Engineering Co, 143

Wakefield Cup Race, 199
Wakefield Prize, 123
Waring, Samuel, 8
Warren, J A C, 218, 225
W D & H O Wills, 27
Westland Aircraft Ltd, 144, 214, 230
Western Aircraft Repair Depot, 39
Worsley, Flg Off O E, 151
Worthy Down, 167
Wright, Sqn Cdr Maurice, 82
Wyndham, Mrs Jill, 216

Yate Aerodrome/Works, 9, 10, 21, 39–44, 46, 48–50, 52–58, 61, 63, 64, 66–68, 107, 110, 113, 117, 124, 125, 127–131, 135, 137, 138, 140–142, 144, 145, 147, 152, 159, 162, 163, 165–169, 171, 173, 175, 177, 184, 185, 187, 190, 194, 197, 201, 202, 205, 216–218, 225, 226, 230
Yendall, Harold, 18
York, HRH The Duke of, 36

Zeppelin airships, 7, 70, 85, 86, 87

Aircraft and Engine Index

ABC engine, 123
ADC Airdisco engine, 140–142
AD Flying-Boat, 18, 19, 89
AD Navyplane, 19, 89
Aichi Sieran, 147

ANEC, 118, 123
Anzani engine, 28, 127
Arado Ar 231, 147
Armstrong Siddeley Genet, 138, 142, 164, 166, 167
  Jaguar, 34, 105–107, 109, 168, 229

Lynx, 179, 180, 231
Mongoose, 150, 152, 153, 158, 159, 160
Panther, 168
Armstrong Whitworth 19, 195
  Ensign, 55
  Whitley, 55, 56, 218
Avro 504, 15, 16, 69, 70, 71, 187, 227
  504A, 70, 227
  504B, 69, 70, 71–74, 227
  504F, 28
  504G, 70
  504J, 70–72, 227
  504K, 13, 70, 72–74, 227, 233
  504N, 73, 228
  529, 28
  Lancaster, 56, 64, 65, 67, 68
  Lincoln, 65, 67, 68

BAC Concorde, 24
Beardmore Wee Bee, 124
Bentley BR2 engine, 20, 90, 97–99
Blackburne engines, 122, 123, 125–127, 130, 132, 133, 230
Blackburn Baby, 80, 83
  B7, 195
  Botha, 56
  Dart, 98
  Kangaroo, 28, 39
  Sprat, 133
Bodyless monoplane, 44, 45
Boulton & Paul Bodmin, 112, 113
  Sidestrand, 34, 35
Bristol Aquila engine, 210
  Badger, 31, 32
  Beaufighter, 22
  Britannia, 24
  Brownie, 124
  Bulldog, 34, 35
  Burney Hydroplane, 146
  Cherub engine, 122, 123, 125–127, 130, 132, 133, 230
  F2A/B Fighter, 28, 41, 144, 194
  Freighter, 24
  Jupiter engine, 32–35, 105, 107, 112, 229
  Lucifer engine, 147, 149, 150, 151, 157, 159, 160
  Mercury engine, 168
  Pegasus engine, 196, 197, 232
  Taxiplane, 149
  Tramp, 112, 113
  Type 120
British Aircraft Eagle/Double Eagle, 44

Caspar U1, 147
Caudron bombers, 78
Cierva C.9, 139
Cierva C.10/C.11 see Parnall aircraft
Cirrus Hermes engine, 51, 181, 186, 187, 189, 199, 200, 204, 205, 207, 230, 231
Clerget engine, 70, 80, 83, 84, 228
Cosmos Jupiter engine, 30–32
Cox Klemin XS-1, 147
Curtiss JN-4, 27, 28
  OX-5 engine, 28

de Havilland DH 9, 143
  DH 4, 85
  DH 9A, 38, 142–146, 230
  DH Comet (airliner), 24
  DH Dove, 23
  DH Gipsy Moth, 44
  DH Gipsy Major engine, 203, 207, 231
  DH Gipsy Six engine, 207, 214, 215, 220, 222, 226, 232
  DH Gipsy Queen 3 engine, 218, 219
  DH Heron, 23
  DH Hercules, 33
  DH Humming Bird, 118
  DH Mosquito, 22
  DH Moth, 189
  DH Tiger Moth, 22, 23
  DH Venom, 23
Douglas engines, 118, 119, 120, 122, 123, 132, 229

Elf see Parnall aircraft
English Electric Wren, 118, 123

Fairey Barracuda, 22
  F.2, 28
  IIID, 98
  IIIF, 152
  F.127, 28
  Flycatcher, 105–107, 109, 110
  G.4/31, 195
  Gordon, 194
  Hamble Baby, 15, 16, 80–84, 228, 233
  Pintail, 101, 103
Farman Longhorn, 28
Fokker F.VIIa, 35

Gloster Gamecock, 33, 35, 171
  Gannet, 118, 124
  Gauntlet, 225
  Grebe, 171
  Meteor, 54, 67
  Nighthawk/Mars VI, 35
Gnome Monosoupape engine, 70, 72, 80, 227
  Rhone Jupiter engine, 112
Graham–White two-seat experimental trainer, 28

Hamble Baby see Fairey aircraft
Handley Page Clive, 35
  Halifax, 22
  Hampstead, 33
  Hare, 35
  Harrow, 56
  Hinaidi, 35
  O/100, 79
  Type 42/45, 33
  Type 47, 195
  Type 14 (R/200), 88
Hansa-Brandenburg Seaplane, 101
Hawker Cygnet, 124, 128
  Demon, 53–56, 214
  Hawfinch, 35
  Hedgehog, 35
  Heron, 35
  Hoopoe, 167

Hurricane, 220, 225, 232
PV4, 195
Woodcock, 35
Hawker Siddeley HS 125, 24
Heinkel He III, 57, 58, 63, 64
Heck *see* Parnall aircraft
Hendy 302/302A, 197–200, 231
  3308, 214
  Heck, 55, 214, 231
Humber engine, 86

Imp *see* Parnall aircraft

Junkers F.13fe, 35

Le Rhône engine, 70
Liberty engine, 143, 146

Macchi, M.53, 147
Martin MS-1, 147
Martinsyde R.G, 28
  F.3, 28
  F.4 Buzzard, 28
Miles Hawk, 220
  M.15, 226
  Magister, 220, 223
  Satyr, 200–202, 231
Mono-Avro, 70

Napier Lion engine, 100, 101, 105, 107, 109, 113, 114, 116, 117, 160, 163, 229, 230
  Javelin engine, 203, 205–207, 231

Parnall aircraft
  (Cierva) C.10/C.11, 137–142, 230
  Elf, 17, 36, 44, 45, 47–49, 48, 51, 181–189, 230
  F.5/33 Fighter Project, 52, 207–213
  G.4/31, 47, 52, 55, 193–197, 214
  Heck 2c, 54, 55, 214–220, 232
  Imp, 44, 164–167, 181, 230
  Panther, 16, 17, 19, 20, 88–99, 100, 105, 228, 229, 233
  Parasol, 44, 175–180, 230
  Perch, 44, 133–137, 230
  Peto, 36, 44, 47, 49, 146–160, 230
  Pike, 44, 47, 160–163, 230
  Pipit, 44, 47, 49, 167–175, 197, 230
  Pixie, 37, 38, 44–46, 118–133, 181, 229
  Plover, 35, 37, 38, 46, 50, 105–112, 197, 229
  Possum, 37, 38, 112–117, 229
  Prawn, 44, 49, 190–193, 230
  Puffin, 37, 100–105, 229
  Scout (Zepp Chaser), 16, 85–88, 228
  Type 382 (T.1/37), 54, 55, 220–226
Percival Gull Four, 47, 50, 203–207, 231
  Gull Six, 206, 207, 231
  Vega Gull/Proctor, 206
Piaggio P.8, 147
Pobjoy engines, 165–167, 200, 201, 202, 231
Port Victoria P.V.5/5a, 88, 89

Royal Aircraft Factory B.E.2c, 39, 85
  B.E.2d, 39
  B.E.2e, 28, 39
  R.E.7, 28
  R.E.8, 39
Renault V-8 engine, 29
Ricardo-Burt engine, 190, 191, 193
Rolls-Royce Eagle engine, 78, 79, 143
  Falcon, 28, 87, 134, 137, 230
  F.XI, 167, 168, 172, 175
  Hawk, 28

Sage Type 3, 28
Salmson engine, 74
Saunders Roe A.4 Medina, 35
Short Bomber, 16, 77–80, 228
  Calcutta, 33
  Kent, 33
  Rangoon, 35
  Scion, 44
  Scylla, 35
  Seaplane, 16
  Stirling, 22
  Sturgeon, 162, 163
  Type 184, 77
  Type 827, 74–77
  Type 830, 74, 75
  Sunderland, 56
  Valetta, 35
Siddeley Puma engine, 113, 143
Sopwith Baby, 80, 81
  Camel, 41, 80
  Cuckoo, 28, 31, 105, 107
  Schneider, 80, 147
  1½-Strutter, 41
Supermarine Spitfire, 19, 56, 57, 67, 219, 220, 225, 232
Sunbeam Maori engine, 87
  Mohawk engine, 78
  Nubian engine, 74–77

Vickers Type 253, 195, 197
Valiant, 35
Vellore I/III, 35
Vendace, 133
Vespa, 35
Viastra VI/VIII, 35
Vildebeest, 35
Wellesley, 197
Wellington, 55, 56, 218
Voisin Biplane, 76

Westland Dreadnought, 112
P.V.3, 35
P.V.7, 195
Walrus, 105
Wapiti, 35, 194
Woodpigeon, 124
Wolseley Aries engine, 232